Praise For Divorce, Simply Stated

"FROM THE KIND OF DIVORCE LAWYER ANYONE WOULD WANT: *funny, kind, laser-focused, nonjudgmental, and extremely informative....* THE BOOK STANDS OUT FOR ITS CALM, DELIBERATE, AND WINNING TONE, WHICH FEELS BOTH REASSURING AND NURTURING."
Foreword Clarion Reviews (October 2016)

"LARRY SAREZKY HAS WRITTEN SIMPLY THE BEST BOOK OF ITS KIND. *Clear, convincing, comprehensive, and straight-forward. A must read for anyone thinking about divorce.*"
Arthur Balbirer, Esq.; past president
American Academy of Matrimonial Lawyers

THIS BOOK IS A MASTERPIECE! *Only Larry Sarezky could have written a book that contains all the divorce essentials plus priceless strategies for success and savings that you won't find anywhere else. And it's all delivered with caring and soul. If you don't think so, check out the illustrations by Larry's granddaughter designed to remind divorcing parents to attend to their children's needs.*"
Joanie Winberg, CEO
National Association of Divorce for Women and Children

"LARRY SAREZKY'S WORK IN THE FIELD OF FAMILY LAW IS AWE-INSPIRING. *Larry's critically acclaimed film about the realities of child custody battles titled "Talk to Strangers" literally brought tears to my eyes. I expected nothing less from this book and he didn't disappoint me. Whether you are divorcing, dissolving a non-marital relationship involving children, attempting to modify post-judgment issues from one of those situations, and whether you intend on representing yourself or working with professionals, this book is a must-read.*
Mark Baer, Esq.
Attorney/Mediator; co-author, *Putting Kids First In Divorce*

"HANDS DOWN, THIS IS THE BEST BOOK OUT THERE *when it comes to learning about the divorce process. Larry Sarezky condenses over 35 years of experience as a family law attorney into practical, easy to read advice. ... IF*

THERE'S ONLY ONE BOOK TO READ AS YOU PREPARE FOR DIVORCE, THIS IS IT!"

Shawn Leamon, MBA; Certified Divorce Financial Analyst, and Host, *Divorce and Your Money podcast series*

"*If you're divorcing, you must read Larry Sarezky's* **Divorce, Simply Stated***. The nuggets in the chapter on "Divorce Pearls and Perils" alone will save you thousands of dollars -- and your sanity!* DIVORCE, SIMPLY STATED DELIVERS NOT ONLY DIVORCE BASICS BUT A DIVORCE INSIDER'S TIPS AND STRATEGIES YOU CAN ONLY GET FROM LARRY. *We know from his Telly Award winning child custody film,* **Talk to Strangers,** *that Larry is uniquely devoted to helping parents and children in their hours of greatest need."*

Terry McNiff, Esq.
Author, *Picture Your Divorce to See The Right Decisions*

DIVORCE, SIMPLY STATED IS THE BOOK TO READ IF YOU'RE LOOKING FOR A CLEAR, WONDERFULLY READABLE EXPLANATION FROM A VETERAN DIVORCE LAWYER WHO CARES! *Sarezky provides valuable insight about how the divorce process works - and how you can make it work for you. And he does it with humor and compassion!"*

Rosalind Sedacca, CCT; Divorce & Parenting Coach
Founder, Child-Centered Divorce Network

"*Larry represented me in a divorce and again in post-judgment proceedings. As a lawyer myself, I was tremendously impressed with his formidable cross-examination and other legal skills. But what I valued most of all was that Larry always had time to listen and calm me in anxious moments. Anyone reading* **Divorce, Simply Stated** *will be incredibly fortunate to get that same blend of knowledge, wisdom and compassion!"*

Jamie G.
Fairfield County, CT

"*I don't know how my young children and I would have survived my divorce without Larry's talent, guidance, and humor while at the same time teaching me much needed life skills. It is exciting to know that Larry will be giving others the benefit of all of that in his new book,* **Divorce, Simply Stated!**"

Helen B.
Fairfield County, CT

This Is *Not* Your Parents' Divorce Book!

Divorce, Simply Stated will empower you to take control of your divorce by maximizing results, reducing costs, and staying in balance during this turbulent time in your life.

With a rare blend of wisdom, wit, and sensitivity, Larry Sarezky explains the mechanics of divorce; principles of divorce law and finance; how to find, afford, and work with the right divorce professionals; how to care for yourself and your children during divorce; and how to avoid the dysfunctional conflict that is *encouraged* in traditional divorces.

But there's much more to this remarkably frank book. In it, you will learn to recognize dangerous divorce myths, avoid divorce's most common mistakes, take advantage of divorce tax opportunities, and save money by sidestepping rarely discussed attorney billing practices.

Divorce, Simply Stated offers a uniquely refreshing approach to navigating divorce—a 9-year-old illustrator to keep your focus on your children; stress-reducing quizzes that make you laugh while you learn; a golden retriever named "Chuck" to guide you through the divorce thicket; and an array of skills to help you cope, organize, relax, and even sleep better.

But perhaps the most unique feature of *Divorce, Simply Stated* is the compassion with which its author shares 35 years of accumulated wisdom to help you overcome divorce's miseries, unravel its mysteries, and emerge better able to meet the future head-on.

About the Author

L arry Sarezky is one-of-a-kind; an accomplished divorce lawyer who uses award-winning creative skills to improve the lot of divorcing spouses and their children.

A practicing attorney for 35 years, Larry has represented clients from the ranks of Fortune 500 CEOs, Major League Baseball Hall of Famers, and Oscar, Grammy, and Emmy Award winners. During that time, Larry developed an approach to divorce designed to maximize results while minimizing financial and emotional costs. Larry has now made that approach available to the public in his new book, *Divorce, Simply Stated.*

Throughout his career, Larry has focused on the care and protection of children of divorce. Acting on that concern, Larry wrote and directed the Telly Award-winning short film *Talk to Strangers,* and wrote its companion guide to help both parents and professionals prevent the harm to children caused by unnecessary child-related litigation. The highly acclaimed film, which is being co-distributed by the American Academy of Matrimonial Lawyers, is currently in use for that purpose throughout the United States and abroad.

Larry has sought to improve the divorce experience in many other ways as well. In 2002 while serving as Chair of the Connecticut Bar Association's Family Law Section, he designed a program to provide divorcing spouses *pro bono* representation by young lawyers mentored by seasoned matrimonial attorneys. The next year, Connecticut Supreme Court Justice Peter Zarella enlisted Larry's help to secure confidentiality for divorcing spouses' financial affidavits, distributing one of Larry's legal commentaries to each of the state's family judges. Larry is currently applying his wisdom and wit to the production of *Become Your Own Star Witness,* an audiobook primer on how to testify in family court cases.

Larry's articles on divorce have appeared in *The Huffington Post,* divorcedmoms. com, ezinearticles.com, and numerous other online venues as well as in professional and consumer publications. Larry has spoken on divorce issues to judges, lawyers, mental health professionals, and consumers throughout the U.S., and has presented *Talk to Strangers* at national meetings of the American Academy of Matrimonial Lawyers, the American Psychoanalytic Association, and the Association of Family and Conciliation Courts. Larry is a member of The American Bar Association, The Association for Conflict Resolution, and The Association of Family and Conciliation Courts.

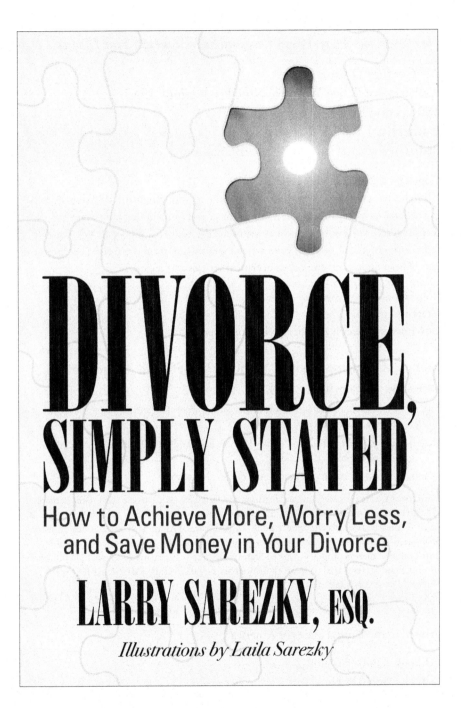

DIVORCE, SIMPLY STATED

How to Achieve More, Worry Less, and Save Money in Your Divorce

LARRY SAREZKY, ESQ.

Illustrations by Laila Sarezky

DIVORCE, SIMPLY STATED

How to Achieve More, Worry Less, and Save Money in Your Divorce

21st Century Divorce Books
A division of When We Were Nine Productions, LLC
180 Inwood Road
Fairfield, CT 06825
http://www.21stCenturyDivorceBooks.com

Illustrations by Laila Sarezky
Graphics by Ethan Sarezky
Cover design by Lewis Agrell: lagrell@commspeed.net

Library of Congress Control Number: 2015907198

Names: Sarezky, Larry, author.

Title: Divorce, simply stated : how to achieve more, worry less, and save money in your divorce / Larry Sarezky.

Description: Fairfield, CT : 21st Century Divorce Books, [2016] | Includes bibliographical references.

Identifiers: ISBN: 978-0-9963809-2-8 | LCCN: 2015907198

Subjects: LCSH: Divorce--Law and legislation--United States. | Divorce suits--United States. | Divorce settlements--United States. | Divorce mediation--United States. | No-fault divorce--United States. | Matrimonial actions--United States. | Alimony--United States. | Custody of children--United States. | Child support--Law and legislation--United States. | Equitable distribution of marital property--United States. | Divorce--United States--Costs. | Divorce--Taxation--United States. | Trials (Divorce)--United States. | BISAC: FAMILY & RELATIONSHIPS / Divorce & Separation.

Classification: LCC: KF535.Z9 S27 2016 | DDC: 346.7301/66--dc23

Printed in the United States of America

ISBN13: 978-0-9963809-2-8
ISBN10: 0-9963809-2-2

To Chuck...

For staying by my side while I wrote this book for as long as he could, taking me outside to play catch when I needed a break, and being so wonderfully, immutably in the moment.

Chuck
9/12/03 – 1/16/14

Acknowledgments

My thanks to all those who gave so generously of their time to help me navigate this book through uncharted and seemingly boundless seas: Clara Batista, Gabriella Cascante, Attorney Jamie Gerard, Brenda Grover, Attorney Deb Grover, Mike Klassen, Attorney Rick Kurshner, Rita Mockler, Sharon Mulligan, Shawn Munday, Amy Rizzo, Ethan Sarezky, and Attorney David Urubshurow.

And special thanks to Attorney Mark Baer for making this book better; to Roz Sedacca, Ginger Marks, and Amy Collins for their kindness and skill in moving the project forward; to my friends Diana Cicero and Attorney Kirk Bennett for their sage advice and assistance; and to my wife Sheryl who no doubt considered seeking a divorce on the grounds of intolerably endless book editing.

Important Notice to Readers of This Book

LIMITATION OF LIABILITY AND DISCLAIMER OF WARRANTY

The law and its interpretation, procedure, and customs regarding divorce and other aspects of family law issues differ significantly among the jurisdictions within the United States and between the United States and other nations. Law, procedure, and customs mentioned in this book apply differently to different facts and may have changed since this writing. Divorce-related and other laws, procedures and customs referenced in this book are intended only as examples of variations among United States jurisdictions.

This book is intended to provide general information regarding the subjects covered within it. It is made available to readers on the express condition, and with the understanding that the author is not rendering legal, accounting, financial, or counseling services. The author, publisher, contributors, and endorsers are not responsible for nor shall be liable for damages arising from, and make no representations regarding the accuracy or completeness of material contained in this book nor appearing at divorcesimplystated.com, witnesstutor.com, 21stcenturydivorce.com, divorceresourcessite.com, childcustodyfilm.com, larrysarezky.com, or linked websites; or the accuracy or completeness of material or the quality of products mentioned at those or other websites or in other resources referenced in this book. The author and publisher expressly disclaim all warranties regarding the accuracy or completeness of such material or the quality or fitness of such products, including but not limited to warranty of fitness for a particular purpose. No warranties shall be deemed to be extended, offered, or created by any material promoting or supplementing this book.

No portion of this book should be considered advice regarding the reader's situation or pending family case, or to be substituted for advice and counsel from an experienced matrimonial attorney licensed by the relevant jurisdiction, or other qualified financial, tax, and mental health professionals. It is the reader's responsibility to seek such advice when and if necessary.

Summary of Contents

Contents

Introduction

Why I Worry About Your Divorce

During 35 years as a lawyer and mediator, I've seen too many people achieve too little in their divorces, while spending and suffering far too much. I don't want that to happen to you, and I wrote this book so that it won't.

A lot can go wrong during divorce, to be sure. Some folks damage their prospects right off the bat by choosing the wrong lawyer, the wrong kind of divorce (yes, you have a choice!), or the wrong divorce goals. Others make poor decisions based on emotion rather than logic. Still others, overwhelmed by anxiety or cost, abandon their goals too early and easily.

And there are even more mistakes that are made much too often. Parents with solvable child-related disputes endanger their children's emotional health by choosing court battles over cooperative problem solving. Self-represented spouses, and even those with attorneys, hurt themselves in court with poorly prepared paperwork and testimony that damages their cases.

This book shows you how to avoid those kinds of mistakes using methods I've developed over the years for my clients.

But you'll learn much more than how to avoid mistakes. The material in the pages that follow will prepare you to reach your goals at the least financial and emotional cost to you and your children.

For example, you'll learn how mediation works. Then you'll find out how to maximize your mediation outcome by finding a qualified mediator, formulating a mediation game plan, and being able to stick to that game plan.

The material on mediation illustrates the 2 types of material provided in this book:

1. The legal rules and financial principles that determine outcomes in family court cases

2. Strategies, tactics, and tips for using those rules and principles to reach your goals

To achieve your divorce goals, you must use your time, money, and energy efficiently. That begins with the learning process in this book. To help you learn efficiently about divorce, I make frequent use of lists to convey information. Much as a straight line is the shortest distance between two points, lists deliver the most information in the fewest words. That's efficient—or put another way—that's *Divorce, Simply Stated*.

For example, the lists in this book will help you:

- Select and work efficiently with skilled divorce professionals
- Decide if mediation or other alternative dispute resolution (ADR) methods are right for you
- Choose realistic divorce goals by getting an idea of the range of likely outcomes in your case
- Increase your chances to achieve your goals by becoming an effective advocate for yourself
- Learn the details of how divorce works in your state
- Enhance the value of your divorce outcome by, for example,
  - Taking full advantage of tax breaks and other divorce "break-upportunities"
  - Identifying hidden costs that can erode the value of property you receive in your settlement
  - Discovering your spouse's undisclosed income
  - Avoiding excessive legal fees by
    - Discovering the "bargain table" of quality divorce lawyers
    - Paying lawyers only for services you need
    - Using non-lawyer professionals who charge substantially less than lawyers
    - Becoming your own paralegal

And if you doubted the efficiency of lists to convey information, consider how much is contained in the one you just read.

Some of the lists in this book summarize typical state laws regarding child support guidelines, alimony formulas, determining what property is in the divorce "pot," grandparents' rights, and numerous other divorce and custody case issues. The lists do not contain the laws of every state. Instead, they illustrate common approaches to issues that arise frequently in family court cases. That information will enable you to identify what more you need to learn about your state's laws.

To help you get any state-specific information that you might need (and to access your state's court forms), you'll have the following tools:

- Links found in Chapter 17 in the section called "Resources For Federal and State Family Law, and For Making Sound Divorce Decisions"
- Appendix 4, a page index of each mention of specific state laws

Notwithstanding these tools, I will remind you periodically—including right now—that your best source of information regarding your state's law is an experienced local matrimonial lawyer.

What's So Funny About Divorce? (Nothing.)

Q. What's so funny about divorce?

A. Nothing.

So why are there jokes and silly dog photos here and there within the chapters, and dopey (yet instructive) quizzes at the end of them?

The occasional silliness in this book is meant to give you a break from the bleakness of divorce and ... despite my best efforts to avoid it ... the boredom you might experience reading about it.

It is *not* meant to make light of what you're going through. Quite the opposite; it's there in recognition of how miserable divorce can be and the importance of getting some relief from it.

Laughter may not always be the best medicine, but psychoneuroimmunological research suggests that it does reduce stress and can even boost the immune system.[1] And hardly anyone questions that research—quite possibly because hardly anyone can pronounce "psychoneuroimmunological."

---

[1] *Alternative Therapies in Health and Medicine* 2003 Mar-Apr; 9(2): 38-45.

I've used humor over the years to assist struggling clients to get through rough patches, to help clients (and myself) keep things in perspective, and even to clear away obstacles to settlement during negotiation sessions. Still, I understand that the humor in this book may not work for you. So I've made it easy to ignore by tagging it with one of these smiling faces:

So if you encounter a smiley and aren't in a laughing mood, simply skip the text that accompanies it!

In case you were wondering, the grinning dog is Chuck, my loyal companion while I wrote this book.[2] I've included pictures of Chuck like his selfie, to give you an occasional healthy... chuckle.

Whether or not you feel like chuckling during this very *un*funny phase of your life, use the silly stuff as a reminder that you need breaks from your divorce. Catch a movie, go on a hike, drop in on a yoga class or meditation group, or even YouTube some *Too Cute* pet clips—whatever it takes for you to get the relaxation you need to stay in balance.

Chuck's selfie

You owe that to yourself—and to your kids.

Speaking of Your Children...

The well-being of my clients' children has always been a priority for me in my law practice, and it remains so in this book. In that spirit, I'll be reminding you from time to time to stay focused on your kids. Children need not be harmed by divorce—conscientious, mindful parents can prevent that.[3]

You might feel you don't need me to remind you to look after your children. And you might be right. But I've seen the most well intentioned

---

[2] Sadly, Chuck passed away while this book was being prepared for publication. There may be a better dog somewhere out there, but you couldn't prove it by me.

[3] From time to time I will refer to a short film called *Talk to Strangers* that I wrote and directed to discourage parents from subjecting their children to custody and access battles. Visit www. ChildCustodyFilm.com to preview the film and its companion parents' guide, and to stream or purchase the film DVD.

divorcing parents become preoccupied with their own concerns, and lose sight of what's best for the young ones around them.

With that in mind, I've illustrated this book with pictures drawn in school by my then 9-year-old granddaughter Laila—a gentle soul offering you gentle reminders of what matters most.

Laila's selfie portrait

Break-Upportunities

After you've completed your divorce journey, you may realize that you learned quite a bit along the way about finance, parenting, handling conflict and other adversity ... and about yourself. Though it might be difficult to imagine while you're in the thick of it, divorce can provide extraordinary opportunities for learning and personal growth. Over the years, I've enjoyed watching people acquire insights, knowledge, and skills that served them well during their divorces and long afterward.

It's my sincerest hope that this book helps you become one of those people.

Finally, if you visit www.DivorceSimplyStated.com for the free updates and supplements available there, use the "Contact Us" page to email me and let me know how you're doing, how this book helped you, or how you think it might be improved for those who use it after you. I'd love to hear from you!

I wish you all the best of luck.

Larry Sarezky
Fairfield, CT

CHAPTER 1

Ending a Dysfunctional Marriage With a Functional Divorce

"I am not afraid of storms for I am learning how to sail my ship."

— Louisa May Alcott

The Functional Divorce

In this chapter we begin gathering the tools necessary to end a dysfunctional marriage with a "functional divorce." A functional divorce achieves reasonable goals at the least financial and emotional cost to you and your children. That requires 2 willing players (you and your spouse) who will:

- Agree upon ground rules to communicate productively, and protect your children from the harmful impact of a high-conflict divorce[1]
- Formulate reasonable goals
- Share all necessary information and documents necessary for a fair and efficient resolution of all issues

What you read in this and the chapters that follow will help you accomplish a functional divorce by:

- Making your children's needs a priority
- Reducing your and your children's stress by
  - Demystifying divorce
  - Enabling you to handle whatever arises during your divorce
- Helping you find affordable divorce professionals who meet your needs
- Showing how to use lawyers creatively to get more for less
- Showing how to save money using the tax code
- Showing how settlement agreement language and seemingly small adjustments can protect you and maximize your divorce results
- Providing you with resources to find

---

[1] See Chapter 10.

  ○ Additional information about your state's divorce laws
  ○ Local lawyers and other professionals
- Showing how to reach a fair agreement that both spouses will want to uphold

Deciding When to File

The decision to "file for divorce" is a momentous and emotionally challenging one. As if that weren't difficult enough, deciding *when* to file involves a number of considerations, namely:

- Whether you are emotionally prepared to proceed and have identified a therapist or divorce coach who you (and your children) can see if necessary
- Whether reasonable attempts to save the marriage have been exhausted
- Whether you have decided between a "court-based" or alternative dispute resolution divorce
- Whether you have chosen a lawyer or mediator, or have at least consulted with one or both
- Whether you have begun the document gathering and other work described in this chapter
- Whether you have reached out to other professionals you may need, such as divorce coaches and divorce financial analysts

Filing Now

If the answer to all of the above is "yes" and you still haven't filed, you may simply be procrastinating. That's certainly understandable given the magnitude of the decision you are making. However, delay might not serve your interests. Below are some reasons you might *not* want to wait:

- Filing protects you by activating automatic court orders prohibiting your STBX[2] (and you) from taking unilateral action regarding finances or your children
- Filing begins resolution of conflict that is stressful for you and your children
- Filing starts the clock ticking toward the beginning of the rest of your life

---

[2] "Soon-to-be-Ex-Spouse"

Filing Later

On the other hand, there may be reasons to put off filing, such as:

- You want to delay your divorce to delay the beginning of the 3-year post-divorce period during which federal law ("ERISA") guarantees availability of health insurance comparable to your current coverage through your spouse's employment.

It's not uncommon to be on the fence about filing for divorce

- Your marriage is nearing the 10-year mark and you wish to preserve your rights to Social Security retirement benefits based on your spouse's income (rather than yours). You can become entitled to those benefits if
    - ⚬ You claim benefits after a marriage of at least 10 years
    - ⚬ You claim benefits at least 2 years after that 10-year marriage
    - ⚬ You and your former spouse are both over 62
    - ⚬ You are not remarried at the time you apply for benefits
    - ⚬ You are not already receiving Social Security benefits
- Your marriage is nearing the 10-year mark throughout which time your spouse has been in military service and you want to preserve your rights to military retirement pay and to receive enforcement assistance through the Department of Defense under The Uniformed Services Former Spouses Protection Act (USFSPA).[3]
- Your marriage is nearing the 20-year mark throughout which time your spouse has been on active duty and remains in the military, entitling you to full USFSPA benefits.[4]
- You need to file joint income tax returns and thus must still be married on the last day of the year.

Alternatives to Divorce

There are two ways for spouses to resolve support, property, and child-related matters without filing for an "absolute divorce":

- **Filing for a "Legal Separation."** If you are hesitant to initiate a divorce action, consult an attorney about commencing a "legal separation" or

---

[3] The Uniformed Services Former Spouses' Protection Act (USFSPA), 10 U.S.C. 1408 et seq.
[4] Ibid.

"limited divorce" action that will resolve all issues just as a divorce or "dissolution of marriage" case does. In most states, these cases can be easily converted to a divorce, so you don't have to start over if you decide you want a divorce. Also, if your soon-to-be-Ex ("STBX") wishes to file for divorce by way of a "counterclaim" or "cross-complaint," the case will then proceed as a divorce action.

- **Signing a Marital or "Postnuptial" Agreement.** A marital agreement settles support, property, and children's issues much in the same way that a divorce settlement agreement does. The differences are that:
  - Because there are no orders from a court, spouses seeking to enforce such agreements will not be able to initiate contempt of court proceedings that divorced individuals use for expedited access to the courts. Instead, enforcement would require a new lawsuit to enforce the agreement just like any other contract. And that could take several years.
  - If spouses later decide to incorporate a marital agreement into a divorce decree, a court usually must find that the agreement:
    - Was fair at the time it was signed, and
    - Remains fair under the circumstances existing at the time it is presented to the court for incorporation into a dissolution decree

States with statutes or case law (court decisions) that have been interpreted to approve marital agreements are: Alabama, Alaska, Arkansas, California, Colorado, Connecticut, Delaware, Florida, Georgia, Idaho, Illinois, Indiana, Kansas, Kentucky, Louisiana, Maryland, Massachusetts, Minnesota, Mississippi, Missouri, Montana, Nebraska, Nevada and New York.

Residence Requirements

One good reason not to file for divorce is that you can't. Nearly every state requires that one of the parties reside in the state for a minimum period before divorce proceedings may be commenced or judgment is entered. Those requirements are as follows:

- 12 months: Connecticut, Iowa, Maryland, Massachusetts, Nebraska, New Hampshire, New Jersey, New York, Rhode Island, South Carolina, West Virginia
- 6 months: Alabama, California, Delaware, District of Columbia, Florida, Georgia, Hawaii, Indiana, Kentucky, Louisiana, Maine, Michigan, Minnesota, Mississippi, New Mexico, North Carolina, North Dakota, Ohio, Oklahoma, Oregon, Pennsylvania, Tennessee, Texas, Vermont, Virginia, Wisconsin

- <u>3 months</u>: Arizona, Colorado, Illinois, Missouri, Montana, Utah
- <u>2 months</u>: Arkansas, Kansas, Wyoming
- <u>6 weeks</u>: Idaho, Nevada
- <u>No statutory requirement</u>: Alaska, South Dakota, Washington

---

Quickie Divorces

States such as California and Connecticut offer expedited or "summary divorces" for short-term marriages with no children, very limited assets, and where neither spouse owns real estate.

Some states also require a couple to be separated before filing for divorce. For example, Maryland and New Jersey require separation periods of 12 and 6 months respectively before filing. Such periods are not to be confused with "cooling off" periods that many states require *after* a divorce is filed. In those states, a divorce can't be obtained until after a specified period.

For example:

- California – 6 months
- Connecticut – 3 months
- Michigan – 2 months
- Rhode Island – 5 months
- Texas – 2 months
- Vermont – 3 months

Parenting During Divorce

A functional divorce in families with children must begin with those children. Decisions regarding them must be governed by *the children's*—not *your*—best interests. Your conduct should be guided by the children's well-being, not your parental "rights."

More on Divorce Parenting

In Chapter 10 you'll find pointers on parenting during divorce, including:
- Do's and Don'ts of Divorce Parenting
- Do's and Don'ts of Breaking the News to the Kids
- Questions Your Children May Ask About Your Divorce

The 10 Steps to a Functional Divorce

Functional divorces require planning. Each of the following 10 steps to a functional divorce is discussed in more detail below.

- Obtaining Professional Advice
- Protecting Yourself with Automatic Restraining Orders
- Protecting Yourself Financially and from Violent Confrontations
- Thinking About Your Divorce Goals
- Locating Key Documents
- Beginning to Plan for the Future
- Creating a Paper Trail to Success
- Educating Yourself About Divorce in Your State
- Caring for Your Children
- Caring for Yourself

Obtaining Professional Advice

Even if you don't feel that you can afford an attorney or other divorce professional, try to consult with one or more of the following anyway. If you can only meet with one, choose a lawyer who is experienced in both traditional divorce and alternative dispute resolution (ADR), which is discussed in Chapter 5.

- **Divorce Lawyers**: An hour or 90 minutes with a local divorce lawyer can be hugely informative. It might also help eliminate those 3:00 AM anxiety attacks. Download from http://www.21stCenturyDivorce. com the Initial Consultation Checklist (ICC) and Statutory Criteria Summary (SCS) that appear in Appendices 1 and 2 to this book. You can make your initial consultation much more productive by bringing a filled-out SCS with you, and selecting a few questions from the ICC to ask. Always ask the lawyer about the benefits of ADR.
- **Mediators & Collaborative Divorce Lawyers**: ADR should always be considered for a more efficient and less stressful divorce.
- **Certified Divorce Financial Analysts (CDFAs) and Certified Financial Divorce Practitioners (CFDPs):** CDFA/CFDPs provide financial advice for less than lawyers charge. They can help with organizing finances, preparing disclosure statements, understanding tax and retirement plan issues, and projecting the impact of settlement alternatives. As discussed in Chapters 3 and 6, you may save even more by having some of this work done *before* hiring a lawyer.

- **Mental Health Professionals**: Consider checking in with a therapist both for your benefit and the benefit of those around you. If you notice any behavioral changes in your children such as declining grades or changes in eating or sleeping patterns, consider counseling for them.
- **Certified Divorce Coaches (CDCs)**: Although not a substitute for an attorney, mediator, CDFA, or CFDP, a CDC can help you:
  - Manage emotions
  - Communicate goals
  - Maximize your attorney/client relationship
  - Transition to post-divorce life
- **Forensic and Other Experts**: Generally, the decision to retain an expert comes later, with the advice of your lawyer. However, you should be aware of the following experts who are sometimes needed in divorce cases:
  - Actuaries used primarily to value defined benefit pensions
  - Accountants to explain (or analyze) tax returns and "financials" of a self-employed spouse's business
  - Business appraisers to
    - Calculate the value of a business interest
    - Calculate the actual compensation a spouse receives from a business

  - Personal property appraisers to establish values for antiques, artwork, collectibles, or technical equipment
  - Real estate appraisers
  - Vocational experts and forensic accountants to determine earnings potential that courts can impute to voluntarily unemployed or under-employed spouses

  A consultation with a divorce professional can help relieve some of the anxiety that keeps you up at night.

  - Forensic psychologists and other mental health professionals to evaluate fitness of parents (and sometimes grandparents and other third parties) in child custody and access cases
  - Computer forensic experts to recover and analyze data that has been deleted or otherwise lost from electronic devices

Why Is There So Much Bad Advice Out There?

The good news is there is a wealth of advice available about divorce.

The *bad* news is there is a wealth of advice available about divorce.

You'll hear a lot about divorce from well-meaning friends, family, and members of divorce support groups. And you'll look at blogs, articles, and unnerving official-looking websites. Information from all of those sources is often misleading because it is offered:

- With no knowledge, or little understanding, of the facts of your case
- With no knowledge, or little understanding, of the relevant laws in your state
- By friends and family members who care dearly about you and whose advice is biased as a result
- By folks who will care dearly about you (briefly) after you buy their products or services, help promote their causes, or "like," "follow," or listen to them grouse about their own divorce experiences

In this Chapter and in Chapters 2–4, we will address the "bad advice problem" by:

- Clearing up common misconceptions about divorce (Chapter 2)
- Sharing basic truths about divorce (Chapter 3)
- Helping you find a competent, affordable lawyer who knows how to apply your state's law to the facts of your case (Chapter 4)

In deciding whether to accept a particular piece of advice, ask yourself if:

- The advice is designed more to make you feel better than to help you achieve your goals
- The advice is consistent with principles that are important to you, such as
  ○ Protecting your children from your conflict with your spouse
  ○ The desire for fairness
- Whether there are other options that
  ○ Are less stressful to you and your children
  ○ Move you more efficiently (and less expensively) toward your goals

Protecting Yourself With Automatic Restraining Orders

In most states, "restraining" or "injunctive" orders take effect automatically upon the filing of a divorce or legal separation case. These orders are designed to prevent either party from:

- Gaining advantage over the other
- Taking action that alters finances
- Taking action that alters children's living circumstances

In situations where one spouse might try to hide money, transfer property, or act irresponsibly regarding the children, automatic orders are a good reason to file for divorce sooner rather than later. These orders typically prohibit:

- Selling, transferring, concealing, wasting, dissipating or encumbering (e.g., borrowing against) marital property
- Failing to maintain, modifying, changing beneficiaries, or assigning life, health, disability, homeowners, or automobile insurance policies
- Spending or incurring debt except in payment of ordinary and normal expenses and attorneys' fees related to the divorce
- Relocating children, except if they are at risk, without written permission of the other parent
- Harassment of the other party
- Destroying, hiding, or spoiling potential evidence including electronically stored material

Some spouses use the period before a divorce is filed to buy big-ticket items, squander or hide cash and other property, or run up debt. Depending upon the severity of the situation, you may need—with a lawyer's advice—to take drastic steps to protect yourself from such conduct, by:

- Freezing or closing joint credit card accounts and home equity credit lines
- Placing in an account in your name
    - 50% of joint bank accounts
    - 50% of available home equity line credit
- Preserving (or improving) your credit rating by arranging with your STBX to pay bills on time
- Triggering automatic restraining orders by commencing a divorce or legal separation action
- Filing a motion for temporary support and contribution to attorneys' fees
- Placing in a safe place items with substantial monetary or nostalgic value

Protecting Yourself From Violence

If you have been the victim of violence in the past or feel that your spouse may become violent, *call 911 at the very first sign of danger*. Before things get to that point however, prepare and protect yourself as follows:

- Inquire at your local courthouse about protective or "restraining" orders that can keep your spouse away from you. Note that under federal law, one who is the subject of a domestic violence protective order cannot possess a firearm while the order is in effect.[5] If you seek a protective order against a gun owner, bring this issue to the court's attention.
- Reach out to additional resources such as
  - Your local domestic abuse hotline for information regarding local facilities and resources available to violence victims
  - National Domestic Coalition against Domestic Violence State Coalition list for local resources, at http://www.ncadv.org/resources/StateCoalitionList.php
  - The National Domestic Violence Hotline at www.thehotline.org
- If you feel violence may be imminent and you cannot move elsewhere
  - Keep your cell phone with you at all times.
  - Keep a spare car key concealed with you or near your car.
  - Establish a code word for texting or calling family members, trusted friends, or co-workers that will prompt them to call for help.
  - Secure your computer with a code.
  - Choose a room in your home with outside access if possible, for you (and your children) to go in a threatening situation.
  - Store with a trusted friend or family member items such as:
    - Jewelry and other valuables
    - Important documents
    - Evidence of past abuse
  - Keep key items such as credit cards and your social security card in a safe place that you can access quickly in an emergency.
  - Arrange with a friend to take you (and your children) in.

Thinking About Your Divorce Goals

It's not too soon to think about what you want to get out of your divorce... besides getting out of your marriage. Below is a list of matters commonly

---

[5] U.S. Code sec. 922(g)(8). Protective orders should never be sought frivolously as they can have lasting emotional impact on children, and can affect job prospects, etc. of those subject to them.

resolved in divorce cases. Child-related issues, support and property distribution will be covered in subsequent chapters, so don't freak out if you don't understand the meaning of everything on the list.

Many of the issues listed will be irrelevant to your case. Similarly, there may be details in your case that are not included. So for now, just scan the items below and as you continue to learn about divorce, return to these pages and use them as a checklist to make sure you've "covered all the bases." You can download and print the list at www.DivorceSimplyStated.com.

Child-Related Issues

- Legal Custody (decision making regarding children)
- Joint vs. Sole Custody
  - Major decisions
    - General health and well-being
    - Education
    - Religious training
  - Day to day decisions
  - Whether either parent has the sole right to make specific decisions
- Physical Custody
  - Joint vs. Sole Custody/Primary Residence
- Parenting Plan Schedules
  - School year weekend and midweek time
  - School year vacations
  - Holidays and three-day weekends
  - Summer vacation
  - Special days: Mother's and Father's Days, parents' birthdays, children's birthdays, traditional family gatherings
  - Access to and communication with children
  - Transportation of children to and from the parents' homes
- Relocation of custodial parent with children
  - Notice requirements
  - Prohibition of move without written agreement or court order
  - Defining geographical area within which agreement or court order is *not* required
- Other Considerations
  - Nurturing parental relationship with both parents
  - Communications with and about children

- ○ Transportation
- ○ Significant Others
    - Grandparents and other third party access
    - Appropriate role of subsequent spouses

Support Issues

- Spousal Support
    - ○ Amount
        - Flat periodic payments
        - Support as a percentage of obligor's income
        - "Base" (minimum) flat amount plus percentage of income exceeding a certain amount
        - Alimony (tax deductible spousal support)
            - Tax considerations and I.R.C. recapture risks
            - Unallocated alimony & support (single tax deductible payment that includes both child and spousal support)
        - Support "floors" (an agreed-upon minimum amount of support)
        - Income "caps" or "ceilings" on the amount of the obligor's income that will be subject to spousal support
        - "Safe harbors:" Income increases that cannot trigger, or be considered in, post-judgment modification proceedings such as, for example
            - New income of a spouse who is reentering the workforce
            - Anticipated increase in obligor's income already factored into agreed upon alimony amount
    - ○ Health insurance – COBRA rights to equivalent coverage for 3 years (at additional cost)
    - ○ Duration of spousal support
        - Transitional ("rehabilitative") and compensatory alimony
        - Permanent alimony
        - Statutory rights to modification due to changes in circumstances, unless limited or prohibited by parties' agreement
        - Nominal alimony ($1 per year) that allows the court to modify if there is a substantial change of circumstances in the future
        - "Wedding Gift:" Alimony payoff or continuing alimony after remarriage in rare circumstances such as recipient's remarriage is anticipated

- Modification upon substantial change in circumstances
  - Limits on modification
  - Termination, modification, or suspension upon cohabitation by recipient
- Child support
  - Child Support Guidelines mandated in every state
    - Deviation criteria for orders outside of the Guidelines
    - Per child amount that allows for automatic reduction upon older children attaining majority; vs. Single amount for several children that may require renegotiation
  - Duration
  - Modification upon substantial change in circumstances
  - "Extras" (e.g. camp, extracurricular expenses, etc.)
  - Private school/college obligations
    - Funding plans (e.g. 529 education accounts)
  - Allocation of responsibility for children's health insurance
- Life insurance on obligor's life to insure spousal and child support
  - Allocation between children and spouse
  - Designation of personal representative to receive life insurance proceeds for minor children
  - Step-downs in amount of required coverage over time as amount of remaining obligation declines

Property Issues

- Property Distribution
  - Identification and valuation of "marital property" that can be distributed by the court
  - Identification and valuation of separate or "non-marital" property in some states
    - Date of acquisition (before or after marriage)
    - Nature of property (e.g., inheritance, gift, etc.)
    - "Transmutation" of non-marital property to "marital property" e.g., through con-mingling of funds or augmentation of an asset's value with joint funds or other contributions
  - Continuing occupancy of family home by 1 party
    - Ownership
      - Legal effect of divorce on joint ownership and rights of survivorship

- Transfer of property to spouse in residence with note and mortgage to other spouse
- Details of eventual sale of residence such as
- Buy-out provisions
- Allocation of responsibility for
  - Pre-sale "fix-up" expenses
  - Necessary repairs and capital improvements
- Mechanisms to resolve disputes
  ○ Valuation, vesting, and tax issues regarding pensions and other pre-tax assets such as 401(k) plan, IRAs, stock options, and stock plans
  ○ Personal property
    - Personal effects
    - Valuables (e.g. antiques, artwork, and collectibles)
    - The rest
  ○ Valuation of spouse's business
    - Whether minority or marketability discounts apply
    - Whether valuation would "double dip" alimony
    - Whether a business's "goodwill" should be valued
  ○ Trusts
    - Established by spouse for benefit of children or third parties
    - Established for others for benefit of a spouse
  ○ Life Insurance Surrender Value
  ○ Frequent Flyer Rewards Points
  ○ Digital assets such as
    - Websites
    - Domain names
- Allocation of debt between the parties
  ○ Credit cards, credit lines, etc.
  ○ Indemnification of other spouse by spouse responsible for a debt

Miscellaneous Issues

- Taxes
    - Filing Status (e.g. head of household) In Current & Future Years
    - Allocation Of Exemptions & Child Tax Credits Between Parents
    - Entitlement To Refunds: Obligations For Payment regarding Past & Future Joint Returns
    - Entitlement To Deductions (e.g. mortgage interest, property tax, and charitable contributions)
- Professional fees
    - Contribution by one spouse to attorneys' fees of other spouse
    - Allocation of other professional fees

Deciding on Your Divorce Goals

Once you have familiarized yourself with the issues requiring resolution in your case (and have learned more about them), you can decide how you'd like to resolve them. When that time comes, use the following approach to formulate your goals:

- **Think long term**: Consider what will matter to you 3, 5, and 10 years from now, rather than focusing only upon immediate cash flow or other current problems.
- **Consult with an attorney**: Even if you plan to represent yourself or use alternative dispute resolution (ADR) methods such as mediation, consult a divorce lawyer for assistance in formulating goals that are realistic in light of your circumstances and your state's laws. Straying too far from the likely range of outcomes can pro-

Don't sacrifice long-term needs to scratch a momentary itch.

long or doom attempts to negotiate settlement. Discuss with the attorney whether the following common outcomes are likely in your case, and whether you might be able to do better:
    - Roughly equal division of marital property in long term first marriages or "principal" marriages that produced children

- ° Restoration of pre-marriage financial positions in short term marriages (equitable distribution states)[6]
- ° Duration of spousal support consistent with your state's law and customs
- ° Child support per your state's Child Support Guidelines
- **Prioritize your goals**: You are highly unlikely to achieve all of your goals, so decide which are the most essential, and which can be "horse-traded" or abandoned if necessary during settlement negotiation.

A Sample Goals Statement

Writing a Goals Statement can help you prioritize your needs. Use the following as an example.[7]

- Shield the kids from our conflict
- Divide our time with the kids in a practical way that doesn't cause them hardship
- Decide if the kids might benefit from counseling
- Alimony thru summer after J.'s high school graduation
- Split cost of kids' extra-curriculars, camp, tutoring, religious training, 60% STBX and 40% me
- We each contribute to college tuition and room and board according to our abilities at the time
- Divide property 50/50, except I get my USB account (including inherited money)
- We each pay our own credit cards and divide the joint Visa evenly
- Give court "continuing jurisdiction" to resolve disputes re sale of the house after the divorce
- Split 50/50 necessary house repairs and roof work if necessary
- Determine off-the-books cash receipts in STBX's business—need expert?
- If there's an IRS audit, protect me from deficiencies resulting from STBX's business
- Protection for me if STBX files for bankruptcy
- Prevent any new home equity line borrowing
- Life insurance to insure support
- Provide for kids' health insurance & non-covered medical expenses.

- **Emphasize needs over positions**: For example, if you wish to maximize your time with your children whose primary residence will be with your STBX, you might decide to demand "joint custody." Joint

---

[6] The differences between equitable distribution states and community property states are discussed in Chapter 13.

[7] Note: Items in this Goals Statement are examples only, and may not apply to your case.

custody is a "position." Your "interest" is to have as much time with your children as possible. Focus on the latter and avoid problematic labels like "joint custody."

- **Familiarize yourself with legal terms**: Learn some "Lawglish" words like "permanent alimony" and "marital property" so that you ...
  - ○ Understand the legal advice you receive
  - ○ Don't take positions based on a misunderstanding of legal terms
  - ○ Don't misunderstand your STBX's positions

Locating Key Documents

Documents have a habit of disappearing once talk about divorce begins. To avoid that, locate and copy important paperwork ASAP. As you gather documents, keep the following in mind:

- Your tax preparer will have some of what you need. But if you don't want to alert your STBX, try initially to locate the documents yourself.

- If you cannot locate, for example, old stock account statements, see if you can find the last 3 year-end statements, and be on the look-out for the next statement.
- If you or your spouse uses Quicken, Moneydance, or other personal finance software, print or transfer on to flash drives current summary reports and year-end reports for the last 3 years.

Gather vital paperwork without delay!

The section of Chapter 7 called "Where to find financial documents and information" shows how to access the following: [8]

- Deeds, mortgages, and other documents relating to real estate
- Information regarding military pay and allowances such as Basic Allowance for Subsistence (BAS) and Basic Allowance for Housing (BAH)
- Estimates of your Social Security retirement, disability, and survivors benefits
- Your filed federal income tax returns

---

[8] For e-book readers, some references in this book will be to chapters or sections rather than pages.

- Wills, trusts, accountings, inventories, etc. relating to pending and closed estates
- Your bank and credit card records
- Local real estate prices
- Loan applications
- Retirement plan information
- Life, homeowners, valuable items, and umbrella insurance policies

Financial Documents You May Need

The following documents are typically needed during divorce:

- Personal and business tax returns for at least 2 years
- Most recent and year-end pay stubs for at least 2 years
- Bank/brokerage statements
- Check registers
- Employment agreements
- Buy/sell agreements, partnership agreements, etc. regarding any business entity in which you or your STBX own a significant interest or actively participates
- Financial statements for businesses you or your STBX own/operate
- Regarding retirement, pension, and other deferred compensation plans such as stock ownership and option plans from current or prior employment...
    - Most recent, and year end statements for the last 2 or 3 years
    - Plan summaries (available from the employer's Human Resources or Personnel Office)
- Major credit card account statements including annual on-line summaries
- Loan applications
- "Closing statements" regarding purchase and sale of real estate
- Powers of attorney
- Appraisals of
    - Real estate
    - Businesses
    - Particularly valuable "personal property" such as collectibles, antiques, and artwork
- Your tax preparer's "cost basis" calculations regarding your home and other real estate
- The deed to your home, or other document such as a mortgage deed, which contains a legal description

- Year-end statements for "529 plans," UTMA/UGMA accounts, and any other accounts maintained for the benefit of your children
- Life insurance policy summary pages ("dec. sheets")
- Health insurance policy summaries
- Homeowner's, renter's, and personal property policies including schedules of covered personal property
- Safe deposit box inventories
- Trust agreements for
  - Trusts that you or your STBX have established
  - Irrevocable trusts set up by others in which you have a legal interest (in states where such trusts may be marital property)[9]
- Resumes

Non-Financial Documents

In some cases, significant non-financial issues are in dispute, such as:

- Child-related matters including custody; allocation of parenting time; access to children by parents, grandparents, or other "third parties;" handling of children's special needs; and disputes regarding decision-making concerning, for example, religious training, private school, extra-curricular activities, therapy, etc.
- Reasons for the breakdown of the marriage in states where those reasons can impact financial orders

If such matters are disputed in your case, the following documents may become important:

- Phone records
- Emails, letters, and transcriptions of texts, electronic communications, and posts
- Print and digital photos and other images
- Children's schoolwork (including younger children's artwork)
- Children's medical records
- Parents' medical records relevant to custodial fitness
- Calendars, schedules, and other documents used by the primary caregiver
- Police records where there has been domestic violence or criminal behavior that bears on custodial fitness

---

[9] See Chapter 12.

Scan and Organize Documents

Consider investing in a scanner to digitize and organize key documents. This can be especially helpful if your lawyer's staff routinely scans such documents. You can recoup the price of the scanner and more with the paralegal time charges you save by doing it yourself.

If your time is limited, you can scan key portions of certain documents. For example:

- Insurance policy declaration ("dec.") sheets that summarize the policy on a single page
- The key parts of personal income tax returns, namely
  - The summary on the first 2 pages
  - Schedule "A" (itemized deductions)
  - Schedule "B" (Interest/Dividend Income)
  - (If applicable) Schedule "C" (Business Profit/Loss)

Beginning to Plan For the Future

It's never too soon to plan for your divorce afterlife. Facing a suddenly uncertain future can be frightening, to say the least. The other side of that coin is the empowerment that comes from taking control of your life. Focus on empowerment as follows:

- Dust off and update your job skills. Start with computer courses offered by local libraries, colleges, and other organizations.
- Begin strengthening your credit rating. Use a credit card in your name only, to build a credit history independent of your STBX. If you don't have your own credit card, apply for one.
- Health insurance provided through your STBX's employment will be available to you for 3 years following the divorce. But the cost might be substantial. Visit your state's Affordable Care Act on-line exchange or the federal site at http://www.healthcare.gov/ to view alternatives.
- Begin assessing your post-divorce financial needs and changes in spending habits that might become necessary.
- Discuss with an estate lawyer the changes to your will that the divorce will require.

Creating a Paper Trail to Success

I can't remember all the court hearings in which I've wished my client had kept better records. But I recall clearly the cases in which my client's documentation helped achieve the desired result. Start creating a paper trail to success with the following:

- Keep a record of how you use your ATM withdrawals.
- If you anticipate receiving child support, hold on to receipts that document your children's expenses—it's nearly always more than you think.
- If issues arise regarding time with the children, keep a log of each parent's time.
- Communicate with your STBX by email to
  - Create a record of significant events
  - Preserve requests you've made or your responses to those of your STBX
  - Confirm any agreements reached

Educating Yourself About Divorce

Universal Divorce Principles

No two states' divorce laws are identical. But, some laws are the same...

- In all jurisdictions because they are governed by federal law
- In many jurisdictions because they are covered by "uniform acts" adopted by those jurisdictions

Below are examples of divorce-related federal laws and uniform acts. They and others are discussed in Chapters 9 and 10.

- Federal law governs divorce issues including
  - Divorce tax breaks such as
    - Alimony
    - Tax exempt property transfers[10]
    - Special rules relating to sales of primary residences
    - Assignments of children's tax exemptions and credits
  - Protecting children and spouses in interstate and international cases[11]
  - Dividing pensions

- Most states have adopted versions of the following uniform acts.[12]
  - The Uniform Interstate Family Support Act (UIFSA), adopted in all states

---

[10] See Chapter 9.
[11] See Chapter 10.
[12] See Chapter 10.

○ The Uniform Child Custody Jurisdiction and Enforcement Act (UCCJEA), adopted in every state except Massachusetts, which uses its predecessor, The Uniform Child Custody Jurisdiction Act (UCCJA)

Basic Family Law Principles[13]

In addition to federal laws and uniform acts, the following basic divorce principles apply to varying degrees in most jurisdictions:

- **Children's Issues**: Decisions concerning children are based on the "best interests of the child."
- **Property distribution**: Except in short marriages, "marital property" is often divided approximately evenly. However, the definition and handling of marital property varies substantially from state to state, and in particular between "community property" and "equitable distribution" states. (See Chapter 13.)
- **Child support**: In every state, child support is calculated according to that state's Child Support Guidelines formula. (A Guidelines booklet should be available on your state's court system or bar association website. See page 24 regarding how to access the Guidelines booklet and related information.)
- **Judges' discretion**: Judges in most states have broad discretion in deciding family case issues, especially ...
    ○ Non-financial orders regarding children's matters
    ○ Financial orders in equitable distribution states
- **Making your own agreement**: Settlement agreement provisions that differ from what a judge might customarily order will usually be acceptable to the court nevertheless, as long as they
    ○ Are knowingly and voluntarily agreed to
    ○ Don't violate state or federal law or policy
    ○ Aren't clearly unfair under the circumstances
    ○ Don't put spouses, especially custodial parents, at financial risk

---

[13] Each of these basic principles will be covered in later chapters.

Types of Case Law

Decisions by a state's highest appellate court are binding upon trial judges. Decisions by lower appellate courts are binding if the state's highest court has not ruled on an issue. Principles established or refined in a decision by a trial judge, and decisions from other states are known as "persuasive authority" that does not bind other courts in the state.

Note that the names of the appellate courts vary from state to state. Most states' highest courts are called "supreme courts." However, in New York, the Supreme Court is the *lowest* or "trial court," where trials and other hearings are conducted. Go figure.

Where State Divorce Law Comes From

There are two kinds of state laws:

- "Statutory law" (including uniform acts) passed by state legislatures
- "Case law" established by state appellate court judges

State laws can differ regarding

- Legal principles
- The factors judges use in applying legal principles

Here are some examples of significant differences among state laws that will be discussed further in later chapters:

- **Children's Issues:** Your state may have "legal presumptions" like for example, a "presumption" that places the burden of proof on a parent who opposes joint custody of the children.
- **Property Distribution:** Most but not all states define "marital property" to exclude inheritances, gifts, and property owned by one of the spouses prior to the marriage.
- **Child Support:** States differ as to what "deviation criteria" judges can use to award child support that differs from the amount calculated under the Guidelines.

Learning About Divorce in Your State

It's important for you to learn the basics of how divorce works in your state. However, be wary of blogs about divorce law written by:

- Non-lawyers about strictly legal issues
- Lawyers outside your state regarding matrimonial law details

Your state's judicial branch or bar association websites are excellent resources regarding divorce law and procedure in your state. To access them, search either of the following:

- Your state's court system (or judicial "branch" or "department") website
- The American Bar Association's directory of state and local bar associations: http://shop.americanbar.org/ebus/ABAGroups/DivisionforBar-Services/BarAssociationDirectories/StateLocalBarAssociations.aspx

Then, to obtain information on a judicial branch or bar association site, follow the following type of path:[14]

- Select a topic such as
  - "For the public"
  - "Public resources"
  - "On-line help center"
  - "Self-Help"
  - "FAQs"

- Then, select a topic such as
  - "Family Law" or "Family Matters"
  - "Divorce"
  - "Alimony"
  - "Child Support"

If the above doesn't get you to the information you seek, select one of the following:

- An index of publications, videos, etc.
- A link to the state bar's Family Law Section
- A link to a Lawyer Referral Service

---

[14] If selecting your state doesn't work, search "[your state] judicial department" or "[your state] bar association" and proceed from there in the same manner as described above.

Divorce Procedure: The Steps to Your Divorce

In addition to "substantive" law on divorce issues like support and property division, each state (and some counties) have their own procedural law and rules. As with substantive law, there are many similarities among the states regarding how most court-based divorce cases proceed, which is generally as follows:

- **Preparation of initial pleading and related documents** (available on your court system website) including:
  - ○ "Complaint" or "Petition" for dissolution of marriage or legal separation[15]
  - ○ Summons
  - ○ Notice of automatic injunctive orders that prohibit unilateral action regarding finances or the children
  - ○ Temporary or *pendente lite* (Latin for "pending the litigation") motions for court action ("relief") that is needed immediately, such as motions for temporary support or custody, award of attorney's fees, or motions for exclusive possession of the marital residence
  - ○ Notice of *Lis Pendens* or other documents to be served and recorded on the land records in the municipality or county in which real estate is owned by both or one of the spouses, in order to
    - Prevent your STBX from transferring the property
    - Give your divorce claims priority over subsequent creditors

- **Filing with the Court**: In some jurisdictions, "service of process" (see below) occurs before filing. In others, the papers are filed and then served.

- **Service of process**: A sheriff, marshal, or other legally authorized person "serves" (usually by handing the papers to the defendant) the following documents signed by the plaintiff or counsel.
  - ○ The Complaint or Petition for dissolution of marriage.
  - ○ A Summons commanding the defendant to appear in court or respond to the Complaint by a certain date. Note that a requirement to appear in court can generally be satisfied by filing a court form called an "Appearance." Court personnel can assist you with this.
  - ○ Where necessary, the additional documents mentioned above.

In amicable situations in some states, service can be pre-arranged between the process server and the defendant. Also, in some jurisdictions the

---

[15] Some states allow filing of a less formal "letter of complaint."

defendant's lawyer can agree to accept service on behalf of his client. (If you are self-represented, make sure that both service of process and filing—no matter in which order they occur—are completed by the applicable deadlines. Assistant clerks at the courthouse can help you with that.)

- **Preparation of a financial disclosure statement**: (also known as a "financial affidavit" and by other similar names).[16] As discussed in Chapter 8, divorcing parties disclose their financial circumstances on forms that summarize income, expenses, assets, and liabilities. The expense section can be time-consuming to prepare so you should begin working on it as soon as you decide to divorce. The disclosure statement is so important that Chapter 8 is dedicated to it.

- **"Cooling off" period**: During this period that lasts as long as 90 days in some states, the case cannot proceed to judgment. Nevertheless, much can be accomplished during cooling off periods, including
    ○ Preparation and exchange of the parties' financial disclosure statements
    ○ "Discovery" (see below)
    ○ Interim agreements
    ○ In the absence of agreement on pressing issues, hearings on *pendente lite* motions for custody, support, attorney's fees, exclusive possession of marital home, etc.
    ○ Settlement negotiation

- **Status or other Court Conferences**: Depending upon state procedure, these conferences may occur during the cooling off period. At a status conference, the court can refer certain issues to ADR, order custody evaluations, or enlist the assistance of parenting coordinators and discovery referees. Subsequent status conferences with a judge or clerk serve to monitor case progress and can include resolution of disputes regarding discovery and other matters.

- **Discovery**: The process by which information, documents, and other material is exchanged between parties to a lawsuit. Discovery in divorce cases consists primarily of the exchange of financial information and documents, though in cases where custody or responsibility for the breakdown of the marriage is at issue, other types of information and documents can be relevant as well. The most frequently used discovery procedures are ...

---

[16] See Chapter 8 for more on financial disclosure statements.

- ○ **Interrogatories**: Written questions directed to a party to a lawsuit. Unless objections are filed or the parties agree to an extension of time, interrogatories must be answered in writing under oath within a specified period of time such as 30 days. The major drawback of interrogatories, as compared with depositions (see below), is that follow-up questions cannot be asked. States like Illinois and Florida use standardized interrogatories. Litigants can ask additional questions only by court order.
- ○ **Document Requests**: The most frequently used discovery tool, document requests are governed by the same rules as interrogatories. Note that document requests apply to electronically stored documents.
- ○ **Depositions**: Proceedings in the office of the examining lawyer who questions a witness (usually the opposing party) under oath. A court stenographer records the deposition. The expense of two lawyers plus a transcript makes the deposition the most expensive discovery tool. But depositions allow the lawyer to pursue a line of questioning until an answer is obtained. Sending out interrogatories and document requests beforehand can reduce deposition time by eliminating the need to ask already answered questions.
- ○ **Requests For Admissions**: The least often used discovery tool consisting of a list of statements that the responding party must either admit or deny under oath.

- • **Pretrial (settlement) Conference**: An informal proceeding conducted by a judge ("judicial pretrial") or by a pair of court-appointed

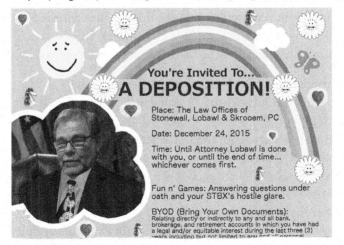

Study the material in Chapter 14 to turn your deposition into a party for you, not for this guy.

matrimonial attorneys sometimes called "special masters." The parties submit financial disclosure statements and often "proposed orders" as well. Counsel and self-represented parties speak briefly in support of the financial and other orders they seek. The pre-trier(s) then recommend how the case should be settled.

- **Uncontested hearing**: If you have settled your case, a judgment or decree dissolving your marriage is entered after a brief hearing at which the allegations in the Complaint are proved, usually by the plaintiff's testimony (see details below). The judge then reviews the parties' settlement agreement for clarity and fairness in light of the financial circumstances reflected on the financial disclosure statements.

- **Trial**: If all attempts to settle the case have failed, evidence including the parties' testimony is presented to the court for adjudication.

From the Bizarro-World Law Dictionary
Complaint \kəm-plānt'\ (1) In many states, the name of the pleading used to commence a divorce proceeding. (2) Dude! You're getting a divorce! Do you really need to know what "complaint" means?

What to Expect at Your Uncontested Hearing

If your divorce case settles as the overwhelming majority of cases do, you will probably be required to attend a final or "uncontested" hearing. Uncontested hearings typically last 15 or 20 minutes. In my state of Connecticut, for example, a judge does the following at an uncontested hearing:

- Receives documentation from the parties including
  - A financial disclosure statement ("financial affidavit") from each party
  - Signed counterpart of the settlement agreement
  - Judgment of Divorce
  - Dissolution of Marriage Report containing statistical information for the State Health Dept.
  - Where applicable,
    - Advisement of rights form informing support recipients of their right to obtain a wage withholding order by which the obligor's

employer deducts the amount of support from the obligor's paycheck and sends it directly to the court or support recipient

- Calculation of child support on a Child Support Guidelines worksheet
- Affidavit regarding custody of children
- Certificate of Completion of Parenting Education Program

- If the defendant is not present, establishes that he/she has been served and has notice of the hearing
- Takes testimony (usually from the plaintiff) to "prove up" the allegations in the Complaint or Petition for dissolution of marriage, including
  - The parties' state of residence
  - The date and place of marriage
  - Names and ages of children of the marriage
  - That the marriage has broken down irretrievably
  - That neither party is receiving public assistance
- Reviews each party's financial affidavit
- Where applicable, reviews the Child Support Guidelines worksheet
- Reviews the settlement agreement and asks questions if necessary to enable the judge to find that the agreement is fair under all the circumstances
- Inquires regarding provision for post-majority educational support (if not covered by the settlement agreement)
- "Canvasses" the parties; i.e., asks each spouse questions such as
  - Have you entered into the Separation Agreement freely, voluntarily, and without duress?
  - Has anyone made any promises that are not contained in the Agreement to induce you to enter into it?
  - Do you fully understand the Agreement?
  - Do you feel that the Agreement is fair under all the circumstances?
  - [If applicable:] Do you understand that by waiving your right to receive alimony now, you cannot come back to court and claim alimony in the future?
- Makes findings on the record that
  - The parties have satisfied the state's residency requirements
  - The parties have established legal entitlement to a dissolution of marriage
  - The parties' settlement or "separation agreement" is fair and reasonable under all the circumstances

- ○ The parties have made suitable provisions for the higher education of their children, or have deferred that decision as permitted under state law
- Restores birth names if requested
- Enters a judgment of dissolution of the marriage and incorporates the separation agreement into the judgment, thus making its terms orders of the court enforceable by the court's contempt power

Caring For Your Children

Many clients worry about how their children will fare during and after their divorce. Certainly not all children are damaged by divorce. A recipe for children emerging from divorce in good health requires the ingredient of parents who:

- Manage their conflict and shield their children from it
- Educate themselves about the basics of child development and shepherding children through divorce
- Agree when and what to tell the children about the divorce (with the help of a therapist or divorce coach if necessary)
- Work cooperatively to quickly resolve all divorce issues
- Stay aware of, and attend to their children's needs

On the other hand children, whether in divorcing or intact families, are at high risk for emotional harm when:

- Parental conflict is intense
- The conflict is witnessed by the children
- The children are the focus of the conflict, as in the case in custody and access battles

Chapter 10 covers methods to build cooperative parenting arrangements that avoid subjecting children to prolonged, acrimonious divorces. In addition, tips for divorce parenting are provided there, including:

- Tell-Tale signs of distress in children
- Do's and don'ts of breaking the news to your children
- Questions your children may ask about your divorce
- Divorce parenting "no-no's"
- Using family therapists and divorce coaches for advice and support

Caring For Yourself

The stress of divorce can pose challenges to your health and well-being. You'll need to be at your best to maximize your divorce results and to support your children during the divorce and afterward. That will take the following, as discussed in more detail in Chapter 16:

- Practice relaxation techniques such as yoga or meditation
- Maintain an exercise schedule
- Keep hydrated and eat regular healthy meals
- Check in with a counselor, therapist or divorce coach
- Avoid isolation
- Get sufficient sleep
- Take free advice for what it's worth
- Have some fun once in a while!

Yes, there *IS* a quiz! Test what you have (or haven't) learned.

1. **The difference between a statute and case law is:**
A. Statutes break when they fall from pedestals.
B. Case law, like anything else that comes by the case, is cheaper.
C. Case law is for those who don't care for potato salad.
D. Statutes are laws passed by state legislatures or Congress, while case law derives from reported decisions by judges.

2. **Unscramble the following key phrases from this chapter!**
olgas mettanest
fatunnolic ridovec
scetenutdotn hragien
dilch poputrs snideluige

CHAPTER 2

Divorce Fact-Checking

"It ain't what you don't know that gets you into trouble. It's what you know for sure that just ain't so."

— Mark Twain

Separating the Wheat From the Cow Chips

This chapter contains basic facts about divorce that you probably didn't know. You may also learn that some of the things you thought you knew about divorce are not accurate. At the end of the chapter you'll find vital truths to bear in mind throughout your divorce—perhaps most importantly: *This Too Shall Pass.*

Divorce BS and Semi-BS

We'll start with the myths. Many folks believe the following statements to be universally true, though none of them are:

"'No-fault divorce' means that family law judges cannot take into consideration the reason a marriage broke down."

FALSE. No-fault divorce means that a spouse is entitled to a divorce without misconduct by the other spouse. Nonetheless, in a number of states the reason for the breakdown of the marriage remains one of the factors a judge can consider when making financial orders. Judges are most likely to take notice when a spouse's conduct is "egregious," such as an extramarital affair that

- Puts the children at risk
- Is flaunted in a way that humiliates the other spouse

- Involves diverting money to a paramour
- Involves other wrongdoing such as concealing or wasting assets

"In community property states, everything gets split 50/50."

FALSE. In community property states, property acquired prior to the marriage or received by inheritance or gift, is separate or "non-marital property," which remains with its owner. Although the remaining marital property is typically divided evenly, extraordinary circumstances can sometimes alter the 50/50 split, even of marital property (See Chapter 12.)

Where No-Fault Divorce REALLY Began

California is considered to have begun the era of "easy divorce" with its 1969 "no-fault" divorce law. But 100 years earlier, divorce may have been even easier to get in Mississippi, where being an idiot at the time of marriage was a ground for divorce. Which, a cynic might say, would have made divorce available to just about all of us!

"In equitable distribution states, everything gets split 50/50."

FALSE. "Equitable distribution" means a fair division of property. That's not necessarily the same as an equal division. Judges in equitable distribution states have the discretion to apply some or all of a number of factors in making financial orders. In addition, many equitable distribution states treat inheritances and property acquired prior to the marriage as separate property that may not be distributed in divorce.

"I don't need a lawyer to figure out child support because any dope can look it up on a Child Support Guidelines chart."

FALSE. It helps if that dope is a lawyer, because it isn't quite that simple. "Deviation criteria" can render Guidelines inapplicable. A spouse's real income on which support is based can be hotly disputed—especially a self-employed spouse's income. Even accurate numbers entered in the wrong spots on Guideline worksheets can create "garbage in, garbage out."

*"If I give up my ownership interest in my home,
I'm no longer responsible for the mortgage."*

FALSE. Such a transfer does not affect your liability to your mortgage lender. The same applies to car loans and other "secured debts."

*"Child and spousal support obligations
can be avoided by filing for bankruptcy."*

FALSE. Neither is dischargeable in bankruptcy. To preserve other support-related obligations against discharge, support recipients' lawyers sometimes classify as "support" obligations such as contribution to
* The support recipient's health insurance premiums
* The support recipient's attorneys' fees.

*"My spouse and I can save on legal fees by
having one lawyer represent both of us."*

FALSE. Lawyers can only represent one spouse in a divorce. The other spouse is self-represented.

*"'Legal separation' is living apart from your
spouse pursuant to a written agreement."*

FALSE. A legal separation is a lawsuit or "action" like a divorce or "dissolution of marriage" action. It is the same as a divorce in that all financial and child-related issues are resolved, and an enforceable judgment is entered incorporating the spouses' agreement or a judge's decision. The difference between legal separation and divorce is that legally separated individuals may not remarry.

If you live in Colorado or North Dakota, "marital agreements" entered into during marriage are governed by The Uniform Premarital & Marital Agreements Act (UPMAA). Other states that have not adopted UPMAA nevertheless honor such agreements in certain circumstances. These agreements resemble what people often think of as "legal separation."

"My STBX is not entitled to any of my pension."

FALSE. The federal statute known as "ERISA" contains exceptions to the general rule that protects pensions from claims by creditors and other third parties. One of those exceptions permits distribution of pension benefits as part of a divorce settlement pursuant to a court order known as a qualified domestic relations order or "QDRO" (pronounced "Kwah-dro").

"'Joint custody' means that parents divide evenly their time with the children."

MOSTLY FALSE. This is true in Louisiana, Georgia, and Arizona. In most states, however, a joint custody order can specify anything from a 50/50 division of child-time to the often used arrangement of primary residence with one parent and every Wednesday evening and alternating weekends with the other.

Note that the term "custody" can be confusing because it can refer to either
- "Legal custody," meaning decision-making, and/or
- "Physical custody," meaning where, when and with which parent the children will reside and spend time. (See Chapter 10.)

"Children benefit when parents 'insulate' them from the divorce."

HALF TRUE. There is a difference between shielding children from the antagonisms of divorce and insulating them from it altogether. It is impossible to "insulate" children from their parents' divorce. And even if insulation were possible, children don't need or want it. Parents who feel they are helping their children by refusing to discuss the divorce, may instead be raising the children's anxiety levels by depriving them of necessary information.[1]

"Children have the resilience to bounce back from child-related litigation."

HALF TRUE. Many children are resilient, but certainly not all of them. And high conflict divorces pose challenges to even the most resilient child.

Studies of children who experience high conflict between their parents, show high incidences of emotional disorder. That experience is particularly damaging in custody battles that place children squarely on the battlefield.

---

[1] The child-related myths discussed here are exposed in the author's Telly award-winning short dramatic film *Talk to Strangers*. Visit www.childcustodyfilm.com.

"If the adults act appropriately during
custody litigation, the children will be fine."

MOSTLY UNTRUE. Some experts feel that custody battles place children unnecessarily at risk except in situations that require court intervention such as those involving abuse, neglect, or untreated mental illness and substance abuse. Child-related litigation can take a toll on children even where parents are not overly antagonistic. And even proper conduct by parents and professionals doesn't guarantee that children will emerge unscathed. Custody litigation is a war, and children are its prisoners.

"The custody evaluation process is designed
to protect children and is implemented by
professionals acting on the children's behalf."

HALF TRUE. While the professionals generally do try to protect children, the process is not designed for that purpose. It is designed to gather information for the court. This unavoidably requires intrusion into children's lives and privacy.

Neither court services personnel, attorneys for minor children (AMCs), guardians *ad litem* (GALs), parenting coordinators nor mental health professionals can protect children from the intrusions, humiliations, and untenable situations that are unavoidable in contested custody cases.

"Judges protect children
during custody battles."

HALF TRUE. Judges protect children when they can. However, judges don't supervise the custody evaluation process that precedes a trial. By the time a judge hears a custody case, that process has been completed and children may have been humiliated, compromised, and frightened along the way.

Seanan Michael Ellis ("Nicky Sherwood") in Talk to Strangers. Photo by Kitryn Ellis

"Lawyers are not allowed to testify in court."

MOSTLY TRUE. As a rule, only witnesses are permitted to testify in court. However, there are 2 instances in which lawyers can be said to testify.

- Lawyers appointed as guardians *ad litem* of children in custody cases may be questioned about what custody arrangement or parenting plan they feel is in a child's best interests and why. The role of lawyers acting as GALs in such situations is similar to that of an expert witness.
- Skilled lawyers use "leading questions" to in effect testify when they cross-examine a witness. Leading questions
  ○ Contain the cross-examiner's conclusions or versions of facts
  ○ Can be answered "yes" or "no"

Cross-examiners typically press witnesses to either agree or disagree with the facts or conclusions in the question by answering it either "yes" or "no." When a witness agrees with those facts or conclusions, the cross-examiner's words have become the witness's testimony. For example:

Attorney Stonewall: So, you sold your jewelry and placed the proceeds in a bank account that you failed to tell your spouse about, correct?

The Witness: I wasn't trying to hide ...

Attorney Stonewall: Can you answer that question "yes" or "no?"

The Witness: Yes.

In Chapter 13, you will learn how to handle leading questions and other aggressive cross-examination techniques.

Divorce BT (Basic Truths)

Here are some important truths about divorce that are often overlooked:

- Being organized won't guarantee that your divorce will proceed efficiently; but being disorganized pretty much guarantees that it won't.
- Asking your lawyer questions throughout the process is critical to maximizing your results.
- Your divorce will give you the opportunity to be a hero to your children by placing their interests above your conflict with your STBX, and by sparing them as much of that conflict as possible.
- Your divorce should also give you the "break-opportunities" to learn or improve important life skills such as
  ○ Parenting
  ○ Communicating effectively in pressure situations
  ○ Budgeting and managing personal finance

- The vast majority of divorce cases are settled. Your case is much more likely to be settled if you
  - Think in terms of your "interests" rather than "positions"
  - Take the high road by avoiding petty disputes
  - Work hard at cooperative parenting
  - Avoid the dozen biggest divorce mistakes listed at the end of Chapter 3
- "This too shall pass:" Keep your spirits up with the knowledge that
  - Your divorce will end
  - You can emerge from it better able to meet life's challenges

---

 Yes, there *IS* a quiz! Test what you have (or haven't) learned.

1. This Chapter is mainly about:
A. Mark Twain's cow chips
B. How to pronounce "QDRO"
C. How many lawyers it takes to spell "QDRO"
D. Distinguishing divorce facts from myths

2. Unscramble the following key phrases from this chapter!
tooverpieca gipennart
yimcunotm yetrpop
diagnaur da mitel
quebaltie tutsinidibor

CHAPTER 3

Divorce Pearls and Perils: Secrets of Saving Money and Avoiding Mistakes

"The wound is the place where the light enters you."

— Rumi

There won't be rainbows at the end of your divorce, and probably not any pots of gold. But along the way, there *will* be some golden opportunities to save money and maximize your divorce results.

In this chapter you'll learn how to take advantage of those opportunities... and how to avoid screwing it all up.

Find the Quality Lawyer Bargain Table!

It's true! There *is* a bargain table out there of quality divorce lawyers who:

- Have practiced principally or exclusively in the field of family law for at least the last 5 years
- Have been trained at either
  - ○ A small "boutique" matrimonial law firm that specializes in family cases, or
  - ○ The matrimonial department of a larger law firm
- Are still firm associates and thus charge substantially less than the firm's partners
- Combine
  - ○ Youthful energy
  - ○ A caring relationship with clients
  - ○ Mentorship by some of the better family lawyers in the area
  - ○ Their own family law experience, which exceeds that of many general practitioners who have been members of the bar for far longer

In Chapter 4 we'll discuss how to find these Bargain Babies!

When More Can Be Less: Learn About "Effective Billing Rates"

Q. When is a 3-minute call to a lawyer who charges $300/hr., more expensive than the same call to a $400/hr. attorney?

A. When Attorney $300 charges in increments of 2/10 of an hour ($60 for 3 minutes) and Attorney $400 charges in 1/10 hr. increments ($40 for 3 minutes). See page 57 to learn how to cope with incremental billing.

Discover the Secret Fount of Family Law Knowledge

Here's how to find lawyers who know your state's family law as well as anyone:

- On your state bar association's website, find "Sections & Committees"
- Select The Family Law Section or similarly named committee
- Find the meeting minutes and locate the names of lawyers who regularly present "recent developments," OR
- Call the office of one of the Section officers and ask for the names of the Family Law Section members who present programs on recent developments in the law.[1]

Learn the Witness's Magic Word

Witnesses can stop a cross-examining attorney in his tracks with a single word: "speculation." For example: "I would just be speculating if I answered that question." Judges don't allow speculation because it has no "probative value." See Chapter 14.

---

[1] If you feel compelled to give a reason for your call, tell the staff person that you are researching an article on Cross-Frontier Surrogacy Issues under the Hague Abduction Convention. That should prevent any of the firm's lawyers from trying to sign you up as a client!

Save Attorneys' Fees With Good Timing

You can save some money by delaying hiring a lawyer for a short period of time while you:

- File for divorce yourself using forms available on your state's court system website
- Consult a certified divorce planner or certified divorce financial analyst to
  - Help you organize your financial paperwork
  - Help you prepare your financial disclosure statement
  - Discuss with you other divorce-related issues such as pensions, alimony deductions, etc.
- Consult a certified divorce coach, if necessary, regarding organizing for divorce and dealing with non-financial issues

Note that this approach is advisable only in the following circumstances:

- You have consulted with a matrimonial attorney who has advised you that there are no pressing matters that require immediate legal representation such as *pendente lite* (temporary) support or custody issues
- You and your children are not at risk of harm
- You have very little funds available for attorneys' fees
- There are experienced CDPs or CDFAs in your area
- You understand that divorce coaches, unlike attorneys, can be required to disclose clients' oral and written communications

Finally, note that there is a related option called "unbundled," "discrete task," or "consulting attorney" representation. In an unbundled representation arrangement, you hire a lawyer to handle only certain parts of your case. Unbundled pros and cons are discussed in Chapter 4.

Settle Your Case Quicker and Cheaper

Fifty years ago, a song called *"What the World Needs Now Is Love"* assured us that love was the only thing the world needed more of.

Not to nitpick, but love isn't the *only* thing the world has too little of. These days, it seems there's an increasingly short supply of empathy as well. And *lack* of empathy can be a serious hindrance to settling your case, whether you choose ADR or a court-based divorce.

Spouses who use empathy to understand and identify with each other's emotions and attitudes have a decided advantage in settling their cases.

Borrowing from another lyric, if you can "walk a mile in your (spouse's) shoes," you're likely to arrive at "yes" that much faster, easier and cheaper. Try to experience emotions and attitudes such as anxiety or entitlement that your spouse may have regarding certain issues. The resulting insights can be of tremendous assistance to you during settlement negotiation.

Staying True to Yourself; Random Acts of Kindness

"You will not be punished for your anger.
You will be punished by your anger."
— The Buddha

It's all too easy during divorce to let anger and anxiety "get the best of you." But that can only hurt you, your children, and your chances for a functional divorce that resolves issues fairly and efficiently.

Besides hindering your ability to achieve your divorce goals, giving in to the divorce furies can leave you feeling out of balance and can even affect your health. You have the responsibility to try to protect your children and your financial future. But try not to let those efforts obscure principles that guide your life.

It won't always be easy. At times, adherence to the Golden Rule, the Buddhist concept of *metta* ("loving kindness"), or a similar creed may seem impossible or senseless. One great way to reconnect with the "best of you" in those tougher moments is through "random acts of kindness." It's amazing how helping out another, even ever so briefly, can help put things back in perspective and get you feeling better about yourself.

Try it! What have you got to lose?

Mess Makes Stress

As noted in Chapter 2, being organized won't guarantee a functional divorce; but a lack of organization usually assures that it won't be. Divorce requires you to get a grip on your finances. Use that as a "break-upportunity" to become more organized and thus more efficient and less stressed during your divorce and afterward by:

• Managing your time more efficiently with electronic To-Be-Done lists linked to smart-phone calendars with reminder alerts

- Using personal finance software such as MoneyDance or Quicken
- Handling paperwork (once) with "one-touch" paper management techniques
- Organizing correspondence, bills, and account statements in color-coded folders
- Keeping that stress-inducing cluttered desktop clear!

Your Lawyer's Secret Weapon: You

In a foreign world of lawyers and judges, you can claim expertise on at least one subject: your spouse. Your knowledge of your spouse can be key in developing an effective negotiation strategy and, if necessary, helping your lawyer prepare for depositions and court proceedings. (See Chapter 7.)

Don't wait for your lawyer to ask you for this information. Schedule a meeting so that you can share it *before* negotiation sessions, depositions or contested hearings. At the meeting, tell your lawyer what you know about your spouse's communication style and his/her relevant personality traits such as motivations and vulnerabilities. Clients can be a terrific resource for lawyers, but only if they are proactive in telling what they know.

"Yes Virginia, There Are Bad Lawyers Out There."

In Chapter 4, you'll learn why the best sources of divorce lawyer recommendations can be their colleagues and other professionals. Of course, a lawyer's clients are also on the list of referral sources. But you'll be cautioned that clients' perceptions of their lawyer's competence are sometimes distorted.

That doesn't mean clients' opinions aren't valuable. On the contrary, they are indispensable regarding matters about which a lawyer's colleagues may know very little. Information from clients about a lawyer's billing practices and responsiveness to clients will be key considerations in your decision whether to retain that lawyer.

For example, you may hear about "divorce mills"—firms that bill out huge amounts of attorney and paralegal time for tasks like document scanning, copying, organizing, analyzing, and review that you can do yourself.[2] And clients can become stuck with such a firm, especially late in cases when it's

- Too close to a trial date to find a lawyer willing to take the case, or
- Prohibitively expensive to start over with a new lawyer

---

[2] See page 100 to learn how to "Be Your Own Paralegal."

You can learn about another key issue by asking former clients: "How is your relationship with your co-parent now? If it's poor, to what extent, if any, did your lawyer contribute to that?"

Don't hire a lawyer until you've spoken with current or former clients regarding the lawyer's billing practices and how the attorney/client relationship worked for the clients.

Divorce Math: Making Sure the Numbers Don't Lie

Sometimes property settlements are tweaked or "adjusted" for money or other property a spouse has already received. Be sure to analyze such adjustments carefully to make sure that what *appears* to be fair... really is.

For example, let's say that during your case you and your spouse agree that you can take $3,000 from a joint bank account for a down payment on a car to replace yours that just died. Subsequently, you agree on a settlement that divides evenly your joint bank accounts. However, your spouse's lawyer argues that your spouse should get an extra $3,000 in order to balance out the $3,000 you already received.

Sounds reasonable, but is it? *No!*

Since you are dividing your cash 50/50, half of the $3,000 you received would have been yours anyway. So your spouse is entitled not to an extra $3,000 but to 50% of that, or $1,500.

The best way to understand and test the accuracy of a divorce calculation is to plug in actual numbers. In our example, let's assume that before you got the $3,000, the joint bank accounts totaled $80,000. Had you divided the $80,000 back then, you and your spouse each would have received $40,000 (50% of $80,000). However, because you already received $3,000, each of you now gets only $38,500 ($77,000 x 50%).

The question is how much extra must your spouse receive in order to get the same $40,000 he/she would have received if you had never taken the $3,000. The answer is the difference between 40,000 and $38,500, which is $1,500, *not* $3,000.

To double-check that answer, look at your side of the ledger. If you add the $3,000 you received earlier to the $37,000 ($38,500 - $1,500 going to your spouse) you are getting now, the total is the $40,000 you would have got had you not received the $3,000.

Now splash some cold water on your face before your head explodes.

Handling Spouses With Personality Disorders

Divorcing someone with borderline personality disorder or narcissistic personality disorder can be especially challenging. Both personality types are likely to exhibit rage during divorce.

Narcissists in particular often react furiously when confronted with divorce. Many of them use the adversarial system as an excuse to act abusively toward spouses who will no longer tolerate their controlling behavior. Principal breadwinners may threaten to quit working to avoid paying support. Parents who have been relatively detached from their children may threaten a custody battle.

For additional information, see Chapter 10 regarding handling difficult spouses in child-related matters, and the resources provided in Chapter 17 under the heading "Dealing with Domestic Violence and Impaired Spouses."

There is no panacea here, but the following should help you prepare for extreme behavior from your spouse and to handle it better:

- Seek counseling to reinforce your feelings of self-worth. This will help counter a narcissistic spouse's attempts to demean and control you. A therapist can also assist you in coping with your spouse by, for example, learning to ignore gratuitous slights and insults, and avoiding unrealistic attempts to appease or change his/her behavior.
- Agree with your lawyer on a plan to establish firm rules and boundaries for your spouse. One way to accomplish that is by obtaining *pendente lite* support orders at the beginning of your case. Your lawyer must also be prepared to rebut your spouse's false claims about you that can plague you throughout your case.
- Get everything in writing. Make sure that any agreements or "stipulations" reached during the divorce contain enough detail to avoid your spouse "gaming the system." Ask the court to enter orders in accordance with any major agreements so that they can be quickly enforced.
- Don't give up on the possibility of mediation especially regarding children's issues that should be resolved outside the courthouse if at all possible. Not everyone who exhibits characteristics of a personality disorder

suffers from one. The severity of these personality traits varies. So it may be possible to find a mediator who commands enough respect from your spouse to enable issues to be resolved. (See Chapter 5.)

- If circumstances permit, consider asking for a meeting with your spouse and his/her therapist to come up with a game plan to help you both get through the divorce.

A Dozen of Divorce's Biggest Perils

Now let's discuss what *not* to do in your divorce. A functional divorce avoids the following serious mistakes:

- <u>Placing your goals ahead of your children's interests</u>. When your goals clash with what is best for your children, the children should come first.

- <u>Choosing the wrong divorce method</u>. If both you and your STBX wish to achieve a fair result more quickly and at less expense, you would be foolish not to consider alternative dispute resolution (ADR), which is discussed in Chapter 5. Conversely, if your STBX is "out for blood" and not open to ADR, choosing a lawyer who is not an experienced litigator could be a costly error.

- <u>Not using a lawyer even though you can afford to</u>. Failure to at least consult with a lawyer at the beginning of your divorce reduces your chances for a successful outcome. In the chapters that follow, you will learn many ways to limit attorneys' fees that don't require eliminating lawyers altogether, such as ADR and unbundled representation.

- <u>Failing to investigate your self-employed STBX's "real earnings."</u> See Chapter 8 on analyzing disclosure statements.

- <u>Trading property in your settlement that is *not* subject to tax, for property that *is* taxable</u>, such as
  o Retirement assets that are taxed upon withdrawal (and subject to a 10% penalty for early withdrawal *if* unrelated to the divorce)

- ° Stocks with low cost bases, subject to capital gains tax upon sale
- ° Depreciated rental real estate, subject to capital gains tax upon sale

- <u>Telling your lawyer only part of the story.</u> Facts you neglect to share with your lawyer have a habit of popping up at the worst possible times... like during depositions and court hearings.

- <u>Driving yourself nuts with advice from sources other than qualified professionals.</u> Accept helpful emotional support, *not* legal advice, from friends and family members. As a matter of common sense, you should avoid divorce advice from non-divorce professionals. But even emotional support can have a downside, which is why I use the phrase "*helpful* emotional support." Your friends and family are likely to "take your side" during divorce. That loyalty may well comfort you. But if coupled with animosity toward your spouse, it can increase and prolong the conflict between you. And *that* can delay or even prevent resolution of the legal, financial and emotional divorce issues that will allow you and your children to begin moving on with your lives. Finally, be wary of divorce websites and blogs that misstate or overgeneralize legal concepts that might not apply to your case in the first place.

- <u>Adhering to rigid "positions"</u> rather than identifying what you need and how best to get it.

- <u>Failing to put together a reasonable set of goals.</u> Even if you mediate or represent yourself, you should obtain legal advice to ensure that your goals are sensible and achievable. Don't fight for a house that you can't carry, or demand a parenting schedule that you can't live up to.

- <u>Allowing emotion to cloud your judgment.</u> Understand the difference between "emotional divorce" and the "legal divorce" process that requires you to understand and deal with legal and financial matters as dispassionately as possible.[3] Don't try to resolve the issues in your divorce if you are in early stages of grief that can hinder your ability to think clearly and make decisions thoughtfully. There's too much at stake to allow anxiety or other emotions to affect those decisions, or to cause you to sacrifice important long-term needs for lesser, short-term ones.

- <u>"Giving in."</u> If you think you might become intimidated by your STBX or exhausted by the divorce process, choose a strong advocate or

---

[3] Visit http://www.divorcemag.com/articles/the-grief-progression to learn more about "emotional divorce."

proactive mediator who will not permit strong-arm tactics or fatigue to dictate results.

- Failing to educate yourself about divorce. Your state's judicial department and/or bar association websites will have material regarding divorce in your state. Check out also the resources listed in Chapter 17.

 Yes, there *IS* a quiz! Test what you have (or haven't) learned.

1. **This chapter is mainly about:**
   A. Ponce de Leon and The Fountain of Youthful Lawyers
   B. Finding your STBX's pot of gold
   C. The penalty for early withdrawal that you wish someone had told you about before you got married
   D. Saving money during divorce and avoiding common divorce mistakes

2. **The legal term *"pendente lite"* is Latin for:**
   A. "Cheap necklace"
   B. An ornament for your Pendente Holiday Tree
   C. A beer popular among courthouse clerks
   D. "Pending the litigation," a term used to designate requests and court orders entered on a temporary basis in family court cases

CHAPTER 4

Choosing the *Right* Divorce Lawyer For You

"Experience is the name everyone gives to their mistakes."
— Oscar Wilde

Your Two Most Important Divorce Decisions

The list of your most important divorce decisions is a short one:

- How do you choose between a traditional ("court-based") divorce and an "ADR" divorce?
- How do you choose the right (and affordable) lawyer for you?

We'll cover lawyer affordability later in the chapter. For now, let's assume that you're hiring a lawyer to handle your entire *court-based* case, or parts of it in an "unbundled representation" arrangement (see below).

The two decisions above are related. There are some skills that all lawyers need. But "court-based" and alternative dispute resolution (ADR) lawyers require different skill subsets. Thus, your choice of a lawyer will depend on whether your divorce is court-based or ADR.

In Chapter 5, we'll discuss the significant advantages of ADR and the skills that mediators and other ADR practitioners must have. If you're uncertain about the type of divorce that is right for you, skip ahead to Chapter 5.

This chapter covers:

- Qualifications that all lawyers should have
- Qualifications that are of particular importance for *court-based* lawyers

Choosing a Traditional "Court-Based" Lawyer

A court-based lawyer's negotiating and courtroom skills can be game-changers. However, less readily apparent skills such as the ability to listen to clients and to understand their needs are also important. Those skills will affect clients not only emotionally but financially as well, because good attorney/client relations save legal fees. Likewise, a lawyer's organizational skills and use of support staff can speed up (or slow down) the progress of your case, and thus reduce (or increase) its cost.

Skills and Attributes to Consider in Choosing a Divorce Lawyer

Below is a list of qualities to consider when choosing a lawyer.

- Knowledge and experience regarding family law
- The power of persuasion
- Family law credentials and reputation
- Law firm affiliation: solo practitioners vs. firm members
- Compatibility, communication skills, and empathy
- Toughness vs. practicality
- Professionalism regarding opposing counsel, clients, and clients' children
- Reasonable fees
- The "X Factor": WISDOM

This list merits further explanation, so here it is:

Knowledge and Experience Regarding Family Law

Keep the following in mind regarding a court-based lawyer's experience.

- You want a lawyer whose practice has been dedicated at least 75% to family law for the last 5 years or more in your jurisdiction.
- The lawyer must have substantial experience with cross-examination and evidentiary rules acquired while handling contested matters.
- Age doesn't necessarily mean family law experience, because

- Some young attorneys in law firm matrimonial departments may have more trial experience than general practitioners who have practiced longer, and
- An increasing number of lawyers have chosen law as a second career

You can find out how long a lawyer has been practicing law at http://www.avvo.com.

The Power of Persuasion

A lawyer's "job #1" is to persuade opposing counsel in settlement negotiations, or a judge in court. To help you assess a lawyer's persuasive powers, ask yourself the following during an initial consultation:

- Does the lawyer appear confident?
- Does the lawyer command respect?
- Is the lawyer knowledgeable about family law?
- Is the lawyer easy to understand?
- Does the lawyer respond fully to questions?
- Does anything about the lawyer's manner suggest a lack of sincerity or sense of perspective?

Family Law Credentials and Reputation

A diploma from a top law school does not guarantee competence. Nor does any single credential. Recommendations from a local lawyer or other professional whom you trust are more useful. One measure of a lawyer's standing in the profession is her "peer review rating" at www.martindale.com. Look for lawyers with "AV" or "BV" ratings who list divorce or family law as a specialty.

The two best credentials for divorce lawyers are

- American Academy of Matrimonial Lawyers (AAML) membership
- Certification as a specialist in family/matrimonial law or family trial advocacy in the states that offer it, namely[1]
  - California
  - Ohio
  - Florida
  - Indiana
  - Louisiana

---

[1]A number of other states allow private organizations to certify attorneys.

° New Jersey
° New Mexico
° North Carolina
° Texas

The Ideal Credentials Bundle

Chances are your case does not require the best divorce lawyer around. Unless your circumstances are unusually complex, there may be many family lawyers in your area who can handle your case quite competently.

But if you are looking for the *very best*, a lawyer with the credentials listed below might qualify. Your biggest challenge would most likely be affording his or her fees.

* Personal recommendation by at least one unaffiliated lawyer
* Martindale Hubbell AV rating
* Contributor to recognized family law publications and lecturer to legal groups
* AAML Membership
* Where available, certification as family law specialist

Law Firm Affiliation: Solo Practitioners vs. Firm Members

The advantage of hiring a "solo" practitioner is "what you see is what you get." You won't be surprised by some kid you've never met "pinch-hitting" for your lawyer at an important hearing.[2]

On the other hand, you save money when a law firm associate with a lower hourly rate than your lawyer, handles a routine court status conference.

Law firms also may have lawyers who can consult with yours regarding other areas of the law—and bill you for their time. A solo conferring with an unaffiliated colleague can get the same advice, and you're less likely to be billed for the colleague's time.

---

[2] However, if you are considering a solo practitioner, make sure there is experienced support staff to help you when the lawyer is unavailable.

If you hire a member of a firm, request that no one else handle settlement negotiations or substantive hearings, and that your lawyer won't involve her partners in your case unless you agree to it.[3]

Compatibility, Communication Skills, and Empathy

You know how some people just don't seem to be on your wavelength? Make sure your lawyer isn't one of them. Clear communication is a must in the attorney/client relationship. To facilitate that, be sure to ask your lawyer questions. Miscommunication leads to misunderstandings, hurt feelings, and smoldering resentments. If that's what you're after, just stay married.

Don't use your lawyer as a therapist. Mental health professionals, including qualified divorce coaches, do it better and cheaper. At the same time, you may prefer a lawyer who displays at least a little empathy. Measure your need for empathy with the three questions below. If you answer question #1 "yes" and questions #2 & 3 "no," you might need a lawyer who is not averse to a little handholding.

The Divorce Need-o-Meter:
Measuring Your Empathy Needs

1. Am I likely to need periodic reassurances on matters such as the following?
   A. My children will be okay
   B. I will be able to deal with new financial realities.
   C. My life will return to normalcy
2. Do I have a therapist or counselor, and/or trusted friends and family members who can help me stay in emotional balance during my divorce?
3. Do I have experience in dealing with lawyers, litigation, or divorce that will make me more comfortable with the process?

Toughness vs. Practicality

You want a lawyer who can be tough *when necessary*. Experienced matrimonial lawyers aren't pushovers, but lawyers known for toughness alone often don't serve their clients' needs. You want an *assertive* lawyer, not a needlessly *aggressive* one. Keep in mind that adaptability and practicality are always essential.

---

[3] Solely for the sake of uniformity, I will refer to your lawyer in the feminine. References to opposing counsel and mediators will be in the masculine. Gender references to judges will be all over the lot... a little like some judges I know.

Be wary of the lawyer called "the barracuda" or the one known as the nastiest SOB with a briefcase. Lawyers with those reputations too often prolong the hostilities at their clients' financial and emotional expense. Moreover, tough guy/gal posturing angers judges who can do without Cruella de Vil blowing smoke out her "*porte-cigarette.*"

The barracuda is not your best choice.

The vast majority of divorce cases are settled. Settlement nearly always saves money and emotional wear and tear for parents and children. Don't hinder settlement by hiring an unreasonable lawyer. Seek one with empathy, perspective and other aspects of "emotional intelligence."[4]

Professionalism With Regard to Opposing Counsel, Clients, and Clients' Children

Courtroom battles occasionally create hard feelings between lawyers. That's *their* problem unless those feelings turn your case into a jousting match between Lord Paynenthass and Lady Stigget-Enyorair. It's unprofessional for lawyers to let grudges cloud their judgment or conduct. Ask your lawyer if she has any problem with the lawyer on the other side. If so, find out the extent of it. Seek an assurance that the lawyers' problem won't become yours.

Your lawyer should treat you respectfully as well. She should also be protective of your children. That means that her tactics should not unnecessarily expose your children to risk of emotional harm.[5]

"Reasonable legal fees" (is there such a thing?)

Divorces cost too much, especially court-based divorces. In Chapter 6, we'll discuss how to work with your lawyer in a way that will limit legal fees. Before you choose that lawyer, however, gather information regarding:
- *Hourly rates.* The great majority of divorce lawyers charge by the hour. How *much* a lawyer charges per hour depends on factors such as experience, reputation, and location. Learn the range of divorce lawyers'

---

[4] For more on emotional intelligence and divorce lawyers, see http://www.markbaeresq.com/Press.aspx.
[5] If your spouse seems intent on battling over child-related issues, use the *Talk to Strangers* short film and parents' guide to help dissuade him/her. Visit www.childcustodyfilm.com.

hourly rates in your area by speaking with divorcing or recently divorced friends, and by contacting some local law firms.

- ⚠ *Billing Increments.* Most lawyers do not charge for the actual number of minutes they devote to a task, but rather for the portion or "increment" of an hour they spend. Increments usually consist of either one-tenth (.1) or two-tenths (.2) of an hour. For tasks that take only a few minutes, incremental billing produces charges at rates that exceed a lawyer's stated hourly rate. The section immediately below on "effective hourly rates" explains why that happens, and what you can do to avoid at least some of those excess charges.
- *Retainers.* Make sure that your fee agreement provides that any unused portion of your retainer will be refunded to you.
- *Hourly Rate Changes.* Find out if the initial hourly rates for your lawyer, paralegals, etc. will remain in effect throughout the case. If not, consider requesting that the rates not be raised for a minimum amount of time such as 6 or 9 months.
- *Location.* Lawyers in affluent communities may charge more than comparable lawyers with offices in more modest areas. There's no need to pay a premium for your lawyer's fancy digs or upscale locale.

⚠ Also, if you are choosing between two otherwise comparable lawyers, limit billings for travel time by selecting the one whose office is closer to the courthouse.

Dealing With Minimum Charges: The *"Effective Hourly Rate"*

Question: When does a 3-minute call from a divorce lawyer who charges $300 per hour cost *MORE* than the same call from a $400/hr. attorney?

Answer: When the $300/hr. lawyer charges in increments of 2/10 of an hour, and the $400/hr. lawyer charges in 1/10 increments.

Wait ... *WHAT?*

Based solely on their hourly rates, you would expect "Attorney 300" to charge you $15.00 for that 3-minute call, and "Attorney 400" to charge $20.00.

But they won't.

Why? Because like most lawyers, they charge in increments. "Attorney 400" charges in increments of 1/10 (.1) of an hour (6 minutes), and "Attorney 300" uses increments of 2/10 (.2) of an hour (12 minutes).

You know how the interest rate on your credit card isn't what you actually pay? That's because banks base interest charges on something other than your card's overdue balance. Most lawyers' hourly rates aren't what you actually pay either. That's because lawyers base their charges on something other than the actual time they spend; namely, increments.

The reason incremental billing adds to your bill is that when lawyers bill in 6 or 12-minute increments, those increments become *minimum charges*. A lawyer using .1 increments charges a minimum of 6 minutes for anything she does on your case—even if it only takes 2 or 3 minutes. And a lawyer using .2 increments, bills even more in extra fees—a minimum of 12 minutes!

Put another way, clients pay more than their lawyer's hourly rate every time a .1 increment lawyer spends less than 6 minutes on a task, or a .2 lawyer spends less than 12 minutes.

Incremental billing creates another problem as well. Because the 6 and 12-minute minimum charges alter lawyers' hourly rates, they make it difficult to compare what different lawyers will actually charge you. A more useful tool for comparison is what I call the lawyer's "*effective* hourly rate" (EHR). EHR takes into account both a lawyer's hourly rate *and* the increments in which she charges.

To illustrate how EHR works, let's use the 3-minute phone call mentioned above.

"Attorney 400," who charges in .1 increments, will charge $40.00 for that call: $400 x .1 = $40.00 ($13.33 per minute).

But "Attorney 300," who charges in .2 increments, will charge *$60.00* for the same 3 minutes: $300 x .2 = $60.00 ($20.00/minute)!

To compare the two lawyers' 3-minute EHRs, simply multiply their per-minute charges by the 60 minutes in an hour. That yields a 3-minute EHR (are you sitting down?) of $800/hr. for "Attorney 400" and $1,200/hr. for "Attorney 300."

While your heartbeat is returning to normal, remember that EHR and hourly rates generally differ only as to tasks that take less than 6 minutes for

.1 increment billers, and less than 12 minutes for .2 increment billers. For example, EHR doesn't apply to a half-hour meeting because it exceeds both the 6 and 12-minute minimum charges. Thus regular hourly rates will accurately measure the cost of that meeting at $200.00 for "Attorney 400" and $150.00 for "Attorney 300."

Nevertheless, minimum charges do add up. While they won't make "Attorney 400" cheaper than "Attorney 300" over the course of a divorce, they will substantially narrow the difference in cost between "Attorney 300" and a lawyer who charges $350.00/hr. but uses .1 increments.

You can't entirely eliminate the extra fees generated by incremental billing. But you can reduce them by:

- Finding out what increments a lawyer uses *before* retaining him. As our example shows, 12-minute increment billers rack up substantially more in extra fees than 6-minute billers. And very few of those 12-minute billers hit enough home runs to be entitled to that big a bonus. If you're considering a 12-minute minimum lawyer, make sure the extra charges will be offset by a lower hourly rate, special expertise, or some other benefit.
- Avoid generating minimum charges. For example, wait to call your lawyer until you have several things to discuss, rather than just one. And don't call your lawyer at all to check whether a hearing has been scheduled; contact a staffer instead.

In Chapter 7 we will discuss a number of additional ways you can save on legal fees.

The "X" Factor: Wisdom

As important as experience, legal knowledge, and credentials combined, is *wisdom*. For example, a smart, experienced lawyer knows all the courtroom tactics. But a wise lawyer knows when *not* to employ hard-nosed tactics that might temporarily

Carefully assess a lawyer's listening skills at the IC.

benefit a client at the expense of more important long-term interests such as preserving a co-parenting relationship. Similarly, while a tough lawyer might "stonewall" to pressure the other side into a single concession during settlement negotiation, a wise lawyer saves time and money by building a path to settlement of the entire case.

Sizing Up a Lawyer: The Initial Consultation

Once you've assembled your short-list of lawyers, you're ready to interview some. When you call up for an initial consultation (IC), ask how you'll be charged for it. Since an IC is partly a "meet and greet," some lawyers charge a reduced rate. Others charge a reduced rate *when asked if they do.*

Be cautious with lawyers offering free consultations, as many lawyers consider that a bad practice that leads to advice based on incomplete information.

Rating How Your Friends Rate Their Lawyers

Test your friends' opinions of their lawyers with the following questions:

- Did the lawyer understand your goals and remember them as your case progressed?
- Were immediate concerns such as temporary support or visitation addressed quickly
- How quickly did the lawyer respond to your emails and phone calls?
- Did you feel your questions were answered frankly and in a way you could understand?
- Were you sufficiently prepared for meetings and court proceedings?
- Did you feel that you were kept informed of the progress of your case?
- Did the lawyer seem confident and persuasive in depositions, hearings, and settlement conferences?
- Did you feel that the lawyer's staff and associate attorneys were knowledgeable?
- Did you feel that the lawyer made a meaningful effort to settle your case?
- Did you feel that your lawyer tried to move the case along?
- Did you feel that the billing practices were fair?
- What did you like most/least about your lawyer?

What to Look For at the IC

Besides providing an opportunity for advice regarding your case, the IC is your chance to learn important things about a lawyer.

- Knowledge & experience regarding your circumstances. The IC gives you the chance to learn specifics about a lawyer's expertise and experience. For example, is the lawyer familiar with matters such as military benefits, royalties, or your spouse's construction business?
- Communication skills. Communication problems that appear in the relaxed atmosphere of an initial consultation will only worsen as your case progresses. Pay attention to whether your questions are answered clearly and thoroughly.
- Listening skills. Poor listening is one of the biggest sources of disconnect in any relationship. (Can you think of a failed relationship where listening skills were an issue?) Many lawyers are lousy listeners, so pay attention to how the lawyer... pays attention to what you have to say.
- Compatibility. You're not looking for a new BFF at your IC. But you must be able to connect with the lawyer well enough to ensure a productive working relationship based on clear communication and mutual respect.

Preparing For an Initial Consultation

Prepare for an IC as follows:

- **Fill out a Statutory Criteria Summary** (see Appendix 1). You can download it from www.21stCenturyDivorce.com. "Updates & Materials" to provide the lawyer a timesaving summary of your case.

- **Select questions from the Initial Consultation Checklist**. Following the Statutory Criteria Summary is this exhaustive checklist of questions that can be asked at an IC. Choose a handful to ask that are of particular importance to you.

- **Bring key documents with you**. Bring along 2 or 3 years of tax returns and a net worth statement (a list of assets and liabilities with estimated dollar values). If you use Quicken or other budgeting software, bring 2 or 3 years' worth of year-end spending summaries.

- **Educate yourself with the right resources**. As discussed in Chapter 1, nearly every state court system website provides information about how family matters proceed there. That's the best place to go for basic information about "divorce procedure" in your state.

Where to Find Attorney Right

Now that you have a better idea of what you want in a court-based lawyer, here's where to look for Attorney GoodBar.[6]

Personal Recommendations

Once you've decided upon the type of lawyer and divorce that you want (ADR vs. traditional), begin assembling your lawyer shortlist with recommendations from attorneys you know personally. If you don't know any lawyers, ask other professionals you trust such as mental health professionals who deal with local divorce lawyers.

It's also important to ask clients about their divorce lawyers to learn how the client was treated. However, be aware that clients can form unsound opinions of their lawyers for many reasons, including:

• Some clients blame lawyers for not reaching (unrealistic) goals.
• Narcissistic clients may blame others (especially their lawyers) for their woes; or conversely, tout their lawyers' brilliance to demonstrate their own brilliance in choosing them.
• Emotionally needy clients may perceive their attorneys as knights in shining armor who can do no wrong.

Institutional Referrals

If you don't know a lawyer or anyone else who can recommend a divorce lawyer, you may wish to try a lawyer referral service. These services are maintained or authorized by state, county, and city bar associations in each state and U.S. territory. To find the closest one to you, visit the American Bar Association website, abanet.org. Select "Public Resource," then "Lawyer Referral Services," followed by the name of your state. However, be aware that many lawyers put their names on referral lists to build their practices, so be sure the lawyer has the experience and skills required for your case.

Bar Association Participation

Lawyers who are active in family law sections of state or county bar associations are likely to be current on developments in the law. Most officers of the state bar association's Family Law Section are above-average family lawyers.

---

[6] Before beginning your search, make sure that you are not forgetting free or discounted legal services that may be available to you through an employment or union provided legal services plan.

As noted in Chapter 3, Family Law Sections contain a little-known "Fount of Family Law Knowledge." To tap into it, obtain contact information on Section officers from your state bar association's website. Call one of them and ask which Section members make presentations to the Section regarding family law recent developments. Those are likely to be energetic lawyers who know your state's family law as well as anyone. And the younger ones who don't yet charge top rates may be a bargain.

Lawyer Rating Services, Professional Memberships, and Directories

- *Martindale Hubbell (www.martindale.com)* with its 1.0-5.0 peer rating system is the most reliable lawyer directory/rating service. Its printed version, available in many libraries and law offices, contains (for those law firms that pay extra for it) information regarding each lawyer's professional achievements and practice areas.

- *American Academy of Matrimonial Lawyers* at www.aaml.org offers a searchable database of AAML membership, which, as noted above, may be the single best credential for top divorce lawyers.

- *State judiciary websites list lawyers certified in matrimonial law.* In the states listed above that offer certification, this is another excellent indicator of family law expertise.

- *National Board of Trial Advocacy* is a non-profit body accredited by the ABA to certify lawyers in family law trial advocacy. Where court proceedings are expected, this is a significant credential. Some states have used it to qualify state-certified family lawyers.

- *"Super Lawyers"* at www.superlawyers.com and *"Best Lawyers"* at www.bestlawyers.com/Search. Inclusion on these lists is a relatively reliable indicator of high competence. The lists are far from infallible, however. For example, "Super Lawyer" partners often promote their associates as promising younger lawyers known as "Rising Stars." That means that some of the "Rising Stars" (who later graduate to "Super Lawyer" status) are designated as such more because of *where* they practice family law than *how well* they do it.

- *Avvo.com.* Avvo and similar on-line sites rely principally upon information supplied by lawyers about themselves. Although Avvo may be the best of the lot, it is not nearly as reliable as Martindale.

- *Phone book advertisements*. Use the phone book to find a lawyer's phone number, not to find a lawyer.

Revisiting the Quality Lawyer Bargain Table

As you might recall, the very first "pearl of wisdom" listed in Chapter 3 was called "Find the Quality Lawyer Bargain Table." Go back to page 41 to review what makes a lawyer a bargain... or at least a bargain compared to other local matrimonial lawyers. Then try the following to find a whole table of them:

- Visit www.aaml.org/find-a-lawyer.
- Select your state to obtain names and contact information for local members of The American Academy of Matrimonial Lawyers (AAML) members. That will give you access to quality matrimonial lawyers in your area. (If there are no AAML lawyers near you, call the closest one and ask for a referral to top matrimonial attorneys in your area who are members of law firms.)
- Visit those lawyers' law firm websites. Make sure that matrimonial law is the firm's specialty—or at least one of them. Then, locate the site's lawyer bio section. Skip past the pricey partners to younger, associate lawyers who practice matrimonial law.

If you find an associate who fits the profile discussed in Chapter 3, you may have found yourself a high quality lawyer at a discount!

Unbundled Representation: Saving Fees With Lawyers *a la Carte*!

In Chapter 5, we will discuss cost savings associated with alternative dispute resolution. For example, mediations conducted without lawyers present can save money with a streamlined process that assigns the bulk of the legal work to one professional—the mediator.

Another valuable lawyer fee-saving technique is available in court-based cases. It's called "unbundled representation."[7] Also known as "discrete task" or "limited scope" representation, unbundled representation

---

[7] Unbundled representation should not be confused with the more traditional limited or "special appearance." The special appearance allows a party to contest the single issue of the court's jurisdiction over him/her without submitting to that jurisdiction. Several states have expanded their limited appearance rules to accommodate the trend toward unbundled legal services.

- Allows clients to control legal fees by retaining a lawyer to provide specified services, rather than handle all aspects of the case
- Allows lawyers to limit their participation in a case to where it can do the most good

Unbundled Representation Tasks

Certain legal services typically provided in matrimonial cases are relatively easy to separate from the others and thus lend themselves readily to unbundling. They include:

- Conducting court proceedings such as temporary custody/support hearings, or trial
- Drafting court filings ("ghost-writing")[8]
- Drafting a settlement agreement
- Providing legal advice and opinions upon request
- Legal research
- Reviewing documents and agreements

A Recipe For Successful Unbundling

Successful unbundled representation arrangements require
- A client who is able to manage certain tasks traditionally handled by lawyers
- A written agreement clearly specifying the responsibilities of attorney and client
- A client fully educated as to how unbundled representation works, its benefits, and its limitations
- Adherence to state law and bar ethical rules

Cautions Regarding Unbundled Representation

Unbundled representation is not for everyone. Before going into an unbundled representation arrangement, make sure that all the specifics are reduced to writing and that both you and your lawyer are perfectly clear as to its scope. Be sure in particular to discuss with your lawyer potential downsides of such arrangements:

---

[8] Note that even in states that allow some form of unbundled representation, "ghost writing" may not be permitted.

- An unbundled representation lawyer handling limited tasks may not be in a position to negotiate an overall settlement of your case
- Clients do not always know when to consult with a lawyer whose role is limited to providing advice, and thus may miss out on important guidance
- Clients who feel they can handle a particular task such as a "routine" court proceeding may find out otherwise when they hit the courtroom
- The line between the respective responsibilities of lawyer and client can become blurred

To find out if your state allows unbundled representation, visit the American Bar Association's website at http://americanbar.org/ and search the phrase "unbundling resources by state."

If You Feel You Cannot Afford a Lawyer...

As austerity budgets shrink legal assistance resources, it is more important than ever to know where to seek free or subsidized legal services:

Publicly Funded Legal Assistance Programs.
- The Legal Services Corporation is the largest funding source of legal assistance programs. You can find the LSC office closest to you at http://www.lsc.gov/.
- The non-profit organization, Lawhelp provides a list of legal assistance resources in each state at www.lawhelp.org.
- Legal aid resources are also available on the American Bar Association website. Go to the "legal help" web page, http://www.abanet.org/legalservices/findlegalhelp/, select your state on the map, and then select "Free Legal help."

Law School Legal Clinics. In these "legal aid clinics," law students supervised by professors provide free legal advice and assistance. You can find a list of your state's law schools at http://lawstudents.findlaw.com/. Then check the schools' websites to find out if they operate legal clinics that handle family cases.

State Bar Association Resources. Many state bar organizations fund or administer groups providing *pro bono* (free) legal services. In some states, residents can access such services on-line. Many state bar associations also maintain the lawyer referral directories mentioned above. Some of the listed lawyers are newer members of the bar, building their practices by charging "below-market" rates.

Limited court-sponsored mediation of child-related issues is free in some states. Other states such as Vermont, offer sliding scale fees to qualifying spouses.[9] In still others, a "court-annexed" ADR program refers cases to private mediators who charge below market rates. To find ADR resources in your state, go to the "family" page on your state's court system website. Search "ADR" or "mediation." And while you're there, look around. Many court system sites offer valuable information about court procedures and links to other useful resources.

---

[9] Visit https://www.vermontjudiciary.org/GTC/Family/Mediation.aspx for more information.

Yes, there *IS* a quiz! Test what you have (or haven't) learned.

1. **Which of the following distinguishes lawyer shopping from food shopping?**
    A. You can always return lawyers, even if they're sour, bloated, or past their expiration date.
    B. You're not allowed to squeeze lawyers before choosing them.
    C. Both of the above.

2. **The best referral source for local divorce lawyers is:**
    A. Your divorced Uncle Billy's website, StrangleShyster.com
    B. Your divorced Aunt Gladys's website, StrangleBilly.com
    C. A Yellow Pages display ad with a headshot large enough to tell if the lawyer really will "fight for your rights"
    D. A local lawyer who can tell you which lawyers command the respect of the matrimonial bench and bar

3. ***Pro Bono* is:**
    A. Cher's PGA golfer daughter
    B. Cher's PGA golfer son
    C. Both A & B
    D. A U-2 tribute band
    E. A Latin term used by lawyers to denote the providing of free legal services

4. **Martindale Hubbell is:**
    A. A male strip club in Hubbell, Michigan
    B. Robert Redford's character in "The Way We Were"
    C. A space telescope manufactured by Martindale, Inc.
    D. A prestigious lawyer directory with peer ratings, information about educational background and length of practice, and for those who purchase it, additional biographical information

CHAPTER 5

Alternative Dispute Resolution: Saving Time, Money, and Your Sanity

"People with clenched fists cannot shake hands."

— Indira Gandhi

ADR in Divorce

The term "alternative dispute resolution" (ADR) refers to several methods of settling legal disagreements outside the traditional "court-based" system. If you and your STBX wish to have more control of your divorce, and settle it fairly and cooperatively, consider ADR.

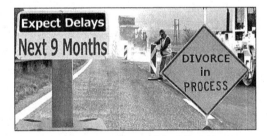

ADR can avoid many of the delays that plague court-based divorces.

In most ADR, lawyers play a smaller role than in court-based divorce.[1] Many feel that's reason enough to try it. But there's more! ADR is usually quicker, cheaper, and less adversarial than court-based divorce, which is why it's usually preferable for the participants—and their children.

Moreover, the court-based process relies on the "adversary system." That system dates back to Merry Olde England where the two not-so-merry methods of dispute resolution were "trial by battle" and "trial by ordeal." Unfortunately, hundreds of years later, court-based divorces retain some of each.

---

[1] That's *not* true of arbitration, which while a form of ADR, is not *consensual* dispute resolution.

ADR Methods Used in Divorce Cases

The following ADR methods are used in divorce cases:

- Mediation
- Collaborative Divorce
- Cooperative Divorce
- Arbitration
- Court-Ordered Parenting Coordination

Mediation

Mediation is the most common form of ADR used in divorce. The two most popular types of divorce mediation[2] are:

- Facilitative mediation in which the mediator guides the participants to identify, analyze, and cooperatively resolve all issues.
- Evaluative mediation in which the mediator assesses the likelihood that the participants would achieve their respective goals if they went to court, and offers settlement recommendations based largely upon the likely outcome if they did.

  Evaluative mediation is very similar to the "pre-trial" process used in court-based divorce. At pre-trials, judges or experienced matrimonial lawyers, sometimes called "special masters," meet with self-represented parties and counsel (and sometimes represented parties as well) and recommend how the case should be settled, based again on likely outcomes at trial.

Neither facilitative nor evaluative mediators can dictate a particular result. If the participants are unable to reach agreement, they are free to proceed with a court-based divorce process.

---

[2] A third, rarely used method is "transformative mediation," a process in which the participants control the course of the mediation and strive for "recognition" of the other party's needs, interests, and points of view.

> ### From the Bizzaro-World Law Dictionary:
> Adversarial system - (1) The Anglo-American model of jurisprudence based on the clash of opponents. (2) The Anglo-American model of marriage based on the clash of opponents.

What Are "Review Counsel" and Why Would I Need One?

Review counsel provide advice upon request during the mediation process, and review the mediation agreement upon its conclusion.

How the Review Counsel Relationship Works

Court-based lawyers control much of the manner in which divorce cases progress. In mediations—at least those conducted without counsel present—review counsel play a vastly reduced role. That role is to:

- Support the mediation process and respect your desire for a fair result.
- Explain your rights and obligations in a way that mediators, who must remain neutral, cannot.
- Request that the mediator obtain any additional information or documents that counsel considers necessary.
- Help you choose reasonable goals. For example, if your review counsel advises that the facts and state law do not justify a claim against your spouse's inheritance, you can select a more realistic goal. Review counsel should *not* encourage clients to go for a "home run" result.
- Help you advocate effectively for yourself in the mediation.
- Propose settlement agreement language changes or new provisions to protect you.[3] For example, counsel might suggest an "indemnification" clause to protect you against your Ex's failure to pay a joint debt. Counsel should *not* try to alter basic terms that are reasonable.

If you are unable to afford review counsel, consider hiring a divorce financial planner or analyst to help you set your financial goals.

How I Mediate: Facilitative Mediation FAQs

Facilitative mediation is the more common of the 2 forms of private mediation, and is mainly what this chapter covers. Below are excerpts from a FAQ sheet I give clients for mediations conducted without lawyers present. Note that each mediator has his own style, and that mediators' and review counsel's roles vary in different locales.

---

[3] Note that in many states, mediators prepare a memorandum of understanding rather than the separation agreement itself. One of the review counsel then prepares an agreement based on the memorandum. The more efficient practice—provided that it is permitted in the jurisdiction—is for the mediator to prepare the agreement. This assumes that the mediator is a matrimonial attorney.

Q. How often will we meet, how long are the mediation sessions, and how many sessions will there be?

A. Sessions are typically 10 to 14 days apart and last about 2 hours. A mediator can't predict the number of sessions needed before knowing the facts of your case and how close you are to agreeing on key issues.

Q. Won't mediation be more, rather than less expensive if 3 lawyers (the mediator and 2 review counsel) are involved?

A. A successfully mediated divorce should be less expensive because one lawyer (the mediator) does the great majority of the work. Mediation also saves fees through quicker gathering of information and issue resolution.

Q. I have been primarily responsible for raising our children while my spouse has pursued a career in finance. How can I compensate for my lack of financial expertise?

A. Part of the mediator's role is to "level the playing field" by explaining legal and financial concepts.

Good mediators don't accept cases if they believe a spouse is
- Severely "overmatched"
- Incapable of understanding the issues
- Unable to meaningfully participate in resolving the issues

If you are concerned that you might not be able to hold your own with your STBX, advise the mediator of that at the outset. Even if you don't have such concerns, make sure to ask questions throughout the process about anything you don't fully understand. If you continue to struggle with a concept, ask the mediator to explain it further after the session.

Q. How do I know that all the necessary information about my spouse's finances will be disclosed in the mediation?

A. Early in the process, mediators require information and documents from the participants. Additional information and documents are typically requested as the mediation progresses. The mediator may also recommend experts such as appraisers, accountants, and actuaries to provide additional information and analysis if necessary. Your review counsel can monitor compliance with, and propose additions to the mediator's requests.

Q. What happens if my spouse and I reach an impasse?

A. Mediators use a variety of techniques to deal with particularly difficult issues. For example, the mediator may suggest
- That participants *reframe* an issue or position in a less confrontational manner.

- Meeting with each participant separately, a process called "caucusing." In caucus, the mediator can explore a participant's goals, concerns, and "bottom line" positions, and candidly help him/her re-think unrealistic positions and goals.

Advantages of Mediation

Mediation offers many advantages:

Mediation cools the hostility that the adversary system encourages.

- Limits the hostility fostered by the court-based adversary system
- Allows clients to maintain much more control than in court-based divorces
- Usually saves money by:
  - Beginning the settlement process immediately
  - Expediting the discovery process
- Dealing quickly and efficiently with disputes that arise along the way
- Usually takes less time than court-based divorce
- Empowers participants to fashion their own creative solutions in which they are more invested and thus more likely to honor
- Attends to details that are often overlooked in court-based cases
- Allows participants to handle their divorce in a private and confidential manner

When Mediation Doesn't Work

Despite its benefits, mediation will not work when:

- Participants are not emotionally prepared to resolve issues cooperatively in face-to-face meetings
- There is too large a disparity in the participants' financial sophistication
- One participant tries to use mediation to work around the legal system and impose his/her will on the other
- A participant insists upon unrealistic goals
- A participant won't agree to anything without first checking with review counsel

General Skills and Attributes Your Mediator Should Have

Mediators should have at least the 5 credentials and attributes listed below that were mentioned in Chapter 2 with regard to court-based lawyers. Note that the last 3 items on the list may be even more important for mediators than lawyers:

- Professionalism
- Family law experience and credentials
- Compatibility with clients
- Communication (including listening) skills
- Empathy

Mediation-Specific Skills and Attributes

In addition to the above, the following are important attributes for a divorce mediator:

- Experience and training in mediating family matters
- Neutrality
- The ability to "reframe" issues in non-contentious ways
- The ability to guide participants to a fair and reasonable agreement
- The ability to get participants to focus on "interests" rather than "positions" that may or may not serve their interests
- Efficiency & practicality
- Familiarity with the range of likely outcomes had the parties chosen a court-based divorce
- Doesn't charge an arm and a leg (or any other body parts)
- Should be a matrimonial attorney (mediations of solely child-related issues can be handled either by mental health professionals or lawyers familiar with the basics of child development)

Finding a Mediator

Use the following resources to find a mediator:

- Referrals from lawyers or mental health professionals who treat families in divorce. As is the case with lawyers, these professionals are the most reliable referral sources.
- Roster of "Advanced Practitioners" of The Association for Conflict Resolution (ACR), available at http://www.acrfamily.org/advanced-practitioners

- Local mediation societies. Contact ACR for information about mediation groups in your state.
- Referrals from former mediation clients.
- Where available, rosters of certified family mediators. No jurisdiction requires certification of private practice mediators. However, the following states require that mediators who receive court referrals meet certain training, experience, and educational requirements:[4]
  - Arkansas
  - California
  - New Hampshire

In addition, the following states offer voluntary certification for mediators:
  - Florida
  - New Hampshire
  - South Carolina
  - North Carolina
  - Virginia
  - Washington

If you live in one of the states above, search your state court system websites for a roster of certified mediators.

What You Need to Know About Your Mediation

Before your mediation begins, you should know the answers to the following:

- Will the mediator provide educational material on mediation, including its voluntary nature, the mediator's impartiality, and confidentiality issues?
- Will the mediator provide forms or checklists to help you organize your financial information?
- In what circumstances will the mediator recommend review counsel?
- Is the mediator familiar with local judges and court customs?
- Who decides the order in which issues will be discussed?
- In situations where one spouse is less knowledgeable about financial matters, how will the mediator "level the playing field?"

---

[4] In other states, such as Massachusetts, confidentiality laws apply only to mediations conducted by mediators who meet training and experience requirements.

The Mediator's Obligations to Participants

As a participant in facilitative mediation, you can reasonably expect the following from your mediator:

- Availability to complete the mediation within a reasonable amount of time
- A written agreement specifying the obligations of participants and mediator, including the fee arrangement
- An unbiased approach to issue resolution
- Clear explanations of relevant legal and financial concepts and their applicability to your circumstances... and the patience to repeat those explanations if necessary
- Recommended rules of conduct such as
  - How and to what extent issues can be discussed outside mediation sessions, including each participant's right to end the discussion at any time
  - Prohibition of *ex parte* (unilateral) discussions between a participant and the mediator
  - Prohibition of threats of court action or other intimidating conduct
- Attention to marital relationship dynamics that affect the mediation
- Facilitation of a reasonable agreement that will pass muster with local judges
- Assistance with promoting your children's best interests, including (where applicable) counseling and other resource recommendations
- Supervision of disclosure of relevant information and documents
- Skillful use of mediation techniques such as caucusing
- If necessary, recommendations of accountants, appraisers, actuaries, or mental health professionals
- Preparation of
  - Settlement agreement, in states where permitted, which accurately memorializes the resolution of issues and contains reasonable protections for the participants
  - Memorandum of settlement in states where mediators do not draft agreements

What You Owe Your Mediator (and Your STBX)

Your mediator and your STBX can reasonably expect the following from you:

- That you enter the mediation with a good faith intention to resolve all issues fairly and efficiently
- That you be willing to compromise when necessary
- That you not try to use the mediation process to obtain unfair advantage over your STBX
- That you not knowingly act against your children's best interests
- That you preserve and fully disclose
  - Relevant information relating to your finances
  - Other pertinent facts relating to your children and other non-financial issues
- That you comply with interim agreements reached during the process
- That you and your STBX agree in good faith upon how and what you will communicate to your children about your mediation and divorce
- That you choose review counsel who support the mediation process
- That you comply with all court orders in your divorce including "automatic orders" that prohibit property transfers, non-routine expenditures, insurance cancellation and removing children from the jurisdiction.
- That you communicate to your STBX and mediator any substantial changes in your financial or other circumstances

Determine Your Goals and Negotiation Strategy, and Avoid Being the Path of Least Resistance

Mediators facing an impasse may look for concessions from participants to help them reach agreement on a particular issue. Consciously or not, mediators sometimes take the "path of least resistance" by seeking more, or larger, concessions from the participant who appears to be more reasonable and flexible.

In mediation, you should be reasonable and flexible. However, you don't want to be considered the "path of least resistance" when difficult issues arise. To avoid that, do the following *before* the mediation process begins:

- Decide on your goals (see pp. 7-11) and how best to achieve them by:
  - Identifying your essential needs, or "must-haves" regarding at least the three main divorce issues:

(1) Amount of child support and/or amount and duration of spousal support
(2) Division of property and debts including mediation and legal fees
(3) (if applicable) Allocation of time and decision-making regarding the kids in a manner consistent with their best interests

Note: You can also include other matters listed in Chapter 1, such as health and life insurance, and higher education expense.

○ Deciding on your initial or "bargaining positions" regarding the issues above that are more favorable than your must-have goals. This will create "wiggle room" for concessions you can make without sacrificing your must-haves.

• Consult a divorce lawyer (even if you can't afford to hire review counsel) or a certified divorce financial analyst before you begin the mediation. Discuss whether and how you should adjust your goals and negotiation approach given your state's law, your circumstances, and how local judges would likely rule on your case if it went to trial.

If You Feel Pressured...

Occasionally, overzealous mediators pressure participants into poor decisions. If you feel that is happening to you and are having difficulty sticking to your game plan, calmly but firmly express that concern. If the pressure continues, state that you'd like to suspend the session in order to consult with your lawyer or financial advisor.

Collaborative Divorce

A second, increasingly popular form of ADR is known as "collaborative divorce." Collaborative divorce addresses the items in the "When Mediation Won't Work" list above. Other than in states that have adopted The Uniform Collaborative Law Act (see below), most collaborative divorces are conducted privately. Private collaborative divorces proceed generally as follows:

• Spouses negotiate settlements directly as in mediation, but in a series of "4-way" negotiation sessions with their lawyers present and participating.
• There is no mediator or other neutral third party to guide the process.

- Participants and their lawyers sign an agreement making settlement their primary goal and further providing that
  - Participants and lawyers will work cooperatively to resolve all issues
  - The parties will provide full disclosure of all relevant financial and other information
  - Aggressive techniques such as threatening litigation are forbidden
  - If the parties fail to reach agreement, the lawyers must terminate representation of their clients, thus providing both participants and lawyers an additional incentive to settle
- A "team approach" is used in which
  - Divorce coaches and child development experts are made available as necessary to help parents understand and deal with children's issues and concerns
  - If necessary, the parties agree upon additional facilitators such as appraisers, certified divorce planners and accountants

The Uniform Collaborative Law Act (UCLA)

State laws differ greatly in their use of collaborative dispute resolution. In 2009, The Uniform Law Commission sought to address this problem with The Uniform Collaborative Law Act (UCLA), which has since been enacted in:

- Alabama
- The District of Columbia
- Hawaii
- Nevada
- Ohio
- Texas
- Utah
- Washington

The Act's provisions (as amended in 2010) include:

- Voluntary referral procedures by state courts, including extended "stays" (delays) of pending cases while the collaborative process is ongoing
- Confidentiality of all communications (and thus prohibition of their use in court proceedings) if the collaborative process fails
- Minimum standards for collaborative agreements

Cautions Regarding Collaborative Divorce

Collaborative divorce can be an efficient way for divorcing parties to control their path to settlement. Nevertheless, the process has several potential downsides:

- Like mediation, it won't work if the parties are not emotionally prepared for face-to-face negotiation
- It won't work if the lawyers behave too much like... lawyers
- Parties who don't reach agreement must start over with new counsel

The third item above, sometimes called the "disqualification requirement," distinguishes collaborative divorce from its sister ADR process, "cooperative divorce." The two processes are essentially the same except that if the cooperative divorce process fails, the parties' lawyers may continue to represent their clients in a traditional divorce. That distinction renders cooperative divorce acceptable to some lawyers who believe that mandatory disqualification punishes clients for failing to resolve all issues, and emphasizes reaching any agreement over reaching a reasonable one.

Court-Ordered Parenting Coordination

Court-ordered parenting coordination ("PC") is another type of ADR available in some states. PC is:

- Used to resolve ongoing parental disputes, to formulate parenting plans, and to try to build durable co-parenting relationships
- Particularly useful where parents have failed to co-parent, comply with court orders, or protect children from parental conflict
- Often ordered by judges to monitor particularly difficult cases, in which case it is
  - Not confidential
  - Involuntary
- Administered by parenting coordinators who typically have
  - Graduate degrees in law, psychology, counseling, or related disciplines
  - Training in conflict resolution, child development, and similar areas
  - Knowledge of state divorce law and procedure
  - Licenses (in states where available)
- A process focused on children's rather than parents' needs

States Using Court-Ordered Parenting Coordination

As of this writing, PC is used in the states listed below. However, its use is expanding, so check with a local matrimonial lawyer to see if it has become available in your locale.

- Arizona
- Colorado
- Delaware (pilot program)
- Florida
- Idaho
- Kentucky (in certain counties)
- Louisiana
- Maryland (in certain counties)
- Massachusetts
- Michigan (some judges order PC despite the lack of an authorizing statute or court rules)
- Minnesota (has "parenting time expeditor" statute similar to PC)
- New Hampshire
- North Carolina
- Ohio (in certain counties)
- Oklahoma
- Oregon
- Texas

Arbitration in Divorce: Pros and Cons

In arbitration, a neutral lawyer chosen by the parties is paid to decide a case. The arbitrator receives testimony and other evidence in a hearing much like a court trial. Arbitration is the one form of ADR in which a resolution can be imposed on the participants.

Experienced arbitrators can be found on The American Arbitration Association website: https://www.adr.org/.

As with all divorce dispute resolution methods, arbitration has its pros and cons:

- Pro: Participants can choose the arbitrator.
- Pro: Participants have more control over scheduling.
- Pro: Arbitration hearings are typically scheduled more quickly than court trials.

- Pro: The pre-trial discovery process is expedited, avoiding the delays in exchanging information and documents that slow court-based cases.
- Con: Arbitration carries an additional expense—the arbitrator's fee.
- Con: Arbitration retains the conflict of adversarial proceedings.
- Con: Most states don't allow arbitration of "ultimate" child-related issues such as custody. In some jurisdictions, arbitration is limited to "post-judgment" issues (disputes that arise after the parties are divorced).[5]
- Con: Arbitration will not prevent the parties from ignoring the arbitration result and seeking a court trial if
  ○ State law does not allow "binding arbitration" of family cases in which arbitrators' decisions become a judgment of the court the same as judges' decisions
  ○ State law *does* allow binding arbitration but the parties will not agree that their arbitration will be binding

---

[5] In recent years, some states have expanded the scope of divorce-related arbitration to include children's issues. A few such as New Jersey even authorize arbitration of custody. Although more states are likely to expand the role of arbitration in family cases, states permitting custody arbitration are likely to remain in the minority. As always, check with a local family law practitioner for the latest on your state's law.

 Yes, there *IS* a quiz! Test what you have (or haven't) learned.

1. **Modern courthouses have the following in common with the castles in Merry Olde England where our judicial system originated:**
   A. Not so merry black-robed figures who decide people's fates from on high
   B. Even less merry guards at the entrance
   C. "Trials by ordeal"
   D. All of the above
2. **ADR won't work if:**
   A. You show up for your 1st mediation session at The Meditation Society
   B. The lawyers in a collaborative divorce are not emotionally prepared to sit down together and behave themselves
   C. Mediation or collaborative divorce participants are not willing to work in good faith toward a fair result
   D. You live in the Middle Ages
   E. All of the above

CHAPTER 6

Using Financial Planners, Coaches, and Other Non-Lawyer Professionals

*"Wise men don't need advice.
Fools won't take it."*

— Benjamin Franklin

Who Needs a Lawyer?

You do. If you can possibly afford to, it's critical to meet with a divorce lawyer even if it's only for an initial evaluation of your case. When you make the appointment, ask what paperwork you need to enable the lawyer to give you a range of likely outcomes.

In any event, fill out and bring with you the Initial Consultation Checklist (See Appendix 1.) that you can download from www.divorcesimplystated.com/updates-materials/. Then go back over the material beginning on page 60 regarding ..

If you can afford a bit more in legal fees, you have options to use "part-time lawyers."

Avoid getting crushed by legal fees. Use other professionals too!

- If your case is mediated, lawyers acting as "review counsel" can advise you as needed during the process, and prepare or review your settlement agreement upon its conclusion. (see page 71.)
- In court-based cases, a majority of states now permit "unbundled" or "discrete task" representation where lawyers perform only specified tasks. These tasks can include contested court proceedings, legal research and settlement negotiation. (see page 64 for more information regarding unbundled representation.)

So don't give up on the idea of having a lawyer. An experienced divorce lawyer's services are critical to achieving positive divorce outcomes. A lawyer is particularly important to

- Evaluate your case and advise you regarding likely outcomes
- Explain how to use the strengths of your case to your advantage, and minimize the impact of any weaknesses
- Explain how applicable law and courthouse customs will affect your case
- Represent you in contested court proceedings and depositions if they become necessary
- Prepare enforceable interim agreements
- Negotiate settlement
- Advise you regarding issues about which you may be unaware, such as
  ○ Tax ramifications of various settlement alternatives
  ○ Valuation and division of retirement plans
  ○ Life insurance to insure alimony and child support
  ○ Protection if your STBX files for bankruptcy
  ○ Enforcement of your settlement agreement
  ○ Protection of your rights as a spouse of a member of the military
- Prepare a final settlement agreement with clear, enforceable language that meets legal requirements in areas such as
  ○ Spousal support that qualifies for tax treatment as alimony
  ○ Impact of cohabitation on spousal support
  ○ Property valuation
  ○ Retirement plans

Limiting Lawyer Time

In Chapter 7 you will learn a host of ways to limit legal fees by
- Choosing the right lawyer for you and your case
- Using the lawyer's time wisely
- Maintaining a functional relationship with the lawyer

Chapter 7 also covers the use of "traditional" professionals such as your accountant and paralegals to perform non-legal or "quasi-legal" work for less than lawyers charge, or at no cost at all. This chapter covers some less traditional types of professionals who can save or generate money in your divorce.

Divorce Coaches

Divorce coaches offer services that most divorce lawyers don't. Coaches do not provide legal advice, and are not substitutes for divorce lawyers. However, a meeting with a divorce coach (and one of the divorce financial professionals discussed below) *before* you hire an attorney will allow you to

* Gain a general understanding of how divorce works
* Begin divorce preparation to make your initial dealings with your lawyer more efficient and productive
* Provide emotional support and if necessary, refer you to counseling[1]

If you do go on to retain a lawyer, your coach can remain involved. In fact, coaches can be highly effective when working with cooperative lawyers.[2]

In addition to the above, divorce coaches can assist you by:

* Helping you make choices, including:
  ○ Whether you should be considering alternatives to divorce, and
  ○ Whether you are emotionally prepared to make life decisions, and if not, how to become so
* Facilitating your recovery from the end of your marriage
* Familiarizing you generally with the divorce process including the types of professional assistance you may need

Divorce coaches can help you organize those mountains of paperwork.

* Helping you organize financial and other documents and information
* Helping you optimize your attorney/client relationship
* Helping you support your children and serve their interests
* Helping you forge a new co-parenting relationship
* Providing you with techniques to manage emotions and resolve conflict
* Helping you make sound, intentional life choices
* Empowering you to transition to a happy and productive post-divorce life

---

[1] Note, however, that your communications with coaches and financial planners/analysts are *not* privileged and thus can be "discovered" by opposing counsel.

[2] This occurs, for example, in the collaborative divorce "team approach" discussed in Chapter 5.

Finding a Divorce Coach

Many divorce coaches come from backgrounds in mental health, mediation and even law. Others are drawn to coaching as a result of their own divorce experiences. As with divorce planners/analysts and private practice mediators, there is no mandatory certification of divorce coaches. Thus, personal recommendations from other divorce professionals and former clients are particularly important in selecting a divorce coach.

Your divorce coach should have substantial experience in the field and have been trained and certified by a private organization such as The CDC College for Divorce Coaching.[3]

Certified Divorce Financial Analysts (CDFAs) and Certified Financial Divorce Practitioners (CFDPs)

Certified Divorce Financial Analysts (CDFAs) and Certified Financial Divorce Practitioners (CFDPs) provide financial advice and assistance during divorce less expensively than attorneys. The main difference between CDFAs and CFDPs is that CDFAs are certified by The Institute for Divorce Financial Analysts while CFDPs are certified by The Academy of Financial Divorce Practitioners. For ease of reference, I'll refer to both collectively as "CDFAs."

Don't be a sad sack! You can limit legal fees by getting help from non-lawyers.

An experienced CDFA can help you by
- Organizing your financial documents
- Evaluating your current financial circumstances
- Helping you prepare your financial disclosure statement
- Explaining retirement plans including
   - Plan elections that determine the type of benefit you want such as whether it includes survivors' benefits
   - What will occur upon the death of the employee spouse
   - How to divide retirement plans using qualified domestic relations orders ("QDROs")

[3] Help locating local divorce coaches is available at the CDC website: http://certifieddivorcecoach.com/

- Explaining tax aspects of divorce such as
  - How the alimony deduction can help both spouses save money
  - The value of your children's tax exemptions and related tax credits
  - How to identify future costs "hidden" in securities, such as
    - Unrealized capital gains
    - Stock and bond fund "back-end" fees, commissions and penalties
- Analyzing current and long-term spending at various income levels
- Projecting the long term effect of various settlement scenarios, adjusted for inflation and other factors

In mediation and collaborative law cases, spouses can agree upon a single CDFA to provide the above-listed services to both of them. Sharing the expertise of a single expert is one of the ways ADR can save you money.

CDFAs should not be confused with experts known as forensic accountants who are hired to value business interests or determine the "real" compensation of a small business owner. Traditionally, forensic accountants have been used most often in court-based cases to
- Help formulate a settlement negotiation strategy
- Provide litigation support if negotiations break down
- Provide expert testimony

Again, however, in circumstances such as where a closely held business must be valued, spouses can try to avoid costly "battles of the experts" by attempting to agree on a single expert.

Other Divorce Consultants

There are other experts with whom you can consult in either an ADR or a court-based case to help you better understand likely outcomes and settlement alternatives. Unlike the use of divorce coaches and CDFAs, using the following experts will generally *not* reduce your legal fees. However, their expertise can help you achieve your divorce goals and save or generate money for you in your settlement.

Forensic and Other Psychologists

Lawyers have long used forensic psychologists as expert witnesses in contested custody cases. But mental health professionals can also be used as consultants to
- Assess parenting issues
- Help improve parenting skills

- Perform psychological testing
- Interpret existing psychological test results
- Recommend options such as
  ○ Individual counseling
  ○ Parenting and family counseling
  ○ Parenting coordination (see page 79)
- Evaluate sexual abuse and other domestic violence

Vocational Experts

Vocational experts perform "employability assessments" to determine a spouse's
- Employability
- Income potential
- Highest level of occupational functioning
- Need for training and education

A vocational expert's services are most often used where a spouse appears to be earning below his/her "earning capacity" (i.e., "dogging it") or otherwise earning less than he/she could be expected to. Vocational experts base their conclusions on factors such as
- A spouse's history of higher income
- A spouse's earnings that fall below industry norms
- Potentially income-producing skills that a spouse chooses not to use

---

Court Rules Regarding Expert Witnesses

Court rules require that expert witnesses be identified and the substance of their testimony disclosed. Failure to meet disclosure deadlines can result in exclusion of your expert's testimony if your case goes to trial.

Appraisers

Listed below are the types of appraisers most commonly used in divorce cases. You can find help locating an appraiser among the resources in Chapter 17. Also, see the material regarding business valuation in Chapter 13.

- Real estate appraisers
- Appraisers of antiques, collectibles and artwork
- Appraisers of business interests

Other valuations are available if you can't afford an appraiser. But the values are less reliable and are inadmissible in court except by agreement.

For example, realtors will provide "opinions of value" of a family home and other real estate. However, values from realtors eager for your signature on a listing agreement typically come in a bit higher than those of appraisers.

Sites like eBay can also shed light on values of antiques and collectibles for use in settlement discussions. However, note that prices from eBay-type sites or any source other than a qualified expert who is available to testify, are inadmissible in court. If you do try eBay, use actual sales results (not asking prices) of items substantially the same as yours in nature and condition.

More reliable sources of information regarding value include:
- Antique and collectible dealers—you can find local antique dealers at: http://www.local.com/results.aspx?keyword=collectibles+shop&cid
- Price guides and valuation services including, for example,
  - Kovels price guides for antiques and collectibles at http://www.kovels.com/
  - Beckett Grading Services at http://www.beckett.com/grading/ or Professional Sports Authenticators at www.psacard.com
- Vendors at antique and collectible shows
- Auction houses offering free appraisals, hoping for a commission if you use them to sell the item

---

On-line Updates
The law is evolving regarding the use of forensic computer experts to search electronic devices during the discovery phase of divorces. For free updates on this and other issues, visit http://DivorceSimplyStated.com.

Forensic Computer Experts

Computer forensic experts are occasionally used in divorce cases to examine computer hard drives in order to

- Locate documents, photos, and videos including emails and other electronic correspondence (including items "deleted" from the device)
- Determine information regarding the origination of computer contents such as
  ° The identity of the preparer or originator of the item
  ° The date of preparation or origination
  ° Whether, when and by whom an item has been modified

As with all divorce professionals, hire only a computer expert with training, expertise and experience that relate to the issues in your case. The following computer experts should have the necessary training to perform divorce-related tasks.

- Certified Computer Examiners (CCE), certified by The International Society of Forensic Computer Examiners (ISFCE)
- Certified Forensic Computer Examiners (CFCE), certified by The International Association of Computer Investigative Specialists (IACIS), which specializes in law enforcement
- Professional Certified Investigators (PCI), certified by ASIS International

---

 Yes, there *IS* a quiz! Test what you have (or haven't) learned.

1. **This chapter is mainly about:**
   A. Finding more professionals to pay
   B. Friending on Facebook that kid Sheldon who you used to give wedgies in high school, after you found out he became a CDFA
   C. Deleting from your draft box those poison pen emails to your STBX that you wrote to feel better but never sent
   D. Saving on legal fees by using non-lawyer professionals for certain tasks; and deciding what other professionals you may need

2. **Unscramble the following key phrases from this chapter!**
   A. tacoviloan sexterp
   B. revcodi shecoca
   C. reinscof slopyhogstics

CHAPTER 7

Embracing the Tiger: How to Work With, and Spend Less on Lawyers

"We are all born ignorant, but one must work hard to remain stupid."

— Benjamin Franklin

The Half-Dozen Best Ways to Save Money During Divorce

There are half a dozen highly effective steps you can take to save money on your divorce:

- Use ADR methods such as mediation or collaborative divorce to begin work on settling your case without delay.
- If yours is a court-based divorce, choose a lawyer who will resolve your case efficiently.
- Choose a lawyer whose fees aren't outrageous.
- Avoid legal fees by using professionals other than lawyers for tasks that are primarily financial or child-related rather than legal in nature.
- Control legal fees with an efficient attorney/client relationship.
- Take advantage of divorce tax breaks.

We've already covered #1 – 4, though we will touch again on #3 here. Item #6, divorce tax breaks (including deductible legal fees) will be covered in Chapter 9. This chapter will focus on item #5; how to work efficiently with your lawyer to achieve a quicker, cheaper, and better outcome in your case.

Financial Considerations
in Choosing a Lawyer, Revisited

Chapter 4 included a list of tips on evaluating the cost of a lawyer. In case you spilled your energy drink on it, here it is again:

- Find out from divorced friends and local law firms what local divorce lawyers charge.
- Make sure that any unused portion of your retainer is refundable.
- Lawyers in affluent communities may charge more than comparable lawyers with offices in more modest areas. Don't pay more for a lawyer's elegant digs.
- All other things being equal, save fees on travel time by choosing a lawyer who is located closer to the courthouse.

Billing Increments. Find out in what *increments* a lawyer charges to learn the lawyer's *real* or "effective hourly rate." Increments are what causes a 3-minute phone call with a lawyer who charges at $450/hr. and bills in 1/10 hour increments to cost less than the same call to a $350/hr. lawyer who bills in increments of 2/10 of an hour. (See page 57.)

Keeping the Long Arm of the Law Out
of Your Pocket: Saving Legal Fees by
Understanding Your Fee Agreement

A lawyer's fee or "retainer" agreement should tell you most of what you need to know about how you will be charged. Most states have ethical rules requiring lawyers to provide written agreements to family law clients. Even if your state doesn't require it, ask for a clearly written description of how you will be charged. Clarity benefits both attorney and client.

When reading your agreement, pay particular attention to the following:

- *Hourly rates.* Most divorce lawyers charge by the hour. The lawyer's rate as well as that of associate attorneys and paralegals must be clearly stated. If the agreement permits increases in the rates, ask the lawyer to keep the stated amount in effect throughout your case, or for at least 6 or 9 months. Finally, look for the billing increment language discussed above—the hidden fee inflator that catches many clients off guard.
- *Flat fees.* Some lawyers charge a flat fee for "simple" divorces. But many of those lawyers handle a high volume of cases, spending little time on any of them. Also, many flat fee agreements allow for additional fees

if the case becomes more complicated than expected—something that may occur more often than not. In that event, make sure you understand
- ○ What constitutes an unexpected complication
- ○ How any increase is to be calculated
- **Non-refundable retainers.** If only some of a retainer (either the initial or any subsequent retainer payment) is used, will the unused portion be refunded? Unless the lawyer is the only competent/sober one in the county, don't agree to a non-refundable retainer. Find an attorney who charges you only for services actually provided.
- **Expenses.** Be sure that your prior approval is required for major expenditures such as hiring an expert.
- **Travel time.** Charges for trips to and from court are appropriate but paying your lawyer to drive home from court... not so much.
- **Premium billing.** Beware of premium billing language that permits an additional charge if the lawyer achieves a "superior result." Lawyers don't hit enough home runs to earn bonuses.
- **"Communication fees."** A few law firms still charge a flat "communications fee" for phone calls, etc. *in addition to* the charge for time spent. These fees were originally intended to limit client phone calls, but lawyers' hourly rates these days compensate them quite sufficiently.

From the Bizarro-World Law Dictionary
Retainer (1) Something your orthodontist puts in your mouth that makes you gag. (2) Something your lawyer puts in her wallet that makes you gag.

Holding Down Legal Fees With a Productive Attorney/Client Relationship

Once you've hired a lawyer, you can save money with a productive attorney/client relationship. The relationship tends to work pretty well for lawyers—they get paid to participate. It's your job to make it work for you.

Avoiding Familiar Relationship Mistakes

There are a number of ways to optimize your relationship with your lawyer. Start by avoiding mistakes from your last partnership—the one that sent you to a divorce lawyer in the first place. For example, DON'T:

- Harbor unrealistic expectations
- Be overly compliant or inattentive—a healthy relationship requires both partners to be engaged and mindful
- Be overly skeptical or contentious—make sure to participate in the relationship in a productive way
- Refuse to admit that you don't understand something
- Listen without truly hearing
- Blame your lawyer for delays and other things that aren't her fault
- Transfer feelings of victimization, betrayal, emotional need, etc. from your marriage to the relationship with your divorce lawyer

---

A Lawyer's Top Ten List of Least Favorite Questions from New Clients

- If you're such a hotshot, why isn't your picture in the phone book?
- Do you mind if my parents, their attorney, and my "godfather" sit in on our meetings?
- Are we on the clock yet?
- Do I get a refund if you like… screw up my case?
- Which one are you, Jacoby or Meyers?
- I thought you'd be … bigger!
- When I put down my income on my financial disclosure statement, should I put what's on my tax returns or the real amount?
- You won't wear that outfit to court, right?
- Do any of the judges maybe owe you a favor?
- My brother-in-law's plumber knows a guy whose girlfriend's cousin only charges $500 for a divorce, soup to nuts. Can you beat his price?

Great Expectations . . . and Reasonable Ones

The first "relationship mistake" on the list above has to do with unrealistic expectations. Understanding the following will help you avoid them:

- Your lawyer can't change the facts of your case. She cannot, for example, magically increase your net worth, or transform your STBX into parent-of-the-year.
- Your lawyer's conduct is constrained by procedural and ethical rules that she must follow whether or not you think they make any sense.
- Your lawyer is neither interested in nor qualified to act as your therapist.
- Nearly everything in your case will take longer than you would like due to scheduling conflicts, court system inefficiencies, and life in general.

Mutual Obligations of Clients and Lawyers

Getting the most out of the attorney/client relationship requires that each of you fulfill certain basic obligations to the other.

Your obligations to your lawyer are to:

- Fully disclose all relevant facts
- Notify your lawyer of any substantial change in your circumstances
- Communicate clearly and concisely
- Ask questions to make sure you understand what's going on
- Ask more questions to make doubly sure you understand what's going on
- Tell your lawyer about any misgivings you have concerning her advice or tactics
- Consult with your lawyer before any direct negotiations with your spouse
- Pay your lawyer's bills promptly, or make alternative arrangements
- Treat your lawyer with civility and respect

Your lawyer's obligations to you are to:

- Listen to and understand your goals, advise you as to their feasibility and where appropriate, suggest alternatives
- Devise a plan to achieve your reasonable goals
- Keep you informed of all developments in your case
- Respond to your calls and emails within a reasonable period of time
- Use her experience and expertise to resolve your case as favorably as possible
- Consult with you before incurring any substantial expenses
- Use her time as efficiently as possible
- Make sure her bills are consistent with her fee agreement
- Keep your communications confidential
- Pay attention to your concerns and address them
- Treat you with civility and respect

Embracing the Tiger:
Keys to a Functional Attorney/Client Relationship
Both you and your lawyer must:
- Agree upon and follow a plan for your case while remaining flexible enough to make adjustments when necessary
- Ask questions to avoid misunderstandings
- Take notes at meetings
- Be respectful
- Be reasonably available to each other
- Keep each other informed

What Lawyers and Clients Should *Not* Expect from Each Other

It is *not* reasonable for you to expect your lawyer to:

- Misuse court procedures to harass your spouse
- Do whatever you ask, whether reasonable or not
- Allow you to act disrespectfully to the lawyer or her staff
- Act as your therapist
- Wait indefinitely to be paid

Likewise, your lawyer cannot expect that you will:

- Accept all of her advice without question
- Tolerate inattention or rudeness
- Allow her to ignore your reasonable goals

Ten Ways to Optimize the Attorney-Client Relationship

Below are specific steps you and your lawyer can take to get the most out of your relationship:

- Put in writing the agreed-upon goals in your case, and any revisions
- Establish ground rules such as an agreement to respond to each other's phone calls and emails within 24 hours.
- Agree that you will receive copies of all substantive correspondence and be kept informed of all developments.
- Limit communications with your lawyer to matters she can actually help you with. To avoid being charged 1/10 or 2/10 of an hour for a 3-minute phone call, don't call your lawyer in non-emergency circumstances until you have more than one topic to discuss.

- Be efficient at meetings with your lawyer by
  - Having an informal agenda of topics to be discussed
  - Making sure that you each have copies of your current financial disclosure statement
  - Listening carefully to your lawyer's questions and answering them concisely
- Don't fret and fume—if one of you does something the other doesn't like, talk about it.
- Don't drown your lawyer in paperwork. Provide accurate information concisely.
- Ask your lawyer to explain legal concepts and terms she uses. Take notes, but if you've forgotten the explanation, ask again.
- With respect to court proceedings, make sure that you understand
  - The reason for the proceeding
  - The potential risks and rewards
  - Whether you might need to testify and if so, the details of the testimony including expected cross-examination (See Chapter 14.)
- Keep copies of key financial documents you've given to your lawyer in a binder for quick access. (This can also be helpful to your lawyer in court or at a deposition if she can't locate her own copies.)

Optimizing the Attorney/Client Relationship Item #11: Skip the Lawyer Basketball Games

There's one more way to optimize the attorney/client relationship. Ask your lawyer to consult you before getting other lawyers in the firm involved in your case. Otherwise, you may find yourself watching "Lawyer Basketball," played by 2 or more lawyers bouncing your case back and forth, and slam-dunking you with their bill.

How to Talk to a Lawyer

If your lawyer seems impatient when you speak with her, she may be behaving poorly. *Or*, you may be communicating poorly.

If it's the latter, try the following to communicate more clearly and concisely:

- If you are recounting a series of events, present them chronologically. The less your lawyer hears, "Wait—I forgot to tell you!" the better.

- If you are expressing a concern, state the concern first and then provide the details.
- Listen carefully to what your lawyer tells you.
- At the end of the conversation, state your understanding of any decisions that have been made.
- As always, ask questions!

Incurring Additional Legal Expenses

The cost of divorce can strain even the best attorney/client relationship. Those costs sometimes involve more than attorneys' fees. Among the most expensive add-ons are depositions[1] and expert witnesses. Before incurring such expenses, you must compare the likely costs with the anticipated benefits.

Deciding Whether a Deposition Is Necessary

Consider the following in deciding whether to take the deposition of your spouse or a third party:

- Can the same information be obtained using less expensive discovery methods such as interrogatories, document requests, or requests for admissions?
- To what extent does your lawyer need to ask follow-up questions that are not available with other discovery methods?
- What does your lawyer estimate the cost of a deposition will be in legal fees (including preparation time) and transcript expense?
- Can you agree with your lawyer on a time limit for the deposition?[2]
- Will taking your spouse's deposition cause the other side to take your deposition too, adding yet more expense?

---

[1] For information regarding depositions, see "Divorce Procedure: The Steps to Your Divorce" on page 25.
[2] Court reporters get paid by the transcript page. If you've ever seen a transcript, you know why. The pages have more white than Mount Everest in the snow season.

Deciding Whether an Expert Is Necessary

Before retaining an appraiser, accountant, actuary, or other financial expert, find out the following:

- The expert's fee or hourly rate for
  - Research
  - Preparation of a report
  - Testimony (in court and at depositions)
- How much of an impact will the expert's opinion likely have on the outcome of your case?
- What are the chances that the expert's opinion could harm your case?
- Should you hire your own expert (typical in court-based cases) or hire an expert jointly with your STBX (typical in ADR cases)?

⚠ Use Providers Other Than Your Lawyer or Paralegal

Another way to save on legal fees is to have someone other than your lawyer or paralegal perform non-legal or semi-legal services. Consider the following:

- **Communicate with office staff** rather than your lawyer on scheduling and "housekeeping" matters such as
  - Checking whether your accountant sent your tax returns to your lawyer
  - Whether a motion has been filed or scheduled for hearing
  - Whether opposing counsel has agreed to, or the court has granted a request for a continuance or extension of time
- **Use a certified divorce planner, divorce financial analyst[3] or accountant** to
  - Help you prepare your financial disclosure statement
  - Analyze tax and other financial implications of settlement options or proposals
  - Advise you as to pension elections regarding survivors' benefits, etc.
- **Use a therapist, or divorce coach** to assist in resolving child-related issues, while the lawyers focus on financial issues.
- **Use an actuary** to value pensions.
- **Use a mediator** to resolve disputes regarding division of personal property.

---

[3] Find a CFDA in your area at: www.institutedfa.com

- **Use a discovery referee** (where available) to resolve discovery issues such as disputes over what information and documents you and your STBX must exchange.

⚠ Be Your Own Paralegal

While paralegals' rates are much lower than those of attorneys, avoid fees altogether by having someone else perform paralegal tasks. Who? You!

Discuss with your lawyer performing tasks yourself such as gathering, copying, scanning and organizing documents. The documents typically gathered in divorce cases are listed halfway through Chapter 1 under the heading "Locating Key Documents."

Don't be a pawn in your divorce. Be your own paralegal!

If you don't have access to a scanner, see if you can arrange to use your lawyer's. Otherwise, consider buying one yourself to organize key documents electronically. You can recoup the cost and more with what you save on paralegal charges.

With some direction by your lawyer or her paralegal, you can also summarize and analyze documents such as bank and credit card statements and even tax returns.

Using Legal Resources Wisely

Talk to staff about:
- Scheduling
- File organization
- Document production logistics
- Billing questions and payment arrangements
- Routine questions regarding your financial disclosure statement such as whether to include your STBX's solely owned property on your statement

Talk to your lawyer about:
- The law and how it applies to your case
- The progress of your case
- Your responses to discovery
- Regarding your STBX's responses to discovery
  - Information obtained that you feel is particularly important
  - Missing information
- Advice or divorce 'war stories" you've heard that worry you
- Substantive questions regarding your financial disclosure statement such as
  - Whether and how to include discretionary bonuses in the income section
  - Whether to deduct selling expenses from the value of your home

Where to Find Financial Documents and Information

Look for financial documents in your home where tax returns, etc. are normally kept. Then look in as many other places as you can ... as soon as you can. While this may not be pleasant to do, it can save time and money down the road having your lawyer track the documents down.

Make copies of as many documents as you can. If you suspect that your STBX will conceal information, strong measures may be necessary. Consider consulting with a forensic computer expert regarding copying computer hard drives.

For documents you cannot locate, there are a number of resources available:

- **Documents recorded on Land Records** such as deeds, mortgages, liens, etc. are located in your Town, City, or County Seat Clerk's Office and should also be accessible on-line. There are also several electronic document retrieval services such as www.fastdeed.com and http://datastore.netronline.com/ that access public records for a fee.

- **Information regarding military pay and allowances** such as Basic Allowance for Subsistence ("BAS") and Basic Allowance for Housing ("BAH") is available at http://www.military.com/benefits/military-pay/allowances/

- **Estimates of your Social Security retirement, disability, and survivors' benefits** are available from the Social Security Administration at http://www.ssa.gov/myaccount/

- **Your filed federal income tax returns** must be retained by the preparer for at least three years. You can also call IRS at 1-800-908-9946 or order them on-line at https://www.irs.gov/taxtopics/tc156.html

- **Probate Court documents (wills, trusts, accountings, inventories, etc.)** relating to pending or closed estates are available in the Probate or Surrogate's Court[4] located in the municipality or county in which the decedent resided at death. Note that "ancillary estates" may also have been opened in other states where the decedent owned property.

- **Your bank and credit card records** can often be obtained on-line through your bank or credit card company for at least the last 12 months.

---

[4] A list of U. S. probate courts appears at http://estate.findlaw.com/probate/state-probate-courts.html

You may also be able to get copies (and sidestep the bank's fee schedule) by asking nicely at your local branch where you've stood in line for years without complaining.

Alternatively, share access to on-line accounts with your STBX using temporary passwords. However, make sure to consult your lawyer first about limitations and safeguards.

• **Local real estate prices and other property information** regarding sale prices of homes similar to yours ("comparables" or "comps") are available from local realtors. Real estate appraisers charge a few hundred dollars for simple appraisal reports.

You might also be able to access recent home sale prices on-line, though be sure that those prices relate to comps. Be wary of on-line services that supply information regarding sales (though not necessarily "comparable" ones) and those that supply "fair market value" estimates.

⚠• **Loan applications** may be found in the files of the attorney who handled the transaction. If you have refinanced your home in the last few years or your STBX has borrowed for a business, these applications containing statements under oath as to income and asset values can be a treasure trove of information.

• **Retirement plan information** and plain language information regarding your account should be available from the plan administrator. Information regarding the largest plans, which are guaranteed by The Pension Benefit Guarantee Corporation (PBGC), can be accessed at http://www.pbgc.gov/wr/trusteed/plans.html.

• **Life, homeowners, valuable items, and umbrella insurance policies** can be obtained from your insurance agent or insurance company.

Begin Organizing For Success With a Goals Statement

One of the basic truths in Chapter 2 is that while organization doesn't guarantee you'll have a functional divorce, disorganization usually guarantees that you won't. The first thing you need to organize is ... *you*. Start with a list of your divorce goals. The Sample Goals Statement provided in Chapter 1 (reproduced below) should help you write your own.[5]

---

[5] Note: The items in this Goals Statement are examples only, and are NOT intended to be used as goals in your case.

Sample Goals Statement

- Shield the children from the divorce conflict as much as possible
- Divide time with the children as practically as possible
- Determine if the children need counseling
- Provide for sufficient alimony and child support to stay in the house until... [the oldest/youngest child leaves for college]
- Allocate responsibility for the children's extra-curricular activities, camp, tutoring, religious training, etc.
- Require each of us to contribute to college education according to our respective abilities
- Divide our assets 50/50, except that I keep my investment account that includes money I inherited
- Allocate the debts fairly between us
- Establish methods to resolve any disputes regarding the sale of our home after the divorce
- Look for off-the-books cash receipts in STBX's business, possibly using a forensic expert
- If there's an audit of our joint tax returns, protect me from paying deficiencies resulting from STBX's business
- Protection for me if STBX files for bankruptcy
- Prevent additional home equity line borrowing except by agreement
- Require life insurance coverage to ensure support
- Provide for children's health insurance and non-covered expenses

Needs vs. Positions

You're more likely to achieve your goals if you can express them in terms of needs rather than positions. For example, let's say you want to maximize your time with your kids who live primarily with your STBX. This might lead you to demand "joint physical custody."

"Joint physical custody" is a position. Your desire is to spend as much time with your children as you can. Focusing on that will help avoid rigid positions (and hot-button legalisms) that can obstruct settlement.

As you can see, a Goals Statement need not specify how your goals are to be achieved. That will be for you and your lawyer to decide, weighing the potential benefits of a course of action against its costs.

How to Prioritize Your Goals

Very few people achieve all of their divorce goals, so it's important to prioritize them. Weigh the importance of each of your goals by asking yourself the following questions:

* Is my goal (e.g., alimony of a specific amount or percentage) realistic given the circumstances?
* Is my goal important enough to me that I would be willing to give up something important to achieve it?
* Might pursuing my goal (for example, getting an item of personal property that has emotional significance to my STBX) harm prospects for overall settlement?
* Is there another way to state my goal that will be less threatening to my STBX?
* Is my goal something that the divorce process is intended or able to achieve?
* Is my goal motivated by what's in my or my children's interests as opposed to malice toward my STBX?
* Might achieving my goal sacrifice long-term interests to a less important "win" in the present? For example, would limiting my STBX's time with the children come at the expense of the children's interest in maintaining strong ties to both parents?

You may need a lawyer's advice to answer these questions. Prioritizing goals is an important task. Don't hesitate to seek help with it.

Questions For Your Lawyer

Writing out a Goals Statement will also alert you to matters you need to know more about. Make a list of those issues for discussion with your lawyer. It might include, for example:

* To what extent should alimony payments be modifiable as to amount or duration?
* What happens if our financial circumstances change substantially?
* How does cohabitation affect alimony?

- What happens if one of us wants to move out of the area?
- Can my settlement agreement include a method for resolving post-divorce disputes without going to court?
- Can penalties for non-compliance with our agreement be established now?
- Can my agreement include provisions for pet care & custody?
- Can I get a contribution from my STBX to my attorney fees?

Organize With a Divorce Binder

Divorces involve a pile of documents. You can make sure you're able to access the important ones quickly with a divorce binder. Even in the electronic 21st Century, binders provide an easy way to organize and share documents with your lawyer, mediator, or collaborative attorney.

Start with a single 1½-inch binder. Pick up numbered binder dividers—a 12-set if your case is court-based; a 10-set if you are in ADR. Set up your Table of Contents as follows:

Divorce Binder Sections

Court-based Cases

1. Financial Disclosure Statements
2. Atty./Client Correspondence/Memos
3. Court filings
4. Discovery Requests & Responses
5. Parenting Issues
6. Support Calculations
7. Assets & Liabilities
8. Financial Exhibits
9. Non-Financial Exhibits
10. Agreements & Orders
11. Tax Return Excerpts
12. Research and Notes

ADR Cases

1. Financial Disclosure Statements
2. Atty./Client Correspondence/Memos
3. Court Filings
4. Parenting Issues
5. Support Calculations
6. Assets & Liabilities
7. Agreements & Orders
8. Tax Return Excerpts
9. Education
10. Research and Session Notes

Writing Your Marital History

Your lawyer may ask you for a "marital history" or chronology. If she doesn't have her own form, prepare one in *outline form* like the one below. You get no points for style, so the fewer words, the better.

1. *Personal background*

- Date of marriage, separation(s)
- Former marriages and ages of children from prior relationships
- Events contributing to the breakdown of the marriage[6]
- Approximate dates of any marriage counseling
- Significant professional achievements such as promotions, awards, and industry recognition
- Health including significant illnesses or disabilities
- Substance abuse or mental health issues

2. *Financial history and highlights*

- Values of assets owned and debts owed at the time of the marriage
- Employment histories with positions held, dates, and incomes
- Significant financial events such as inheritances,[7] acquisition of property, and squandering or waste of assets
- Bankruptcy
- Educational background

---

[6] Before doing this, see the material below regarding whether a chronicle of spousal misconduct is worth your time and money.

[7] In a majority of states, inheritances are not considered "marital property" that a court can distribute. Connecticut and Massachusetts are exceptions to the rule.

3. *Children's issues*

- *Pendente lite* parenting plan
- Areas of co-parenting agreements and disagreements
- Children's talents and achievements
- Children's special needs and related matters such as individualized education plans (IEPs), physical therapy, or counseling
- Children's expressed desires regarding sharing time with parents
- Anticipated significant child-related expenses such as orthodontia, car purchase, tutoring, *Bar/Bat Mitzvah,* travel for athletics or other events or competitions

Mess Makes Stress: More Organizing Tips
For Your Divorce and Divorce After-Life

- Check out personal finance software such as MoneyLine or Quicken. Besides helping you organize, PF software can save you lots of that fun time you spend paying bills.
- Consider using your financial disclosure statement to help take control of your finances. Though totaling up your expenses can be disheartening, use what you learn to stay within a budget in the future.
- Manage your time efficiently with electronic or actual To Be Done Lists.
- Handle paperwork (once) with 1-touch paper management techniques.
- Organize your correspondence, bills, and account statements in color-coded folders.
- Keep your Divorce Binder handy . . . to you, not your kids!

Staying Relaxed and Healthy

Obviously, good health and stress reduction involve more than organization. The steps listed below are not only good for you; they will foster a more productive, efficient, and thus less expensive attorney/client relationship.

- <u>Learn relaxation techniques such as yoga and meditation</u>. If you haven't tried meditation, there are, of course, apps and sites to show you how, such as Headspace ("the world's first gym membership for the mind") at https://www.headspace.com
or "Headspace-on-the-go" (IOS & Android) at
https://www.headspace.com/headspace-meditation-app.
- <u>Maintain an exercise schedule</u>. If you're not the gym type, there are plenty of apps for cardio, core exercises, etc.
- <u>Eat well</u>. You don't have to shop at high-end organic grocery stores to
  - ᵒ Eat a balanced diet with plenty of fresh fruits and vegetables
  - ᵒ Lay off soda and other sugar-laden products
  - ᵒ Drink lots of water
- <u>Seek counseling</u>. If you don't need therapy during a divorce, you probably never will. Check with a qualified therapist to see if you might.
- <u>Have some fun once in a while</u>!
- <u>Avoid isolation</u>. Nothing good comes out of brooding at home. And

your networking opportunities there are pretty much limited to mail carriers, repairmen and the kid from down the street selling magazines.

- <u>Sleep like Chuck</u>. My dog Chuck is a very accomplished sleeper. He's much better at it than I am—and he doesn't worry half as much as I do, so connect the dots. Try the following to help you sleep like Chuck:
  - ᵒ Establish a pre-sleep routine built around relaxation, such as a hot bath, meditation, or light reading. Avoid bright lights, including TV. And turn off all electronics.
  - ᵒ Don't drink alcohol, smoke cigarettes or drink caffeinated beverages within 4 to 6 hours of bedtime. Try not to take in liquids for a few hours, so you don't wake up in the middle of the night to get them back out.
  - ᵒ Experiment with the thermostat to find your best sleep temperature—a degree or 2 can make a big difference.

Chuck, an accomplished sleeper, avoids ill health associated with the lack of it.

- ° Don't nap within 8 hours of your bedtime. However, if you've had a bad sleep night, a 20 or 30-minute nap sometime the next day can be surprisingly rejuvenating.
- ° If possible, catch up on lost weeknight sleep with extra sleep on the weekends.
- ° If nothing else gets you to sleep, try reading Chapter 9 on taxes. That should do it.

Keeping an Eye on Yourself

Wouldn't it be cool if there were apps to monitor your sleep and other lifestyle habits? Well, there are, of course. Check out a fitness-tracking app such as Jawbone UP, Fitbit, or Pillow-Neybox to chart your physical activity, as well as sleep and eating habits.

Avoid Unnecessary Confrontations That Damage the Attorney/Client Relationship

No matter if your arrangement with your lawyer is traditional, ADR-based or unbundled, problems can arise. Some of your lawyer's conduct may seem insensitive, lazy or inattentive to you.

But her conduct may not be as inappropriate as you think. Below is a list of things lawyers do that might irritate you, accompanied by possible explanations for them. If you encounter such conduct, discuss it with your lawyer. It may turn out to be justified or at least explainable.

- At the beginning of your case, your lawyer may be busy with other matters. If there are no urgent issues early in your case, it makes sense for your lawyer to be giving priority to court hearings, settlement negotiations, or trial preparation in cases that are further along.
- Your lawyer may appear insensitive to you. Veteran divorce lawyers often become desensitized to the emotional aspects of divorce. However, this may be a blessing in disguise if it sends you to a mental health professional who does emotional support better and cheaper.
- Your lawyer will not always agree with you as to which details of your case are important. She may be right to focus on the "big picture" that is likely to decide your case.

- Even if you have emphasized that you wish to settle, your lawyer may continue to reference what a judge might do in your case. This is simply a "yardstick" that lawyers use during settlement negotiations.
- You might feel that your lawyer is either too friendly or too antagonistic to opposing counsel. However, your lawyer may simply be using the tactics she feels will be most effective.

Deciding Whether to Fire Your Lawyer

Despite your best efforts, your relationship with your lawyer may continue to be unsatisfactory. Changing lawyers isn't the end of the world; if there's one thing the world has no shortage of, it's divorce lawyers. However, changing lawyers invariably causes duplication of effort and thus additional expense. So how do you know if it's time for a barrister trade-in?

A Half-Dozen Ways to Drive Your Lawyer Nuts
- Calling your lawyer at home after hours
- Calling your lawyer certain other things at any hour
- Acting on advice from others that conflicts with your lawyer's advice
- "Goin' Rogue:" negotiating directly with your spouse without first consulting your lawyer
- Failing to disclose important information to your lawyer
- Drowning your lawyer in unnecessary paperwork

Confronting Attorney/Client Relationship Problems

Make a list of the things that bother or worry you about your lawyer. They might include, for example, hefty bills that have brought little result, or your lawyer failing to:

- Return phone calls or reply to emails quickly enough
- Fully explain legalities
- Fully explain her strategy
- Update you on developments
- Attend to pressing needs such as temporary support

Before throwing back your barrister and reeling in another...

- Discuss your concerns candidly with your lawyer in an attempt to fix the problems, including finding out how your own conduct may be contributing to the dysfunction

- Weigh the cost of paying another lawyer to get "up to speed" on your case

- Get a 2nd opinion from another lawyer regarding whether
  - ○ Your current lawyer is pursuing necessary discovery
  - ○ Your current lawyer's settlement "game plan" is valid
  - ○ Your case is proceeding at a reasonable pace
  - ○ Your case has become unnecessarily contentious
  - ○ Your lawyer has been responsive to your reasonable needs and goals
  - ○ Your lawyer has kept you informed and prepared for what may come next
  - ○ Your lawyer's assessment of likely outcomes in your case is accurate
  - ○ Reasonable *pendente lite* orders and agreements have been obtained
  - ○ The lawyer would be willing to take your case, or can recommend competent counsel who will

You might find that there are reasons for the conduct that has bothered you such as a temporarily heavy case-load or some of the explanations mentioned above. If not, you have to consider making a change. As Chuck would say, there are plenty of tennis balls in the sea.

 Yes, there *IS* a quiz! Test what you have (or haven't) learned.

1. Alternate titles to this chapter could be:
   A. "Mission Impossible"
   B. "Death by Divorce: How to Avoid Choking on Retainers, Drowning in Paperwork and Being Mauled by Tigers"
   C. "How to Sleep Like a Dog"

2. [Activity] To make absolutely sure your children won't leaf through your divorce binder, slip a sheet of paper between the front cover and the plastic overlay, bearing any one of the following titles:
   A. *"Sweat Equity:* Jobs Kids Can Do Around the House."
   B. "Why Algebra Matters"
   C. "*SQOOMBA!* 25 Zoomba Square Dance Routines for Cardio, Core, and Cornpone"

CHAPTER 8

Preparing and Analyzing Financial Disclosure Statements

"Seldom, very seldom, does complete truth belong to any human disclosure."

— Jane Austen

Introduction to the Financial Disclosure Statement

The financial disclosure statement, or "financial affidavit," is the most important document in your divorce. It is heavily relied upon by divorce lawyers negotiating settlement, and by family court judges deciding cases.

Disclosure forms provide a summary of each spouse's financial circumstances. The forms typically require detailed information regarding income, expenses, assets, and liabilities.

The following states provide a short form disclosure statement for "lower income" individuals:

- Florida for individuals whose gross annual income is less than $50,000
- Connecticut for individuals whose gross annual income and net assets total less than $75,000.00
- Massachusetts for individuals whose gross annual income is less than $75,000

Proper preparation of a disclosure statement takes time. You can save attorney and paralegal fees by preparing a solid first draft yourself early in your case, or even before it begins. In this chapter, you'll learn how to:

- Prepare your disclosure statement accurately
- Show your finances in the most advantageous way
- Analyze your spouse's disclosure to make sure it shows
  - All income, including "perks" and "add-backs"
  - The *full* value of all assets

Finding Your Financial Disclosure Statement Form

You can access disclosure statement forms on your court system's website.[1] Your search of the site should go something like this:

- Locate the "Forms" page.
- Select "Family" or "Domestic Relations" forms.
- Find "Financial disclosure statement," "Financial affidavit," "Net worth statement," or something similar.
- If necessary, choose the "short" or "long" form that applies to you.

> ⚠️ **Saving Lots of Time on Your Disclosure Statement**
>
> Some state financial disclosure forms automatically add numbers in each section and post them to the form's subtotal summary. Test your state's form to see if it contains these functions. If so, you're in luck! You just saved yourself a bundle of time having to recalculate subtotals each time you change a number.
>
> CAUTION: Print and save your work frequently using the "Save As" feature to make sure your work is preserved.

Before beginning work on the form:

- Review it in its entirety to avoid inserting numbers in one section that belong in another.
- Ask your lawyer, financial planner or divorce analyst questions such as
  - Can I use all of my payroll deductions to reduce my income?
  - How do I deal with self-employment income?
  - Can I reduce my income with expenses like child-care?
  - For expenses like food, clothing, etc., should I separate what is for the kids and what is for me?
  - Can I include as expenses items that I have been putting off because I can't afford them, like home repairs and auto repair?
  - Should I include my house on my statement even though it's in my STBX's name?

---

[1] Many states permit use of manuscripted disclosure statements as long as they substantially conform to the court form. If you have retained a lawyer, check to make sure your lawyer uses the court form before beginning to fill it out.

- ○ Can I show 50% of the value of jointly owned property?
- ○ Should I include
  - ▪ Jointly owned property?
  - ▪ My STBX's retirement plan?
  - ▪ Trusts or inherited property?
- ○ How do I handle the discretionary bonus that I might or might not get this year?
- ○ I haven't earned much yet this year from my seasonal business. Should I put what I've earned or base my income on last year's totals?
- ○ Should I include, as a liability, money my parents gave me during the divorce that they told me to pay back when I can?
- Gather the information and documents discussed below

Documents You Will Need to Prepare Your Disclosure Statement

The following documents will contain much of the information you will need to prepare your disclosure statement:

- 24 to 36 months of
  - ○ Checkbook registers
  - ○ Bank and security account statements
  - ○ Credit card statements
- Your most recent retirement account (including IRA) statements
- Summaries from amazon.com, PayPal, and other on-line stores and payment resources
- Statements for bills that you are paying in installments
- Income and business tax returns (2 to 5 years' worth)
- Most recent mortgage interest and property tax payment records
- Appraisals of real estate or other property you own
- Homeowners' insurance valuable item schedules

Save yourself grief on your disclosure statement: Ask your lawyer, financial planner, or divorce analyst any questions you have before you begin!

Filling Out Your Disclosure Statement

Disclosure statements include the following 4 areas, each of which will be discussed below:

1. Income
2. Expenses
3. Assets
4. Liabilities

Income

Because support is "income-driven," your income is the single most import-ant number on your disclosure statement. It is crucial to show it accurately and in a way that is not unfair to you.

⚠ Pay Stub Pitfalls

Divorce clients and lawyers alike often use an income figure based on the client's most recent paystub. That can be a serious mistake. If you are a wage earner, discuss with your lawyer how to:

- Avoid understating the taxes you will pay for the year based on a paystub that claims too many exemptions.
- Present in a manner that is fair to you income that varies due to commis-sions, discretionary bonuses, overtime, seasonal work, etc.
- "Back out" deductions on your paystub that are impermissible for sup-port calculations, such as voluntary pension contributions.
- Include the FICA deduction that is omitted from a late year paystub if you have reached the maximum annual income amount subject to FICA ($118,500 in 2016). In such situations, show your annual net income more accurately by dividing the total FICA paid (based on "year-to-date" figures on the paystub) by the total number of pay periods in the year.
- In determining your weekly or monthly income (some states require weekly numbers, some monthly), use the proper number of pay periods; e.g. does the paystub of a wage earner who is paid "twice a month" rep-resent 1 of 24 or 1 of 26 pay periods per year?

If you are self-employed with irregular income, your year-to-date numbers at any point in the year may not accurately forecast your annual income. If so, discuss with your lawyer, accountant or a certified divorce planner how to show your income in a way that is fair to you. Your options include basing your income calculation on:

- Your previous year's income, especially early in the year
- Year-to-date income and expense numbers
- Where permitted, a projection of the current year's numbers

---

What Does "Net Income" Mean?

"Net income" can be a misleading term for the self-employed because it can be used to mean either:

- Gross revenues less business-related expenses, OR
- Gross revenues less
  - Business-related expenses AND
  - Personal income taxes

If you are self-employed, make sure that you have deducted all business-related expenses from the income number shown on your disclosure statement. Then, in states where support is based upon "net income," ask your lawyer or tax preparer to calculate the amount of income taxes to be deducted from THAT.

Expenses

Calculating your expenses will likely be the most time-consuming part of preparing your disclosure statement. Use your check register, credit card statements, amazon.com account, online payment services such as PayPal, etc. to identify your expenses. Find out if you can include expenses that you've incurred traditionally but have been unable to afford recently, by using footnotes to note that fact.

You may well have expenses that don't appear on the disclosure form. If so, add a supplemental page to list such expenses and then "bring forward" the total of the expenses on that page to a line on the form for "other expenses."

Children's Expenses

If you are seeking child support:

- Identify and separate your children's expenses from your own
- Jog your memory regarding child-related expenses with a foray into your children's rooms. Don't worry. It's not snooping. It's *research*.

- Visit http://www.cnpp.usda.gov/tools/CRC_Calculator/default.aspx to get USDA child-raising cost estimates based upon factors such as number of children, locale and income.

Typical child-related expenses

Use the list of children's expenses below to avoid leaving anything out.

- Child care
    - Day care and pre-school facility fees and activity expenses
    - Babysitters
- Medical/Health
    - Unreimbursed expenses (not covered or subject to insurance deductibles)
    - Unreimbursed costs of medications, vitamins, inhalers, etc.
    - Unreimbursed therapy, dental, and orthodontia (including appliances)
- Clothing
- Education
    - Private school tuition
    - Boarding school room & board
    - Books, supplies, and activity fees
    - Religious school
    - Tutors
    - Field trips and special functions (school dances, proms, performances)
    - Lunches
- Extracurricular activities
    - Athletics (lessons, fees, uniforms, equipment)
    - Arts (lessons, instruments, supplies, clothing)
    - Group activities (clubs, Scouts, orchestras, etc.)
    - Hobbies (lessons, equipment, materials, etc.)
- Summer and vacation camp activities and programs
    - Room, board, and fees
    - Transportation
- Entertainment
    - Movies
    - Special events (theatre, athletic events, etc.)
    - Toys, books, magazines, CD & DVDs, electronic games, downloads, etc.
    - Trips (skiing, etc.)

- Special celebrations (graduations, religious functions, etc.)
    - Gifts, outfits, supplies, and accessories
    - Birthday & holiday expenses
    - Gifts for other children's birthdays and special celebrations
- Automobile expense
    - Insurance
    - Registration
    - Gas, maintenance, and repair
- Travel
- Miscellaneous
    - Electronic/wireless device expense and fees (smart-phones, computers, iPads, chargers, flash drives, internet fees)
    - Grooming, haircuts, toiletries/cosmetics
    - Gym fees

Don't Lose the Forest For the Trees

Take a step back from your disclosure statement and consider whether the income and expense totals make sense. For example, if your expenses are substantially more than your income, see if the difference can be explained by

- Unpaid credit card balances and other unpaid bills
- Other money you've borrowed
- Inclusion of expenses that you normally have but have not been incurring lately because the divorce has caused a cash shortage
- Inclusion of expenses paid by your STBX, parents or others. (Ask your lawyer about providing an explanation in such circumstances with a footnote or attachment.)

If you cannot account for the disparity between income and expenses, consider revising your figures.

Liabilities

Making a list of your debts or "liabilities" seems easy enough to do. Painful perhaps, but easy. However, things can get complicated if you fail to:

- Understand the difference between expenses and liabilities. Expenses are costs that you continue to incur regularly. Liabilities are debts you already owe, such as medical bills or credit card prior balances.[2]
- Avoid "double-dips." These often appear on disclosure statements inadvertently, for example where
    - An auto loan balance listed in the liability section has already been deducted from the car's value in the asset section
    - A mortgage balance listed as a liability has already been deducted from the fair market value of the family home

Showing such loans again as liabilities in the liability section has the effect of reducing your net worth twice for the same loans.

Assets

In the majority of states, your disclosure statement should only include assets in which you have an ownership interest.[3] Thus, your spouse's retirement plans, leased cars and the like probably don't belong on *your* disclosure statement.

Below are some ways to show particular assets in the most favorable light to you.

- Real estate. If your marital home or other real estate is being sold and you will get the proceeds or the majority of them in the settlement, you may be able to reduce the value of what you will receive by the amount of
    - Certain fix-up expenses incurred
    - Realtor's commissions
    - Projected capital gains taxes

- Retirement accounts. Retirement funds are generally subject to income taxes when withdrawn.[4] (And if you make a withdrawal from a retirement account prior to age 59½ that is *not* related to your divorce, the IRS has another surprise for you: a 10% penalty!) It is generally permissible

---

[2] Note that while a credit card prior balance is a liability, accruing interest and fees can be included in your expense section.

[3] As with all aspects of your disclosure statement, confirm that your state law is consistent with the general rules mentioned here.

[4] The Roth IRA is an exception. See Internal Revenue Service Publication 590.

to reduce retirement account values on your disclosure statement by estimated future income taxes so long as you note the amount of the reduction on the statement. As always, however, check with your lawyer to determine the practice in your state or locale.

- Partnerships. If you are a member of a partnership, ask your lawyer whether your ownership interest must be valued. In this connection, try to find out whether a recent appraisal is available.

Bear in mind that if you own a minority interest in a partnership, the value of your interest can be reduced or "discounted" because you can't control partnership business decisions such as whether to sell the company or property that it owns. That makes your interest less valuable and your disclosure statement should reflect that lower value.

- Assets with nominal or undetermined values. Assets that have little or no value may still need to be included on your disclosure statement. To avoid claims that you failed to fully disclose all assets, err on the side of caution regarding property such as collectibles that you think have little or no value. Depending upon local custom, state that the value of such assets is "undetermined" and/or "believed to be nominal."[5]

Reviewing and Revising Disclosure Statements

Once you have completed your draft disclosure statement, review it carefully. Step back from the details to see if it jives with your overall financial circumstances. Check in particular for the common mistakes and issues listed below. (Apply the same analysis when you get your STBX's statement.)

Mistakes to Avoid and Issues to Consider Regarding Your Disclosure Statement

- If spending exceeds available cash (take-home pay, credit card charges, loans, gifts, bank withdrawals, etc.), *where's the money coming from?*
- Why is there no mention of a retirement plan in the asset section even though the income section shows a retirement deduction?
- Have you double-dipped mortgage or car-loan balances?
- Do you show earnings for assets you list such as stock accounts?

---

[5] Note that term life insurance policies generally believed to have no cash or "surrender" value, may have "return of premium" features allowing refund of a portion of premiums upon expiration.

- Is the amount of taxes deducted on your disclosure statement substantially different from what your tax return reflects because, for example:
  - The number of exemptions you claim does not take into consideration your mortgage interest and property tax deductions, etc.
  - Your STBX's income has substantially altered your effective tax rate on joint tax returns
- Did you use a monthly figure for a weekly expense or vice versa?
- Did you treat a semi-monthly paycheck (24 pay periods per year) as if it were bi-weekly (26 pay periods per year)?
- Did you neglect property such as savings bond wedding gifts in your safe deposit box?

Most of the mistakes and inconsistencies above are caused by sloppiness rather than dishonesty. But it may not appear that way if you are cross-examined regarding your disclosure statement at a deposition or court hearing. So be sure to:

- Review your draft disclosure statement carefully before turning it over to your lawyer
- Update your disclosure statement to reflect any substantial changes while your case is pending

Analyzing Your Spouse's Disclosure Statement

Determining Income of a Self-Employed Spouse

It can be difficult to determine the "real income" of self-employed spouses. Your knowledge of your spouse's business can be a huge help to your lawyer. Income and expenses are found in a business's financial statements ("financials") and on various tax returns depending on the nature of the business entity.

Take your time and prepare your disclosure statement carefully to avoid mistakes.

Tax Reporting by Various Types of Businesses

The manner in which income is taxed and reported to IRS depends on the type of business:

- Unincorporated businesses such as sole proprietorships and limited liability companies ("LLCs"): Income and expenses are shown on

"Schedule C" of the individual's Form 1040 income tax return; no other federal income tax returns are required.

- C Corporations: Form 1120: The corporation files a tax return and is subject to tax. C corporations can create "double taxation": a tax on the corporation's earnings and a second tax on dividends received by the shareholders. However, shareholders of a C corporation who receive a share of the company's profits as dividends rather than compensation, typically pay taxes on those dividends at a lower rate than they would have paid on salary or other compensation.

- Subchapter S Corporations: The corporation files a Form 1120S. However, the corporation is not taxed. Instead, the income is "passed through" to the shareholders and taxed at ordinary income tax rates, much like unincorporated sole proprietorships, partnerships, and LLCs.

- Partnerships: Partnerships file Form 1065 "informational" tax returns but it is the partners, not the partnership, who are taxed. Note that a partner is taxed on his "distributive share" of income whether or not he receives it. This can create "phantom income" that is shown on tax returns and taxed as income even though the partner doesn't receive it.

⚠ Income Add-Backs: Increasing Income With "Disallowed Expenses"

Business owners are permitted to reduce the business' income by deducting expenses that are "ordinary and necessary" to production of business income. IRS disallows deductions for expenses that are only partly business-related or not related to the business at all. Disallowed expenses such as the following may be "added back" to taxable compensation both for income tax purposes and for purposes of calculating support:

Stay awake! We're nearly done with disclosure statements!

- Home and family members' cell phone bills
- Vehicle expense such as
  - Gas, repair and maintenance for non-business vehicles
  - Gas, repair and maintenance for business owned vehicles not being used for business purposes
  - Depreciation and insurance on non-business vehicles

- Commuting expense
- Primarily personal travel and lodging expense[6]
- Personal expenses incurred on combination business and pleasure trips[7]
- Expenses of family members or other companions during business trips
- Personal meals and entertainment
- Dues to clubs and fraternal or veterans' organizations
- Expenditures not "ordinary and necessary" to the business
- "Consultant" and other fees paid to family members who perform no services for the business
- Inflated home office expense
- Travel expense purchased with frequent flyer miles
- Hobby losses (losses generated by a "business" that has operated at a loss for 3 of 5 years)
- Personal legal expenses
- Political contributions
- Fines and penalties such as automobile moving violations and parking tickets

⚠ Business Expense Deductions That Family Judges May "Add Back"

Judges determining child or spousal support are not required to accept all business deductions that IRS allows to reduce taxable income. Deductions that are permissible for income tax purposes but which a judge may nonetheless "add back" to income for purposes of calculating support can include the following:

- Accelerated Depreciation. Some courts will disallow certain "paper deductions" such as accelerated depreciation that don't involve an outlay of cash in the current year[8]
- Entertainment and travel allowances deducted from business income to the extent that such allowances reduce the taxpayer's usual expenses
- Voluntary contributions to retirement plans
- Home office deduction

---

[6] Note that IRS has different rules for travel within, and outside the U.S.

[7] IRS Publication 463 contains specific rules for allocating time between business and personal days on combined business and pleasure trips.

[8] This applies particularly to "accelerated depreciation" as opposed to "straight-line depreciation." Don't panic over the terminology—ask your tax preparer, for further explanation.

- Excessive auto expenses[9]
- Some amount of travel and entertainment
- Any other expenses that appear excessive or inappropriate to the business

Scrutinizing Wage and Salary Earners' Incomes

It's not only self-employment income that should be analyzed in connection with support calculations. In the circumstances listed below, it is also important to scrutinize a wage earner's income.

Factors in Determining a Wage Earner's Income For Support Calculations

- Whether and how to factor in overtime
- Whether discretionary bonuses and other incentives should be included
- The impact of work hours that vary from one pay period to another
- The impact of seasonal work
- Non-cash perks such as use of company car
- Expense accounts
- Commissions and tips
- Whether payroll deductions such as mandatory retirement account contributions (generally a permitted deduction for support purposes) vs. elective contributions (generally not permissible) can be used to reduce income available for child or spousal support

Analyzing Your Spouse's Assets

In addition to scrutinizing income, consider the following regarding the asset section of your STBX's disclosure statement:

- Whether the asset values are consistent with information you have (or will obtain through the discovery process) including information appearing on
  - Loan applications
  - Homeowners' or renters' insurance personal property schedules
  - Safe deposit box inventories
  - Tax returns
  - Statements from financial institutions
  - Receipts and bills of sale

---

[9] Note that if a taxpayer attempts to deduct both actual auto expense and the IRS business mileage rate ($.54/mile in 2016), IRS will disallow one of them.

- Whether the asset values have been reduced by projected taxes, selling expense, etc. and, if so, whether such reductions conform to state law and customs of your local courthouse
- Whether any mortgage or other loan that has been deducted from the asset value has been double-dipped as a liability
- Whether any assets are missing
- Whether the values add up – check the arithmetic!

Reporting Inaccuracies on Your Spouse's Disclosure Statement

Once you've completed your review of your spouse's disclosure statement
- Prepare a list of comments and questions for your lawyer (arranged in the order in which the items appear on the disclosure statement) and/or annotate a copy of the disclosure statement itself
- Make your comments concise and your annotations legible.

If you've found major discrepancies between your spouse's statement and the real world, consider meeting with your lawyer to underscore their importance.

 Yes, there *IS* a quiz! Test what you have (or haven't) learned.

1. This chapter is mainly about:
   A. Snooping around my kids' rooms to find out what they manage to spend their allowance on within hours of receiving it
   B. How to stay awake reading unbelievably boring stuff about disclosure statements—what's next, a chapter on taxes?
   C. How to prepare my financial disclosure statement properly and consistent with my goals, and to test my STBX's statement for omissions and inaccuracies

2. Unscramble the following key phrases from this chapter!
   A. Thros morf lessudirco meettants
   B. Snesubis Snepexes
   C. Emicon dad-kacbs

CHAPTER 9

Taking Advantage of Divorce Tax Breaks

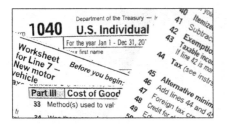

"Anyone who lives within their means suffers from a lack of imagination."

— Oscar Wilde

Thumb Tax: A Thumbnail Sketch of Divorce Tax Savings

You can save tax dollars and make the tax code work for you during your divorce in a variety of ways:

- Deducting qualifying legal fees
- Using the alimony deduction properly
- Identifying tax costs of assets to be transferred in the property settlement
- Taking advantage of special divorce tax rules
- Including tax-friendly language in your settlement agreement

All of the above will be covered in this chapter. If at all possible, seek help from a qualified professional to make sure you do what's necessary to make these tax saving techniques work for you.

How to Grow Tax Deductible Legal Fees

Personal (non-business) legal fees are generally *not* deductible from taxable income. But some very cool exceptions to that rule can save you an IRS auditor's briefcase full of taxes, and thus substantially reduce the cost of your divorce.

You may be entitled to deduct a portion of legal fees incurred for:

- Creating taxable income such as alimony
- Obtaining an interest in your STBX's retirement plan
- Obtaining other taxable income such as royalties and residuals
- Tax planning advice
- Identifying and collecting tax refunds

Legal Fee Deduction Requirements

Since we're talking about IRS rules, there are, of course, conditions and requirements involved in deducting legal fees:

- You must file tax returns separately from your STBX for the year in which you take the deduction.
- You must obtain an "allocation letter" from your lawyer stating which of your fees are tax deductible and why.
- The deductible portion of your fees must exceed 2% of your adjusted gross income ("AGI"), subject to high-income phase-outs.

Making the Legal Fee Deduction Work For You

To maximize and protect your deduction for certain legal fees & expenses, take the following steps:

- Pay as much of your fees as possible in a single calendar year to exceed the 2% of AGI threshold
- At the beginning of your case, ask your lawyer if it is possible to segregate potentially deductible services on her bills
- Don't go overboard with the legal fee deduction

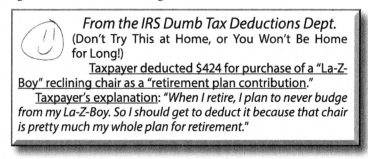

From the IRS Dumb Tax Deductions Dept.
(Don't Try This at Home, or You Won't Be Home for Long!)
      Taxpayer deducted $424 for purchase of a "La-Z-Boy" reclining chair as a "retirement plan contribution."
   Taxpayer's explanation: *"When I retire, I plan to never budge from my La-Z-Boy. So I should get to deduct it because that chair is pretty much my whole plan for retirement."*

The Alimony Tax Deduction

Spousal support structured in accordance with IRS alimony rules is deductible to the obligor and taxable to the recipient. If a recipient pays taxes on the alimony in a lower tax bracket than the bracket in which the obligor deducts it, substantial tax savings occur. In Chapter 12, we'll discuss more about how alimony can save both spouses money.

> ⚠ NOTE: The exemption, tax credit and income thresholds discussed below apply to 2016 taxes. Most exemptions change annually and some 2016 amounts may have been revised slightly. Check for updates at https://www.irs.gov/credits-deductions.

More Divorce Tax Savings Opportunities

In addition to the alimony and legal fee deductions, there are other tax savings available to you during and after your divorce.

- Allocation of children's exemptions: You can allocate between you and your STBX exemptions for your children and related child tax credits. The exemptions belong to the parent having custody of a child for more than half the calendar year while providing more than half the child's support. However, the non-primary custodial parent can be entitled to a child exemption if the child lives with him/her more than half the year.

  In addition, a custodial parent can assign to the other parent exemptions for children on a temporary, permanent, or alternating basis, using IRS Form 8332.[1] This is particularly useful if the custodial parent's income exceeds the AGI levels at which exemptions begin to be phased out ($259,400 for individuals and $285,350 for Heads of Household in 2016).

- Head of Household income tax filing status: The custodial parent is entitled to Head of Household ("HOH") filing status that results in lower taxes than filing as "Single" after the divorce or "Married Filing Separately" (the least desirable filing status) prior to the divorce decree. Except in split custody situations where each parent can claim HOH

---

[1] See IRS Publication 504, *Divorced or Separated Individuals*.

status based on having custody of one or more children, only one parent is entitled to HOH status.

NOTE: It is not necessary to claim the "qualifying child" as a dependent. This allows allocation between spouses of dependent exemptions in a way that maximizes their benefit. To qualify for Head of Household status, you must

- Have a child living in your home for more than half the calendar year
- Provide more than half the cost of maintaining the household
- Be unmarried as of December 31st or have lived separately from your spouse for more than 6 months
- Have been a U.S. citizen or resident alien for the entire tax year
- The child has health insurance as required by law

• Child Tax Credit: Worth as much as $1,000 for a dependent child if
  - The child is under 17 as of December 31st

Your Tax Deduction Coupon Book

Think of the Internal Revenue Code as a coupon book—but with discounts on taxes instead of pizza. You won't need the cardiologist that too many free pizza promotions might require, but you *will* need a tax professional to make sure you qualify for the savings.

Buy 10 Pizzas Get One FREE

Al's Grease Pit & Fructose Emporium

- You claim the child as a dependent on your income tax returns
- The child is your child, stepchild, foster child, adopted child, brother, sister, stepbrother, stepsister, or a descendent of one of these individuals (e.g., grandchild, niece or nephew)
- The child did not provide more than half of his/her own support during the year
- The child is a U.S. citizen, U.S. national, or U.S. resident alien
- The child does not file a joint income tax return for the year except to claim a refund

• Child and Dependent Care Credit: Worth up to 35% of child care expenses to the custodial parent, with maximums of $3,000 for one child and $6,000 in all, if

- The child is under age 13 or disabled
- The child lived with you for more than half the year
- You incurred child care expenses to allow you to earn
- Child care payments are not made to your spouse, the child's parent or a child under age 19[2]

- Lifetime Learning Credit: Subject to income limits, you can claim a lifetime learning credit of up to $2,000 for qualified education expenses paid for each dependent eligible student. The LLC is available for an unlimited number of years, provided that you do not elect the American Opportunity Credit (see below) in the same year for a particular student.

- American Opportunity Credit (formerly The Hope Credit): Subject to income limits, you can claim a credit of up to $2,500 per eligible dependent student (including yourself) for whom you claim an exemption on your tax return. Unlike the lifetime learning credit, 40% of the credit may be refundable, but it is available for only 4 years per student.

> ### What's the Difference Between a Tax Credit and a Tax Deduction?
> A tax deduction reduces the amount of your income that will be taxed. Tax credits are worth more because the amount of the credit is subtracted <u>directly from the taxes you owe</u>.

- Earned Income Tax Credit: In 2016, low-income families can claim up to the following amounts, depending on income level:[3]
  - $6,269 with 3 or more qualifying children
  - $5,572 with 2 qualifying children
  - $3,373 with 1 qualifying child
  - $506 with no qualifying children

Additional Tax Savings Tips

Careful drafting of your settlement agreement, proper preparation of your tax returns and even the timing of your divorce can help you realize additional tax savings and protect those for which you've negotiated.

---

[2] See IRS Publication 503 for numerous additional restrictions on using this credit.
[3] See IRS Publication 596 for more information including entitlement calculations.

- Make sure that your settlement agreement allocates the following between you and your STBX:
  - Mortgage interest deductions on jointly owned homes
  - Property tax deductions
  - Entitlement to income tax refunds
  - Responsibility for deficiencies on past joint tax returns, making sure that you are "indemnified and held harmless" as to any taxes for which your STBX is responsible

> *More from the IRS Dumb Tax Deductions Dept.*
> (Don't Try This at Home, or You Won't Be Home for Long!)
> <u>Taxpayer deducted $329 in airfare as "tax advice"</u>
> <u>Taxpayer's Explanation:</u> *"I flew to Charlotte to have Thanksgiving with my Cousin Sheldon the accountant. During halftime of the Dallas-Seattle game I said, 'Tell you what, Shelly—taxes is a bitch.' And Sheldon tax-advised me: 'No sh*t'!"*

To avoid a tax audit, your tax return must be consistent with your STBX's return as to the preceding items, as well as how much alimony was paid/received during the calendar year.

- If your final hearing date is near the end of the year and a joint tax return would save you a substantial amount of taxes, consider
  - Postponing a late-year final hearing until the following January
  - Going forward with your final hearing but asking the judge to delay the effective date of the dissolution until January 2nd

Protecting Yourself From Your STBX's IRS BS

You may be concerned that your STBX has exposed you to IRS problems on joint tax returns by under-reporting income, overstating deductions or other tax misbehavior in connection with his/her business. You may be particularly worried if you are a company officer or director.

If you have such concerns, take the following steps to protect yourself:

- Provide in your settlement agreement that your STBX "indemnify and hold you harmless" against any tax deficiencies (and accountants' or attorneys' fees and expenses you incur as a result) relating to his/her income or deductions.

- If you remain married at the end of a calendar year during the pendency of your divorce, consider filing separately to avoid any potential liability for your STBX's tax reporting shenanigans. Get advice before making this election because married filing separate status can disqualify you for other tax benefits such as the lifetime learning credit.
- Resign in writing as an officer or director of companies controlled by your STBX to avoid personal liability that corporate officers and directors may have in the following situations.
  - Failure to pay wages within the time periods required by state law, which under some states expose corporate officers and directors to liability for as much as three times the wages owed ("treble damages") and attorneys' fees

---

Still Another Divorce Tax Break!
With proper planning, you can get the full $500,000 capital gain exclusion on the sale of your *jointly owned* home, even after your divorce. (see page 218.) As with all the tax tips here, have a divorce financial analyst or CPA show you how.

  - Failure to properly withhold income and FICA taxes
  - Failure to pay minimum wages (e.g., to "interns") or overtime, which can also result in treble damages and attorneys' fees
  - Failure to pay Workers' Compensation insurance
  - Liability for corporate debts incurred after the corporation's privileges have been forfeited for failure to pay taxes or file reports.

Common Tax Mistakes During Divorce

Beware of the following common tax traps for the unwary:

- Failing to provide that alimony terminates upon the death of the recipient (unless state law requires such termination).
- Failing to consider tax consequences of an "alimony payoff" by which the obligor terminates his obligation by paying a year or more worth of alimony all at once

- Dividing up securities in a way that results in one of the parties receiving a disproportionate share of unrealized taxable gain
- Assigning dependency exemptions (and related tax credits) to a party who cannot maximize their use or use them at all due to the Alternative Minimum Tax (AMT)
- Mixing "apples & oranges" by trading retirement assets subject to tax for tax-free assets
- Creating a "taxable event" by a separation agreement that provides for a property transfer to occur more than six years after the divorce
- Relying upon pay stub tax numbers for your financial disclosure statements where a history of tax refunds reflects inflated withholding that ignores deductions such as mortgage interest and property taxes
- Where a separation agreement substitutes "unallocated alimony & child support" in lieu of separate payments of child support and alimony, ignoring IRS regulations that can disallow the alimony deduction and re-characterize or "recapture" unallocated alimony as non-deductible child support

 Yes, there IS a quiz! Test what you have (or haven't) learned.

1. This chapter is mainly about:
   A. Why we have to watch the Dallas Cowboys on TV every Thanksgiving
   B. Remembering to invite an accountant to Thanksgiving dinner so you can deduct your Butterball
   C. How to take advantage of divorce tax-saving opportunities

2. The reason that alimony, but not child support, is taxable to the recipient and deductible by the obligor, is:
   A. Because some Congressman who was getting divorced, wanted a tax break
   B. Because some divorcing oil company executive reminded Congress that the Constitution guarantees oil company executives tax breaks for everything
   C. Because child support, unlike alimony, is considered an absolute obligation and thus not appropriate for tax incentives

3. Unscramble the following key phrases from this chapter!
   yanimol ciddonute
   builddecet galle sefe
   drow beljums

CHAPTER 10

Child Custody, Care, and Comfort

"'Would you tell me, please, which way
I ought to go from here?'
'That depends a good deal on where you
want to get to,' said the Cat."

— Lewis Carroll, *Alice in Wonderland*

Caring For Your Children During Divorce

One of the most difficult aspects of divorce is that your children need extra attention just when you may be least able to provide it. Your challenge as a divorcing parent is to attend to your children's fears and anxieties despite feeling preoccupied if not overwhelmed by your own problems.

Telltale Signs of Distress in Children

Be on the lookout for the following behavioral changes that may indicate anxiety, stress, insecurity, or depression in children:

- Altered sleep patterns or eating habits
- Declining performance in academics, athletics, or other activities
- Frequent and/or broad mood changes
- Acting out through anger, aggression, defiance or other misbehavior with peers, teachers or family members
- Withdrawal from family and friends
- Lethargy or disinterest
- Regressive behavior
- Becoming accident prone
- Excessive catering to parents, which may signal self-blame for the divorce

Dos and Don'ts of Breaking
the News to Your Children

How, what, and when you first tell your children about the divorce will affect how they see and understand everything that comes thereafter. So, to use legal terminology... don't screw it up.

Here are the Dos and Don'ts of your first discussions about the divorce:

- Don't talk to the children about the divorce until you are emotionally prepared to discuss it in a calm, reassuring manner.
- Agree with your STBX about when and what the children will be told—initially, at least, by the two of you together.
- Try to anticipate questions the children might ask and agree upon the answers.
- See a therapist or divorce coach if you can't agree with your spouse on how, when, or what to tell the children.
- Consider telling teenage children about the divorce before the younger ones because children in different stages of development require different approaches; for example
   - Older children should be told before they hear it elsewhere or figure it out themselves.
   - Younger children often don't need to know until separation or some other event that requires explanation.
- Gather materials for your children and yourself about assisting children through divorce, such as
   - The American Bar Association's (ABA) handbooks: "My Parents Are Getting Divorced" and "What Your Children Need Now!"[1]
   - The American Academy of Matrimonial Lawyers' "Children's Bill of Rights" (See Appendix 3.)
   - For a story-book approach for younger children, see also http://www.childcentereddivorce.com/kids/
- Together with your STBX, be positive and reassure the children that
   - Both of you will continue to be involved in their lives.
   - You can work cooperatively as their parents.
   - The divorce is not their fault and has nothing to do with anything they have done (a message that bears repeating during the divorce).
- Be honest but DON'T discuss things that are unnecessary or that are likely to upset or worry them, such as

---

[1] Available at http://shop.americanbar.org/ebus/

- ° An extramarital affair or other fault for the divorce
- ° Money problems
- Tell your children about arrangements you've made for both parents to spend time with them. (Avoid Lawglish terms like "custody," "visitation," or "primary residence.")
- Assure them that you will try your best to answer any questions they have.

Breaking the news, from
Talk to Strangers (2014)

Questions Your Children
May Ask About Your Divorce

One thing you can expect is that your kids will ask you about your divorce when you least expect it. So be prepared ahead of time for questions like:

- "What does divorce mean?"
- "Why do you have to get a divorce?"
- "Is the divorce my fault?"
- "Will you and Mommy [Daddy] get back together again?"
- "Why can't you make up?"
- "Will we have to move?"
- "Can we all still live here together in the house?"
- "Will I have to change schools?"
- "Is Mom/Dad going to move away?"
- "Will we still go to Grandma's for Thanksgiving?"
- "Who will be home when I get home from school?"

The "right" answers depend upon your children's ages, maturity and temperament. Mental health professionals and divorce coaches can help you formulate those answers. If at all possible, do this with your co-parent for the sake of consistency and to demonstrate to your children that you will continue to co-parent after the divorce.

Divorce Parenting No-No's

Try to avoid making the following mistakes with your children during your divorce. But even if you do have bad moments (it's okay; everyone does), use those experiences to strengthen your resolve not to let it happen again.

- Don't complain to your children about their other parent.
- Don't use the children to convey messages to their other parent.
- Don't ask the children (directly or indirectly) to choose with which parent they prefer to live or spend time.
- Don't try to "insulate" the children entirely from the divorce because
  ○ It won't work
  ○ Depriving children of basic information will only increase their anxiety
- Don't arbitrarily make rules that are inconsistent with their other parent's reasonable rules.
- Don't give the children false hope that you and your STBX might reconcile.
- Don't treat children as confidants or therapists. Children (and not only the younger ones) need to be reassured that normalcy will return to their lives and that they can feel safe and loved. Maintain the boundaries that will allow you to continue to fulfill those needs.

What is Child Custody?

The term "child custody" involves two concepts:

- **Legal custody:** Determines who makes decisions—and how—regarding the children
- **Physical custody:** Determines how much time the children spend with each parent and thus how much day-to-day child-care responsibility each parent has

Types of Legal Custody

The types of legal custody are:

- **Joint legal custody:** The parents share decision making regarding the health and welfare of the children, including schooling, extracurricular activities, medical decisions, and the like. Joint legal custody also entitles each parent access to their children's educational, health, and other records.
- **Sole legal custody:** One parent has the right to make child-related decisions.
- **Hybrid legal custody: Arrangements such as one of the following**
  ○ One parent has the right to make child-related decisions except as to certain matters.

- ○ Parents share decision-making except as to specified matters.
- ○ Parents share decision-making, but one parent has the right to decide in the event of an impasse.

Orders and Disorders

Some psychological traits, whether or not they are considered disorders, make settlement both difficult and perilous. But settlement is still worth a try, especially if children are involved. If you do manage to agree on some children's issues in such a case, also do the following:

- Immediately put the agreement in writing.
- Avoid any vagueness or "wiggle room" in wording. Parents suffering from Narcissistic Personality Disorder, for example, will exploit to their advantage any lack of clarity, so be specific and precise regarding matters such as
  - ○ Pick-up and drop-off times and places
  - ○ Responsibility for transporting the children
  - ○ Exactly what "day-to-day" decisions can and can't be made by the parent who has the children with him/her
- Submit any agreements to the court with a motion for a court order so that the agreements can be quickly and effectively enforced with the court's contempt power.

If a court hearing becomes necessary because agreement can't be reached, ask your lawyer to prepare detailed "proposed orders" to submit to the court. This will:

- Underscore your concerns about your STBX's penchant for manipulation and/or avoidance of responsibility
- Provide the detail you need (if the court rules in your favor) that court orders often lack

Legal Presumptions Regarding Custody

In the states listed below, it is presumed that joint legal custody is in a child's best interests. That means that parents arguing *against* joint custody in those states have the burden of proving that it is more likely than not that joint custody is *contrary* to the children's best interests. Evidence that joint custody is not in a child's best interests would include, for example, a history of the parents being unable to parent cooperatively.[2]

---

[2] Some judges feel that legal presumptions are unimportant in child-related matters where the ultimate issue is what's in a child's best interests. An experienced local attorney knows which judges those are and thus can help you weigh probable outcomes in your case.

States With Joint Custody Presumptions[3]

- Alabama
- Arizona
- California
- Connecticut
- Florida
- Idaho
- Louisiana
- Minnesota
- Mississippi
- Nevada
- New Mexico
- Tennessee
- Texas
- Wisconsin

Types of Physical Custody

Just as there are several forms of legal custody, there are several forms of *physical* custody:

- **Sole physical custody**: One parent has the great majority of
  - Time with the children, and
  - Day-to-day child care responsibilities

  Note that in extreme situations when a parent poses a risk to a child, the other parent may have *exclusive* care of the children and the other parent's time with the children, if any, will be ordered to be supervised by a capable third party.

- **Joint physical or "shared" custody**: Each parent has specified rights to have the children with him/her. This can range from a "50/50" time split to the children having their "primary residence" with one parent, subject to a parenting plan schedule of time with the other parent. Note that an agreement or court order regarding physical custody can determine a child's school district.

---

[3] In states such as Alabama, California, Connecticut and Mississippi, the court has no authority to award joint custody unless at least one parent requests it. In Oregon, joint custody can be awarded only if both parents request it.

- **"Primary physical custody"** or **"primary residential parent:"** These terms usually refer to the fact that the children's "home" is with one parent.

- **Alternating custody:** A joint custody arrangement in which the parents take turns living with the children for extended periods of time, such as two weeks with one parent followed by two weeks with the other parent. Input from a mental health professional is especially helpful with alternating custody, as it is not appropriate for all children.

- **Bird-nesting:** A type of alternating custody in which the children remain in the home and the parents alternate residing there. This requires that each parent have an alternate residence.

- **Split custody:** An arrangement in which not all the children have their primary residence with the same parent, resulting in the children being "split up" from each other.

The Shortest List of All: How Judges Decide Child-Related Issues

In making decisions regarding children, the standard used by judges is
- The best interests of the children ("BIC")

That's it, plain and simple. The devil, as they say, is in the details.

"BIC" Factors Judges Consider

Among the most significant "details" of the BIC standard are the factors judges may consider in applying it:

- The child's age and gender
- The parent's ability to provide the child with basic necessities such as food, shelter, clothing, and medical care
- The parent's ability to meet the child's physical, emotional, developmental, educational, and special needs
- The parent's mental and physical health
- The emotional ties between parent and child, including a parent's history as primary caregiver
- The parent's ability to provide a loving, stable, consistent and nurturing relationship
- The parent's lifestyle and ability to provide a stable environment

- A history of child abuse or neglect by a parent or household member
- The preference of a child of suitable age (often age 12 and up) and maturity
- The quality of the child's established home, school and community environments, and the importance of maintaining continuity
- The child's sibling relationships
- Whether a parent is likely to foster the child's relationship with the non-custodial parent
- Whether a parent has attempted to alienate a child from the other parent
- The availability of extended family
- Logistical considerations such as the ability of each parent to make appropriate child-care arrangements (or to provide child-care themselves), and the distance between the parents' residences
- The application of principles of developmental psychology
- Any other factors relevant to the child's best interests

Avoiding Battles Over Child-Related Issues

Despite their marital break-up, most parents must co-parent after divorce. Except in situations in which cooperation is impossible such as when a parent poses a risk to a child, parents have the responsibility to cooperate in creating a parenting plan that is in the children's interests.[4]

If you are unable to resolve children's issues with your co-parent, a judge will do it for you. Here are some reasons to avoid that if at all possible:

- The custody evaluation process can humiliate, frighten and compromise your children, and cause them enduring emotional harm.
- Custody cases are tremendously expensive. Parents must not only pay their own lawyers, but in some cases, they must also pay attorneys to represent the children and/or guardians ad litem (GALs). GALs can be appointed for children unable to act in their own interests due to age or other factors or who are otherwise in need of protection.
- Trial outcomes are difficult to predict.
- A judge's orders after trial rarely contain the crucial details and fine-tuning that parents who resolve the issues themselves include in their agreements.

---

[4] If you feel that you and your co-parent may be unable to resolve child-related issues, see my short film *Talk to Strangers* (available at www.childcustodyfilm.com). Encourage your spouse to do the same. The film is accompanied by "The *Talk to Strangers* Pocket Guide for Parents" from which some of the material above is excerpted, and which contains additional strategies for sparing your children the trauma of court battles regarding them.

Avoiding the Custody Evaluation Process

Talk to Strangers (2014) portrays how intrusive and humiliating the custody evaluation process can be for the children trapped in it.

DR. HARDIN
Your mother loves you very much, you know. She always will.

EMILY
Yeah, she always loved my Dad too … until she didn't anymore.

DR. HARDIN
I'm curious. Why do you feel it's your mother's fault that your parents can't agree on custody? Did your father tell you that?

Custody Battles: A Perfect Storm For Harm to Children

Children need very specific things from their divorcing parents. A "Kids' Top 4 List" of divorce needs would read something like this:

- An end to their parents' fighting
- An end to uncertainty about where and with whom they will be living
- A return to some degree of normalcy
- Security in knowing their parents will continue to love and care for them

Custody battles put children at risk for emotional harm because they delay or prevent children from getting the very things that they need most during divorce. That's because custody battles:

- Increase the parents' conflict.
- Require children to suffer through evaluation procedures that frighten, humiliate and compromise them.
- Add months to divorces, thus prolonging the children's anxiety and delaying any return to normalcy.
- Leave parents hostile to each other for years, severely damaging prospects for cooperative post-divorce co-parenting. Even children who receive assurances of their parents' love may question why that love isn't strong enough to create cooperative parenting in place of hostility.

So perhaps the first question to ask yourself if you are considering a custody battle is this: Do you love your children enough *not* to fight over them?

Hopeful, Out-of-the-Box Solutions

Hope Fuller knows that her husband's proposal to evenly divide time with the children would be a logistical nightmare. Her lawyer has told her not to negotiate because she will "win" at trial. But Hope knows how custody battles damage children and that there are no guarantees that she will get the result she wants. So she asked her lawyer for some out-of-the-box solutions. He suggested:

- "Flip schedules" that reverse the school year plan for all or some of the summer, allowing for more quality time for the "out parent" without disturbing school week routines
- "Bird-nesting" arrangements in which children remain in the family home and the parents rotate in and out of it
- Trial parenting plans lasting for a month or two while the divorce is pending that reveal quickly what will and won't work

Ten Questions to Ask Before Fighting Over the Kids

For many years, I have required clients considering custody litigation to answer ten questions. If it's your co-parent who seems intent on fighting over the kids, see if he or she has answers to the following:

1. Do you want your children to endure months of anxiety and uncertainty as to where they will be living and whether they will have the relationship they want with each of their parents and their siblings?

2. Do you want your children subjected to interviews by attorneys, mental health professionals and court personnel in which they will feel afraid, conflicted, and pressured to be loyal to both their parents?

3. Do you want your children subjected to the possibility of inquiry by these professionals about the most personal aspects of their lives, including their fears and frailties?

4. Clinical studies have shown that exposure to high conflict between parents places children at risk for serious psychological harm. Do you want to risk harming your children with a high-conflict custody battle?

5. Do you want your inability to resolve your differences to serve as a model of parenting for your children?

6. Do you want intimate details of your life to become a matter of public record?

7. Do you want a stranger deciding how much you will see your children and how you will make decisions concerning them?

8. Do you want a substantial portion of your assets used as fees for attorneys and expert witnesses with no guarantee that you will be happy with the result?

9. Do you want to give up attention to detail that a negotiated agreement will have but that a judge's decision will not?

10. Do you want to engage in costly, time-consuming and rancorous litigation that can make future cooperation between you and your co-parent extremely difficult at best and the resumption of amicable joint parenting nearly impossible?

Improving Communication With Your Co-Parent

In the early days of a divorce or separation, before lawyers are hired and positions harden, you and your co-parent can establish a spirit of cooperation with productive discussions of child-related issues. Consider the following ways to accomplish that:

- Keep your conversations under control by agreeing ahead of time what issues will be discussed.
- Focus on current issues without dredging up old problems, conflicts or vulnerabilities.
- Don't assume that your co-parent's motivations or intentions are hostile.
- Remain calm, and try to understand your co-parent's standpoint.
- Ask questions to better understand how your co-parent feels about an issue—and why.
- Don't interrupt. Make your co-parent feel that his/her concerns are being heard.
- If the conversation deteriorates to the point that further discussion will only make things worse, express that concern and politely end the conversation.

Parenting Goal Statements

If you are able to communicate productively about your kids, begin your new co-parenting relationship by agreeing upon some shared parenting goals and beliefs. Writing a "Parenting Goal Statement" redirects the focus from the parents' conflict to the children's needs. A Parenting Goal Statement can also create momentum for the ultimate goal; a "Parenting Plan" that will become part of your settlement agreement.

Parenting Goal Statements should include most if not all of the following:

Sample Parenting Goal Statement

- We will shield our children from our conflict.
- We will not use our children as messengers.
- We will not use our children as confidants.
- We will not put our children in a position of "choosing sides."
- We will keep child-related issues completely separate from financial ones.
- We will not criticize each other to or in front of, our children. (Devaluing each other can cause children to wonder what is wrong with <u>them</u> for loving such unworthy parents.)
- We will each nurture our children's love for the other parent.
- We will agree beforehand what information we will share with the children regarding the divorce.
- We will encourage our children to express their feelings, but we will make the decisions.
- We will share information about our children's well-being, schoolwork, activities and schedules.
- We will make our best effort to have similar, consistent rules for the children.
- We will reassure our children that they will continue to have two parents who love them.
- We will reassure our children that the failure of our marriage is not their fault in any way. (This is especially important when child-related issues are in dispute and children may feel that if not for them, their parents wouldn't be fighting.)
- Because our children will suffer as long as issues remain unresolved regarding them, we will try to resolve those issues quickly and in a way that reflects the values stated above.

Parenting Plans: What Should Be Included?

Parenting plans should address all non-financial matters regarding the children, including:

- Legal custody
- Physical custody, including
  - An allocation of each parent's time with the children
  - Where applicable, a designation of the children's "primary residence"
  - A parenting schedule (see discussion below)
- Statement of shared parenting goals or beliefs regarding matters such as religion, health, and safety issues, etc.
- Obligations to parent cooperatively in the children's best interests, including
  - Sharing school, extracurricular, medical and other information
  - Being flexible in handling scheduling and other issues that arise unexpectedly
- Relocation: What happens if the primary custodial parent wishes to move from the area with the child?

Parenting Plan Schedules

Parenting plan schedules should cover:

- School year weekend and midweek time
- School year vacations
- Holidays & three-day weekends
- Summer vacation
- Special days: Mother's and Father's days, parents' birthdays; children's birthdays; traditional family gatherings
- Language regarding flexibility in handling changes in parents' or children's schedules
- If desired, a review of the schedule periodically or by a certain date

Virtual Visitation

More and more non-custodial parents are supplementing time with their children using Skype, FaceTime and other electronic means. Florida, Illinois, North Carolina, Texas, Utah and Wisconsin have virtual visitation laws and another 20 or so states are considering them. Even if your state doesn't have a statute, you can include virtual visitation in your settlement agreement or ask a judge to order it.

Additional Parenting Plan Provisions

Depending upon the degree of specificity desired or deemed necessary in an agreement, additional provisions can be included to preserve the children's well-being and to ensure continued, meaningful involvement in their lives by the non-custodial parent. Such provisions can cover:

- Bedtime and homework routines
- TV and on-line restrictions, etc.
- Responsibility for transporting children
- Phone and virtual parenting time via texting, message boards, Facetime, Skype, etc.
- Religious upbringing and training
- Counseling or therapy for children
- Access of grandparents and other relatives
- A parent's first option or "right of first refusal" to have the children if the other parent can't be with them as scheduled per the parenting plan
- Shared approach to discipline
- Transferring clothes, school material, special toys, etc.
- Matters of concern such as dangerous activities and travel limitations
- Restrictions regarding housemates and access of relatives or others who may put the children at risk
- Role of subsequent spouses and significant others in communications regarding the children
- Appointment of a child therapist or other third party to mediate or otherwise help solve problems that arise

Parenting agreements can include a wide range of topics beyond scheduling; from activity choices, to bedtimes, to transporting the kids.

When You May Need the Court to Be Involved

Parents should settle child-related differences as soon as possible. Children's interests are served by speedy resolution of divorces and an end to, or at least a reduction of their parents' acrimony. However, the court's intervention may be necessary to protect children when there is:

- A history of or verifiable potential for domestic violence or neglect
- Untreated mental illness or continuing substance abuse
- The presence of third-parties in the household who put a child at risk
- Parents who are chronically unable to parent cooperatively
- Any other circumstances that pose a risk to a child's health or welfare

When Child-Related Issues Remain in Dispute

If, despite your best efforts, child-related issues cannot be resolved by agreement, you may have to testify at

- A deposition during which you will be questioned by opposing counsel
- A *pendente lite* child custody or access hearing

No one looks forward to being a witness. But if you are required to testify, think of it as an opportunity to show that you will be an effective witness if your case goes to trial. Strong testimony can also help persuade your STBX to settle. In Chapter 14, you will learn how to help your case with effective testimony.[5]

The Inside Scoop: What You Might Be Asked at Trial About Child-Related Issues

In order to testify effectively, you must prepare for the types of questions you are likely to be asked. You can expect questions regarding custody and other child-related issues to include the following:

- Your and your spouse's strengths and weaknesses as parents
- Whether you consider your spouse to be a good parent and the reasons for your opinion
- Whether one parent has been the "primary" parent
- Which parent has been chiefly responsible for child rearing tasks such as
  - Meal preparation
  - Buying the children's clothing and necessities
  - Assistance with homework and school projects
  - Getting the children up and out in the morning

---

[5] For a comprehensive guide on testifying in family court cases, check out my audiobook *Become Your Own Star Witness,* available at www.WitnessTutor.com.

- ○ Nighttime routines including baths, bedtime stories, etc.
- ○ Transporting the children to activities
- ○ Participating in parent/child activities such as coaching, scouting, and field trips
- ○ Communicating with teachers, coaches, health care providers, instructors, tutors, etc.
- ○ Providing guidance and religious training
- ○ Selecting and scheduling extracurricular activities
- ○ Setting up play dates
- The children's preferences regarding spending time with their parents
- The children's current routines (including temporary parenting plan) and what changes might be beneficial
- The likely impact on a child of a change in the current living situation
- Whether you have the workplace proximity and work schedule flexibility to attend teachers' conferences, athletic, music, etc. events, and other children's activities
- Health issues, disabilities or habits of either parent that affect the ability to parent
- Whether either parent exhibits conduct or characteristics that may put the children at risk, (e.g., emotional disorders, anger issues, or substance abuse)
- Specific events (including altercations between you and your STBX) that demonstrate either fitness or unsuitability as a custodial parent
- What support systems (grandparents, child care providers, etc.) are available to each parent
- Details of your children's lives regarding schools and teachers, academic performance, children's hobbies and interests, identities of their close friends, etc.
- The nature of your and your STBX's relationships with the key adults in your children's lives such as teachers, physicians, therapists, tutors, music and arts teachers, and coaches
- Your children's special needs, if any
- Similarities and differences among your children
- Which parent is more likely to provide a stable environment and continuity in the children's education, home life and community involvement
- Sensitivity of both parents to the impact of the divorce on children and appropriateness of conduct during the divorce (e.g., not using children as messengers, disparaging the other parent, arguing in front of the children, etc.)

- What more could be done to help the children handle the divorce, including your position on counseling for them
- Whether joint decision making is feasible given your relationship with your STBX
- How you feel you and your STBX will co-parent after the divorce, including what each of you could do to improve the co-parenting relationship

---

A Testimony Pearl

Among the questions above that you might be asked in a custody or child access proceeding is one concerning your child's preferences regarding spending time with you and their other parent. If you do testify about the children's preferences, be prepared for the next area of inquiry regarding how you know what those preferences are, and whether you have influenced them.

On the other hand, such a question may "open the door" for you to repeat what others, such as teachers or neighbors have told you the children have told *them*; testimony that might otherwise be excluded as "hearsay." See Chapter 14 for much more on testifying.

Modification of Child Custody

Either parent can ask a court to modify child custody, access and related orders, either prior to or after a divorce decree is issued. Generally, the requesting parent must establish that:

- There is a substantial or "material" change in circumstances
- As a result of the changed circumstances, a change in custody or access would be in the child's best interest

Substantial changes in circumstances can include the following:

- The non-custodial parent requests a change after the child has lived with the non-custodial parent for a substantial period of time by agreement

- The custodial parent has engaged in conduct detrimental to the child, such as criminal activity or substance abuse
- The custodial parent's judgment or ability to care for the child has substantially declined due to illness or some other reason
- The preference of a child of suitable age and maturity has changed
- The child's residence is not safe for the child physically, mentally, or emotionally, and it would be more harmful to leave the child where he/she is than to move him/her to the other parent's home
- One parent alienates a child from the other parent
- A parent habitually fails to abide by the parenting plan[6]
- The custodial parent has or wishes to relocate (see "Relocation" below)
- Any other change in circumstances that jeopardizes a child's health, safety or welfare

Limitations on Custody Modification

Some states limit how many times a parent can attempt to modify custody. For example, in Minnesota:

- Except in extraordinary circumstances, "or as agreed to in writing by the parties, no motion to modify a custody order or parenting plan may be made earlier than one year after the date of the entry of a decree of dissolution or legal separation containing a provision dealing with custody...."[7]
- If a prior modification motion has been heard, "no subsequent motion may be filed within two years after disposition of the prior motion on its merits."[8]

Find out if your state has rules like Minnesota's, and what, if any, exceptions there are to those rules.

---

[6] Note, however, that custody will not be changed simply to punish a parent.
[7] Minnesota Statutes sec. 518.18(a). The exceptions to Minnesota's limitations on frequency of child custody modification proceedings are: "persistent and willful denial or interference with parenting time, or has reason to believe that the child's present environment may endanger the child's physical or emotional health or impair the child's emotional development. Minnesota Statutes sec. 518.18(c)
[8] Minnesota Statutes §518.18(b)

Relocation

One of the most heart-wrenching controversies regarding children arises *after* a divorce when a custodial parent wishes to move a significant distance away from the other parent. These cases arise most often when:

- The custodial parent or his/her new spouse is transferred
- A custodial spouse who cannot find work locally is offered a job a substantial distance away
- A custodial spouse wishes to relocate to be closer to family or other support systems

Many states require that parents wishing to relocate with children file in court a notice of intent to move. The other parent is then entitled to a hearing. All states use the BIC standard in determining whether to allow the relocation.

Illegal Relocation Provisions

The following provisions regarding relocation, even if agreed to in writing by both parents, are illegal and thus unenforceable:

- While agreements may require that a parent who wishes to relocate with a child obtain court approval, provisions flatly forbidding a custodial spouse from moving out of state after the divorce violate the parent's constitutional right to travel among the states. [Note that Wyoming is an apparent exception to this rule. See *Watt v. Watt*, 971 P.2d 608 (Wyo. 1999).]
- Also void are provisions that automatically change custody if a custodial parent improperly relocates. Such provisions are deemed to impinge upon the court's right to decide custody issues.

Key Relocation Case Facts

As noted above, judges' decisions generally come down to the BIC standard. State statutes (laws passed by state legislatures) and case law (law made by judges) enumerate factors such as the following for determining a child's best interests:

- Whether the relocation is proposed in good faith and is necessary
- The primary custodial parent's reasons for wishing to relocate and the other parent's reasons for opposing relocation
- Whether the child's health, educational and extracurricular activity opportunities would be comparable to her current situation if relocation occurs
- The preference of a child of suitable age and maturity
- The extent to which the child's relationship with the non-custodial parent might be damaged
- The distance of the proposed relocation
- Whether the child's special needs or talents will be sufficiently attended to if relocation occurs
- The hardship and expense the non-relocating parent would experience
- The extent to which the custodial parent is likely to foster the child's relationship with the noncustodial parent if relocation occurs
- Whether it is feasible for the non-custodial parent to relocate as well
- How relocation is likely to impact extended family relationships
- Any other factors relevant to the child's best interests

The Toughest Question

A parent wishing to move in a relocation case can be put in an impossible position when asked whether he/she will move regardless of whether the child is permitted to relocate. Answering either "yes" or "no" can both unfairly prejudice the parent. As a result, the American Academy of Matrimonial Lawyers has proposed that the question not be allowed in relocation cases and state legislatures have begun amending their statutes accordingly.

Key Relocation Case Legalities

Besides weighing the facts listed above, judges must be aware of two key legal principles:

- Definitions of "relocation:" State law definitions of relocation vary, with some statutes focusing on the distance the parent has or wishes to take a child, and some on the duration of time:

- ○ <u>Florida</u>'s definition: "relocation of a child to a principal residence more than 50 miles away from his or her principal place of residence . . ."[9]
- ○ <u>Missouri</u>: "a change in the principal residence of a child for a period of ninety days or more . . ."[10]
- ○ <u>Michigan</u>: ". . . a parent of a child . . . shall not change a legal residence of the child to a location that is more than 100 miles from the child's legal residence . . ."[11]
- • <u>Burdens of proof</u>: As discussed above in connection with joint custody, language in statutes regarding "presumptions" or "burdens of proof" puts one of the parties at a disadvantage. Various state relocation laws allocate the burden differently:
  - ○ <u>Missouri</u>: "The party seeking to relocate shall have the burden of proving that the proposed relocation is made in good faith and is in the best interest of the child."[12]
  - ○ <u>Wisconsin</u>: ". . . the burden of proof is on the parent objecting to the move or removal."[13]
  - ○ <u>Indiana</u>: "The relocating individual has the burden of proof that the proposed relocation is made in good faith and for a legitimate reason.[14] If the relocating individual meets the burden of proof under subsection (c), the burden shifts to the non-relocating parent to show that the proposed relocation is not in the best interest of the child."[15]

Third Party Visitation Claims

The U.S. Supreme Court's 2000 decision in *Troxel v. Granville* made it more difficult for grandparents and other "third parties" such as other relatives to gain visitation rights with children.[16] The Court emphasized the rights of fit parents who objected to grandparent visitation and indicated that "special factors" must be shown to justify visitation by grandparents over the parents' objections. After the *Troxel* case, approximately half the states made it more difficult for grandparents to obtain visitation rights. These states either:

---

[9] Fla. Stat. §61.13001(a)
[10] Missouri Statutes §452.375
[11] Mich. Comp. Laws §722
[12] Missouri Statutes §452.375
[13] Wisconsin Statutes §767.481(3)(a)(3)
[14] Indiana Code §31-17-2.2-5(c)
[15] Indiana Code §31-17-2.2-5(d)
[16] 530 U.S. 57 (2000)

- Established a presumption that the parents' denial of visitation was reasonable, or
- Increased the grandparents' burden of proof to show otherwise

Standing of Third Parties to Seek Visitation

In a number of states, courts will not entertain third party visitation claims unless the claimants establish their right or "standing" to seek visitation by establishing one of the following facts:

- The parents are divorced, legally separated, or a divorce is pending
- A parent has been missing for a specified period of time
- A parent has abandoned the child
- The child was born out of wedlock
- A parent is deceased, incarcerated, incompetent or has had his/her parental rights terminated
- Neither parent is raising the child[17]

Once a third party makes it over the standing threshold, he/she bears the burden of establishing the right to visitation. Either by statutory or case law,[18] third parties are required to show both of the following:

- Visitation is in the child's best interests.
- Additional circumstances that rebut the presumption favoring parents.

What Must a Third Party Claiming Visitation Prove?

The "additional circumstances" a third party seeking visitation may be required to prove in the post-*Troxel* era include the following:

- That the parental determination is not in the child's best interest (Colorado)
- That grandparent visitation would not significantly interfere with any parent-child relationship (Maine, Minnesota, North

[17] By contrast, New York is particularly permissive regarding "standing," allowing a non-parent access to the courts where "equity would see fit to intervene. N.Y. Dom. Rel. Law § 72(1)

[18] This is an area where you will need a lawyer to advise you regarding your state's law. Reading a statute can be misleading. For example, many state statutes require simply that visitation be in the child's best interests. However, case law interpreting those statutes has added additional requirements consistent with *Troxel*. Those states include: Alaska, Arizona, California, Colorado, Delaware, Idaho, Kentucky, Louisiana, Massachusetts, Michigan, Missouri, Montana, North Carolina, Ohio, Vermont, Virginia, and Wisconsin.

Dakota, Pennsylvania, South Carolina, South Dakota, West Virginia, and Wyoming)
- That a substantial relationship has been established between the grandparents and the grandchild or, at the least, the grandparents have attempted to establish such a relationship (Alaska, Arkansas, California, Iowa, Kansas, Maine, Mississippi, and Oregon)
- That grandparent visitation has been unreasonably denied or restricted (Nevada, Alabama, Illinois, Mississippi, Missouri, and South Dakota)
- The parent objecting to grandparent visitation is unfit (Iowa, Montana, and Oklahoma)

Factors Considered in Third Party Visitation Claims

Judges consider some or all of the following in determining whether a grandparent or other third party is entitled to visitation:

- The nature and stability of the relationship between the child and the grandparent seeking visitation
- The amount of time grandparent and child have spent together
- The potential detriments and benefits to the child from granting visitation
- The effect granting visitation would have on the child's relationship with the parents
- The physical and emotional health of parents and grandparents
- The stability of the child's living and school arrangements
- The wishes and preferences of the child
- Parental unfitness
- Significant harm that would result to the child in the absence of a visitation order

Third Party Custody Claims

Although state statutes and case law vary widely, some rules regarding the rights of grandparents and others to seek custody—rather than simply visitation—have gained acceptance in a majority of states:

- Parents who are not unfit, and are able and willing to care for a child are usually presumed to be more appropriate custodians of their child than non-parents.[19]
- As a result of the presumption in favor of the parents, grandparents usually have the burden of establishing some degree of unfitness on the part of a parent against whom they are claiming custody.[20]
- If the court makes a finding that a parent is unfit, the court will apply the best interests of the child standard.
- There is a built-in tension between the "parental preference rule" favoring parents' rights, and the best interests of the child rule that is the ultimate standard in child custody matters.
   - Some courts resolve this conflict by holding that the parents' rights must yield in situations where a non-parent can better serve the child's interest.
   - Many courts, however, will not consider a grandparent's claim until the presumption in favor of parental custody has been rebutted.
- Asserting a close and nurturing relationship with a child is generally not sufficient. However, grandparents with whom a child has been living for an extended period can make a persuasive case for custody. The grandparents' claim is further strengthened if the child was placed with the grandparents by agreement with the parents. In those circumstances, it is the parent who may bear the burden of proving both of the following in seeking a custody change.
   - A change in circumstances has occurred (see modification below).
   - The best interests of the child require a change in custody.
- A parent's lack of financial resources will not be considered unless it reflects a lack of fitness such as substance abuse or emotional problems.

"Standing" Rules Regarding Custody

A number of state statutes provide that third parties do not have standing to seek custody unless they can show at least one of the following:

---

[19] An exception is Iowa's statute that grants grandparents with whom a grandchild resides in a stable relationship, the same standing as parents. In *Hernandez v. Hernandez*, 265 P.3d 495 (Idaho 2011), The Iowa Supreme Court upheld the statute's constitutionality.

[20] States where parental unfitness need not always be proved include New York and California. In California, if granting custody to a parent would be "detrimental" to a child who has been living in a stable environment with a person "who has assumed on a day-to-day basis, the role of his or her parent, fulfilling both the child's physical needs and the child's psychological needs for care and affection, and who has assumed that role for a substantial period of time," the court may transfer custody away from parents without a finding that they are unfit. Cal. Fam. Code sec. 3041(a).

- The third party has acted as a "*de facto* parent" or stands "*in loco parentis*" to the child[21]
  - Arizona
  - Delaware
  - Kentucky
  - Minnesota
  - Montana
  - Oregon
  - Pennsylvania
  - South Carolina
- The child is living with the third party claimant: California, Idaho
- Death of both parents: Texas
- The child is not in the custody of one of the natural parents: Illinois

---

Is It Easier For a Third Party to Get Custody Than Visitation?

Not really, but it might appear that way.

Some state third party visitation statutes contain requirements that seem more difficult than those in custody statutes. That's partly because visitation sought with children of parents who are not unfit is seen as an incursion on the parents' rights. Custody claims, on the other hand, arise most often where there is reason to believe that one or both parents are unfit and thus the children's interests are considered more important than the rights of such parents. And proving these more serious allegations of lack of fitness are more likely to result in a custody change.

Factors Favoring Third Party Custody

Certain circumstances strengthen a grandparent's custody claim:

- Lack of fitness or persistent neglect by the objecting parent(s)
- Abandonment of the child by the objecting parent(s)

---

[21] The Latin terms "*de facto* parent" and "*in loco parentis*" are often used interchangeably. Technically, there is a difference. Grandparents who are *in loco parentis,* meaning that they are acting in the place of a parent, have taken control of a child's upbringing in the temporary absence of the parents, but with the parents' permission. A *de facto* parent is simply a third party acting as the child's parent.

- The grandparents have raised the child for a significant period of time
- One of the parents consents to the grandparents' custody
- Other extraordinary or exceptional circumstances

Factors Considered in "Grandparent Custody" Cases

Once grandparents (the term "grandparents" is often used as shorthand to include all third parties claiming custody) have hurdled the standing obstacle, judges may consider the following factors in custody cases:

- The fitness of parents and grandparents
- The respective abilities of the parents and grandparents to attend to the child's safety, welfare, and physical and emotional health
- The history and nature of the relationship between the grandparent(s) and grandchild, including any periods when the child has resided with the grandparents
- The wishes of the child, if the child is of sufficient age and maturity to make decisions for himself or herself (often beginning around age 12)
- Evidence of abuse or neglect by the parent(s) or grandparent(s)
- Evidence of substance abuse by, or emotional disturbance or mental illness of, the parent(s) or grandparent(s)
- The child's present living situation, including potential threats to the child's well-being from members of the household, neighbors, etc.
- The child's adjustment to the home, school, or community, and importance of maintaining continuity
- The respective abilities of the parents and grandparents to foster the child's love and affection for, and contact with, the other
- The geographical distance between the child and the parent(s) or grandparent(s)
- Any other factors relevant to the child's best interests

Federal Laws Regarding Custody, Safety, and Rights of Children and Spouses

State laws govern the majority of divorce-related issues. However, two other types of laws seek to bring uniformity to disputes where two or more states or countries are involved:

- Federal laws enacted by Congress: Where federal and state laws conflict, federal law prevails under the constitutional law doctrine of "preemption." Federal laws can be found in The United States Code, which contains all laws enacted by Congress.

- "Uniform laws:" These are laws proposed for state adoption by The National Conference of Commissioners on Uniform State Laws (NC-CUSL), also known as the "Uniform Law Commission." They contain the word "uniform," and strive for
  - Predictability
  - Avoidance of disputes over which jurisdiction's law applies
  - Equal treatment of litigants regardless of where they reside

Unlike federal law, "uniform acts" may be adopted by state legislatures in whole or in part. Since a uniform act is not a federal law, your state's version of any uniform act can be found among your state's "Statutes" or in its "Code," usually with the word "uniform" as part of the title.

Issues relating to well-being and safety of children and spouses, and to child custody are particularly likely to be the subject of uniform acts and federal law. Such issues are covered by the following:

- The Uniform Child Custody Jurisdiction and Enforcement Act (UC-CJEA) Adopted by all states (and the District of Columbia) except Massachusetts, the UCCJEA complements and is often applied together with a federal statute, The Parental Kidnapping Prevention Act (PK-PA).[22] Together, these laws seek to
  - Thwart interstate kidnapping of children by a parent
  - Establish rules to determine which state has jurisdiction and which state's law applies in custody disputes where the parents live in different states
  - Provide uniform procedures to register and enforce custody orders across state boundaries
  - Avoid conflicting custody decrees in different states
  - Avoid repetitive litigation of custody orders
- The National Child Search Assistance Act[23]
  Eliminates waiting periods for missing child reports including family abduction cases.
- The Hague Convention on the Civil Aspects of International Child Abduction ("Hague Abduction Convention")
  An international treaty enacted to speed the return of a child who has been abducted from the country of habitual residence to another country,

---

[22] 28 USC Sec. 1738A et seq.

[23] 42 USC 5779 et seq.

and to ensure that each country respect the custody and visitation laws of the others. Signatories include the U.S., Australia, Canada, Israel, The Russian Federation, South Africa, Zimbabwe Mexico, and most other Western Hemisphere countries, and most European countries.

- The International Child Abduction Remedies Act (ICARA)[24]
  Implements The Hague Abduction Convention in the U.S.
- The Uniform Deployed Parents Custody and Visitation Act
  Addresses issues regarding deployed members of the military by
  - Requiring a deployed custodial parent to notify the other parent within 7 days of notice of the deployment
  - Establishing expedited procedures to address child-related issues of deployed parents
  - Allowing deployed parents to grant temporary custody rights to grandparents and other third parties
- The Uniform Parentage Act
  Intended to facilitate the identification of fathers in order to obtain child support orders, including actions brought by non-parent "interested parties."
- The Uniform Interstate Enforcement of Domestic Violence Protection Orders Act
  Intended to expedite the enforcement of out-of-state restraining orders against abusive spouses.
- The Uniform Status of Children of Assisted Conception Act
  Intended to provide uniform rules for establishing parentage by defining the legal mother and father in cases of assisted conception.
- The Indian Child Welfare Act
  Intended to limit the removal of children from custody of Native-American families.

---

[24] 42 U.S.C. 11601

Yes, there *IS* a quiz! Test what you have (or haven't) learned.

1. **This chapter is mainly about:**
   A. International children's uniforms
   B. Whether grandparents should be left standing
   C. Whether visiting a third party in one weekend is too much partying
   D. Caring and making suitable arrangements for children of divorce

2. **Unscramble the following key phrases from this chapter!**
   A. drith taryp griths
   B. nijto stuydoc stipumperon
   C. tincoolear assec

CHAPTER 11

Child Support

"If you think you will, you might. If you think you won't, you're right."

— Unknown

Child Support Guidelines

Federal law requires each state to maintain Child Support Guidelines (referred to here as "Guidelines" or "CSG") that calculate the amount of child support to be ordered in a particular case. Those calculations are based primarily upon

- The parents' incomes
- The number of minor children

There's more to it than arithmetic, however, because a number of variables come into play:

- State laws vary as to how long child support is required.
- "Deviation criteria" in a particular case can render the Guidelines inapplicable.
- Since CSG support depends on income, calculation of a spouse's "real income" is critical and requires analysis of (for example)
  - An employee spouse's bonuses, commissions, overtime, use of a company car, and "perks" such as reimbursed expenses that include personal as well as business related items.
  - The total benefit that a self-employed spouse derives from a business that pays personal bills.

Duration of Child Support

In many states, the child support obligation lasts until a non-emancipated child graduates high school or reaches age 18, whichever comes later.

In states like Texas, parents remain responsible for child support so long as a child remains in high school, regardless of age. More often, however, parents are not required to support indefinitely a child who remains in high school past his or her 18th birthday. Typical child support "end-dates" include:

* Arizona, California, Connecticut, Delaware, Florida, Illinois, Ohio, South Carolina: High school graduation or age 19
* Michigan: High school graduation or age 19 ½
* North Carolina, Georgia: High school graduation or age 20
* Missouri: High school graduation or higher education graduation

In New York and Indiana, child support can extend to age 21 whether or not a child has graduated from high school.

In still other states, child support is not deemed to end at a single age:

* New Jersey: Unless an existing support order specifies a termination date, child support does not end until the court determines the extent to which child support should extend beyond age 18.
* Massachusetts: Child support will end at age 18 unless the child remains principally dependent on the custodial parent, is employed full time, or is in the military. Thereafter, it ends at age 21 or 23 for full-time students in college or a trade school. As in a number of states, child support can be required for longer for disabled children.

Child Support That Ends
Prematurely or Extends Indefinitely

Emancipation terminates child support even prior to the state's termination age. A child's emancipation usually occurs as a result of one of the following:

* Marriage
* Military enlistment
* Financial independence
* Court order of emancipation

At the other end of the spectrum, many states provide for indefinite child support for physically or mentally disabled children.

Amount of Child Support Under Child Support Guidelines

Typically, state Child Support Guidelines
- Provide a formula for calculating child support based on the income of one or both parents and the number of children
- Include instructions as to how the child support amount is affected by factors such as health insurance and child care expense
- Require the judge to order the amount of child support determined by the CSG formula unless the judge finds that it would be inequitable or unjust due to "deviation criteria"
- Define deviation criteria (see below) and specify in what circumstances the Guidelines will not apply
- Define
  - Whether items such as future bonuses and other employment-related "perks" should be included in income for purposes of CSG calculations
  - What can be deducted from the parents' incomes (e.g., mandatory pension contributions, union dues, etc.) to determine the incomes to be used in CSG calculations
- Calculate payment of child support arrearages
- Require periodic revisions to insure that the Guidelines reflect changing economic realities in the state
- Require publication of a booklet (available on many state court websites) explaining the state's rules regarding the items above and including
  - A chart showing the support payable according to number of children and incomes
  - A support calculation worksheet
- Provide for a child support amount based on the state's census income data when there is no reliable information regarding the obligor's income

Child Support Guideline Formulas

At this writing, 34 states use the "Income Shares" formula to calculate child support:

Alabama, Arizona, California, Colorado, Connecticut, Florida, Hawaii, Idaho, Indiana, Kansas, Kentucky, Louisiana, Maine, Maryland, Michigan, Missouri, Nebraska, New Jersey, New Mexico, New York, North Carolina, Ohio, Oklahoma, Oregon, Pennsylvania, Rhode Island, South Carolina, South Dakota, Utah, Vermont, Virginia, Washington, West Virginia, and Wyoming

The Income Shares formula:

- Determines a total child support obligation for both parents based on their incomes
- Calculates the obligation of the non-custodial parent ("the obligor") based on the percentage that his/her income bears to the total of both incomes

Delaware, Hawaii, and Montana use the "Melson Formula," which is a more complicated version of the "Income Shares" formula. The remaining states use the "Percentage of Income" formula that calculates child support solely upon the income of the non-custodial parent.

CSG Deviation Criteria

As mentioned above, certain factors called "deviation criteria" allow a judge to order more or less than the amount calculated under the CSG. Typical deviation criteria include the following:

- Extraordinary expenses for medical care and/or maintenance of the child
- Extraordinary parental expenses
- Extraordinary child care expenses for medical or other reasons
- Atypical amounts of time spent with the parents, such as 50/50 arrangements
- The paying (non-custodial) parent's income is so high that the formula amount would exceed the needs of the children
- Extraordinary disparity in parental income
- Extraordinary assets or debts
- Contributions or gifts of a spouse or domestic partner
- Needs of a parent's other dependents such as their own parents or children of a prior marriage or other union
- Child support paid for children of other relationships

- Shared physical custody that either substantially reduces the custodial parent's expenses for the child or substantially increases the noncustodial parent's expenses[1]
- Low-income obligor and custodial parent
- A child's special needs (e.g., a disabled child) or special expenses (anything from special medical needs to special activities that aid the child's development, such as art or music lessons, travel, and school extracurricular activities such as athletics, band and clubs)
- Income of other adults in the household, which some states such as Texas, require to be coupled with an additional deviation criterion)
- A child's extraordinary income (stranger things have happened!)
- Travel expenses for exercising parenting time

Defining Income For Support Calculations

Federal law requires that all of the child support obligor's income be included for purposes of calculating child support. State Guidelines and cases interpreting them have deemed that to include:

- Salary, wages, tips, overtime, commissions (including draws against commissions), profit sharing, deferred compensation
- Bonuses and severance pay
- Non-cash "perks" and reimbursements such as free housing, meals and vehicles that reduce personal living expenses
- Independent contractor income
- Retained earnings of Subchapter S corporations
- Interest, dividends and partnership distributions, and recurring capital gains[2]
- Trust income
- Pensions and annuity income
- Armed Forces Reserve and National Guard pay
- Social Security, veterans', and G.I. benefits
- Workers' compensation, unemployment and disability insurance benefits
- Scholarships, fellowships, and living expense subsidies
- Forgiveness of a debt or use of property at less than market or customary cost

[1] An *equal* time-sharing is typically *not* required for a finding of shared physical custody.
[2] A capital gain is essentially the profit made when property is sold, with some adjustments. "Recurring capital gain" is profits from, for example, investments, and is distinguished from one-time capital gain such as the profit realized upon sale of a principal residence, which should not be included in income when calculating support.

- A new spouse's income to the extent that it directly reduces a parent's expenses
- Alimony from a former spouse
- Money, goods, or services provided by friends or family
- Prizes and winnings from gambling and lotteries

Reducing an Obligor's Income When Calculating Support

Some state statutes provide for specific *reductions* of the amount of income used in support calculations. For example, New York's Child Support Standards Act allows income to be reduced by the following:

- Certain unreimbursed employee business expenses
- Spousal support paid per an order or written agreement in another case
- Child support paid per an order or written agreement in another case
- Public assistance
- Supplemental security income

Determining Income of the Self-Employed

CSG calculations can be complicated for self-employed business owners whose "real income" is hard to determine. Income and expenses can be found in the business's financial statements ("financials") and on various tax returns, depending on the nature of the business entity.

In Chapter 8, we looked at how those entities report income. Chapter 8 also includes techniques for identifying the "real income" of self-employed individuals that is not readily apparent from financials or tax returns. Since determining "real income" is so crucial to calculating support correctly, you might want to revisit that material.

Additional Child Support

Many spouses negotiate settlement agreements that provide for child support in addition to the CSG amount. Such additional child support can include contributions to:

- Health insurance premiums and coverage of uninsured or partially insured expenses such as mental health therapy and counseling
- Private school and tutoring

- Extracurricular expenses such as athletics (including participation fees and equipment), art and music lessons (including instrument/material expense), related travel and other expenses
- Post-high school education, including contributions to tax sheltered college savings accounts such as "529 accounts"

Negotiation of such "extras" can also include allocation between the parents of valuable tax benefits, including:

- Tax exemptions for children ($4,050.00 per dependent child in 2016) subject to phase-outs at higher income "threshold levels" that vary according to the taxpayer's filing status

- Federal child tax credits (CTC) for low and middle income families of as much as $1,000 for a dependent child,[3] available if

Child Support Guidelines don't prevent parents from negotiating "extras" such as sports activity and equipment fees.

  - The child is under 17 as of December 31st
  - You claim the child as a dependent on your income tax returns[4]
  - The child is your child, stepchild, foster child, adopted child, brother, sister, stepbrother, stepsister, or a descendent of one of these individuals such as a grandchild, niece, or nephew
  - The child did not provide more than half of his/her own support during the year
  - The child is a U.S. citizen, U.S. national, or U.S. resident alien
  - The child does not file a joint income tax return for the year except to claim a refund
- State child tax credits in New York, Oklahoma, North Carolina and California
- Assignment by one parent to the other of Head of Household income tax filing status in shared custody cases

---

[3] Note: The CTC begins phasing out at $75,000 of adjusted gross income for single income tax filers ($110,000 for married filers and $55,000 for married individuals filing separately.) If you have 3 or more "qualifying children," you may be entitled to the "additional child tax credit" that allows a refund if the tax credits exceed the amount of taxes you owe.

[4] The requirement that you claim the child as a dependent distinguishes the child tax credit from the Child and Dependent Tax Credit (DTC) for children who are under age 13 or disabled, or the Earned Income Tax Credit (EITC) designed for low-income individuals and families. Neither the DTC or the EITC can be transferred in a divorce settlement; only the custodial parent may claim them.

Modification of Child Support

Family courts can modify child support amounts that the parties have agreed upon or a judge has ordered when the following occur:

- There has been a substantial or "material" change in the parents' circumstances and abilities to support the child—typically a change in income.[5] In some states, a substantial change is defined as a change that would cause a deviation from the Child Support Guidelines of more than a certain percentage. For example
    - In Connecticut, a change in circumstances requiring the child support amount to be modified by more than 15% will trigger modification.
    - A Minnesota court has held that a 20% (and $75) variance from the Child Support Guidelines created a presumption of a change in circumstances requiring modification.
- There has been a substantial change in the needs of the child, including educational or health expenses.
- The child support being paid does not comply with the current Guidelines.
- There has been a change in custody or primary residence.

Parents cannot limit the court's power to determine child support. Thus, settlement agreement provisions prohibiting child support modification are generally invalid.[6]

Enforcing Child Support Orders

A number of laws offer assistance in enforcing child support orders:

- The Uniform Interstate Family Support Act (UIFSA) makes it much easier for custodial parents to obtain initial child support orders and/ or to modify or enforce them when the obligor parent lives out-of-state. UIFSA facilitates enforcement of out-of-state orders by establishing a "home state" with continuing exclusive jurisdiction over the case. Judges from two states often confer by phone to decide which of their states will be the home state. Note that UIFSA was amended in 2001 and 2008, so different states apply different versions of it.

---

[5] In states such as Oregon and Washington, the change must be "unforeseen" or "unanticipated."
[6] Some state courts, in limited circumstances, will uphold such a provision if agreed to by a child's attorney or *guardian ad litem*.

- State "long-arm jurisdiction" statutes can be used by an "initiating state" to keep child support proceedings in the state where the child support recipient lives. This can occur even when the obligor lives elsewhere if the obligor had at some point established "sufficient contacts" with the initiating state. In deciding whether a state may exert authority over a non-resident under UIFSA, a court can consider whether [7]
  o The obligor has resided with the child in the state
  o The obligor has resided in the state and provided prenatal expenses or support for the child
  o The child resides in the state as a result of the obligor's actions
  o The obligor engaged in sexual intercourse in the state and the child may have been conceived as a result
  o The obligor asserted paternity in the putative father registry filed with the appropriate agency within the state
  o Any other legal basis exists for the state's exercise of personal jurisdiction over the obligor to obtain this result
- State support enforcement agencies assist in both intra-state and inter-state child support proceedings. These agencies have an array of weapons to enforce support orders, including the ability to
  o Summon the obligor to appear at court proceedings in which an agency representative represents the recipient at no or nominal cost

> ⚠️ **A Child Support Enforcement Pearl**
> Qualified Domestic Relations Orders (QDROs) are court orders that allow assignment to one divorcing spouse of some or all of the other spouse's retirement plans. What most people (including most lawyers) don't know is that under The Employee Retirement Income Security Act ("ERISA"), QDROs can also be used to enforce child support orders out of retirement plan assets.

  o File property liens
  o Report child support debts to credit agencies
  o Suspend drivers' and other licenses
  o In UIFSA cases, ask the obligor's state to begin proceedings there

Some state agencies will also assist obligors to reduce support in appropriate circumstances.

---

[7] Because state long-arm statutes differ, judges' application of the UIFSA factors differ as well.

Protecting Rights of Child Support Recipients

If you will be receiving child support, protect your rights as follows:

- Wage Garnishment. Many states allow child support recipients to elect a "wage garnishment" or a "wage order" by which employers deduct child support directly from the obligor's pay and forward the support to the custodial parent. Especially where there is a history of failure to comply with temporary orders, ask for a wage order.

- Direct deposit. If you don't use wage garnishment, provide in your settlement agreement that child support be paid via direct deposit from your Ex's account into yours. This will increase dependability and eliminate lost or late checks issues.

- Life Insurance. Require in your agreement that your Ex maintain life insurance naming you trustee or guardian of the children until child support (including college education expense) terminates. Your attorney, accountant, or an actuary can calculate the "present value" of the stream of child support and thus the amount of insurance needed to insure it. Your agreement can provide for one or more reductions of that amount as the remaining child support obligation is reduced over the years.

- Security Orders. Where there is reason to believe that the obligor may not comply with a spousal support order, courts in some states can require the obligor to provide security for payments.

- Attorneys' Fees. Most state statutes provide that attorneys' fees may be awarded in contempt proceedings. But it generally remains up to the judge whether to award fees—and to decide the amount. If you are a support recipient, provide in your agreement that the obligor will pay your reasonable attorney's fees in any proceeding in which an arrearage is established.

- Interest and Penalties. Support recipients may seek language in their settlement agreements providing for interest and even an additional monetary penalty to be assessed for willful (and perhaps repeated) failure to honor the support obligation.

- Motions for Contempt. Support orders, whether resulting from a judge's decision or a settlement agreement incorporated into a divorce decree, are enforceable by the court's contempt power. Post-judgment motions for contempt give support recipients a streamlined remedy to collect arrearages. Penalties in contempt proceedings include imprisonment of chronic offenders.

- <u>Maintaining Accurate Records</u>. Both spousal support recipients and obligors should keep records of all payments made. Documentation will be necessary in proceedings to collect arrearages.

 Yes, there *IS* a quiz! Test what you have (or haven't) learned.

1. **This chapter is mainly about:**
   A. How to garnish the salad at your Divorce Celebration Party
   B. Making a last minute material change to your Divorce Celebration outfit
   C. The factors that affect the calculation of child support orders, and ways to protect your rights with respect to it

2. **What phrase used in this chapter might have been most helpful in avoiding your failed marriage?**
   A. Uniform acts
   B. Retained earnings
   C. Deviation criteria

3. **Unscramble the following key phrases from this chapter!!**
   A. votinaide iritacre
   B. dilch poputrs snideluige
   C. dilch poputrs ridutoan

CHAPTER 12

Spousal Support

"There is not a woman born who desires to eat the bread of dependence."
— Susan B. Anthony

Trending in Spousal Support: How Much and For How Long?

Spousal "support" or "maintenance" is intended to assist the less financially secure spouse after a divorce or prior to the divorce if the spouses have separated. In the latter case, the support is referred to as "temporary" or "*pendente lite*" support and lasts until final orders are entered in the divorce case.

The *amount* of spousal support depends on the spouses' past financial and non-financial contributions to the marriage, current circumstances and future prospects, plus a list of other factors a judge may consider under state law.

The *duration* or "term" of spousal support has been hotly debated in recent years and a number of states have shortened duration.

Types of Spousal Support

Many of the states that have changed their spousal support laws distinguish among several types:

- Permanent periodic or "lifetime" spousal support: Paid on a regular (usually monthly) basis until the death of either party or the recipient's remarriage. Reserved for long-term marriages, permanent alimony is typically subject to modification upon retirement or other substantial change in circumstances and is subject to state law regarding cohabitation discussed below. In some states, the term "permanent alimony" also refers to alimony awarded at the conclusion of the divorce as opposed to temporary or *pendente lite* alimony awarded while the divorce is pending.

- Transitional support: Also referred to (regrettably) as "rehabilitative alimony," transitional support is paid for a limited period after divorce to enable job training, certifications, etc. leading to employment intended to render assistance unnecessary. It can also be awarded to parents working part-time while raising young children.

- Lump sum support: A fixed amount that is usually, although not always, paid at one time. Because the amount is fixed, it does not terminate upon remarriage. It remains in effect even if the obligor dies, becoming a debt of the obligor's estate.

- Reimbursement support: Paid to compensate an ex-spouse who supported the obligor through school or job training.

- Unallocated alimony and support: A single payment that includes both spousal support and child support, and makes both child and spousal support deductible by the obligor. To qualify for the deduction, unallocated alimony payments must adhere to a complex set of IRS requirements or be subject to "recapture" of the tax benefits (discussed below).

What's the Difference Between "Spousal Support," "Maintenance," and "Alimony"?

The term "spousal support" as used in this book includes payments to or on behalf of a spouse or ex-spouse by agreement or court order in a family case.

"Spousal support," "spousal maintenance" and "alimony" all appear in state statutes, but their meaning varies. For example, in some states "spousal maintenance" refers to temporary support only. Those distinctions are important so be sure to familiarize yourself with your state's terminology.

"Alimony" is also the term used in The Internal Revenue Code (IRC) for spousal support that qualifies for the tax treatment discussed in Chapter 12. Thus payments can be both alimony under the IRC and "maintenance" or "support" under state law.

Spousal Support Formulas

In recent years, the idea of uniform alimony guidelines has gained in popularity in some states. In addition, The American Academy of Matrimonial Lawyers (AAML) has proposed that judges and lawyers use the following formula to calculate the amount of spousal support:

30% of the obligor's gross income minus 20% of the recipient's gross income, provided that the recipient's total income including alimony does not exceed 40% of the parties' combined gross income.

As of this writing, only a handful of states (including those listed below) have adopted statutory formulas or rebuttable presumptions regarding alimony amount and/or duration. In some other states, courts in particular counties use alimony formulas. While each state's approach to alimony is different, the sampling below gives you an idea of the range of those approaches. *As always, your best source of information regarding your state's law is an experienced matrimonial lawyer.*

Lawglish lesson: What's a presumption?

A legal presumption allows a court to assume a fact to be true or requires a court to reach a certain conclusion until evidence disproves the fact or the reasonableness of the conclusion. For example, Maine has a statute containing a presumption that spousal support cannot last longer than half the length of the marriage. That presumption can be overcome or *rebutted* by evidence that it would be unreasonable or unfair under the circumstances of the case.

States That Use Spousal Support Formulas, Guidelines, or Presumptions

- California: California Family Code Section 4320(k) states that one of the goals of alimony is for the supported party to be self-supporting within a reasonable period of time. While the reasonable period of time is defined as half the length of the marriage, the statute further states that its goal is not to limit the court's discretion to order support for a greater or lesser length of time. California Family Code Section 4336 requires the court to retain jurisdiction indefinitely for purposes of alimony in marriages of "long duration," which is presumed to mean marriages of at least 10 years. Read together, these sections create the possibility of lifetime alimony after 10 years so long as the recipient is working toward self-sufficiency.

- Colorado: Pursuant to Colorado's alimony guideline statute effective January 2015,[1] in a marriage of at least three years where the parties' combined gross income is less than the greater of $240,000 or the highest income contained in the Child Support Guidelines (currently $124,000), "spousal maintenance" is calculated at 40% of the higher income party's monthly adjusted gross income less 50% of the lower income party's monthly adjusted gross income provided that the amount paid does not exceed 40% of the parties' combined monthly adjusted gross income.

- Maine: Maine has a rebuttable presumption that, absent unusual circumstances, no spousal support will be awarded in marriages of less than 10 years. General spousal support awarded in marriages exceeding 10 years is subject to a rebuttable presumption that its duration can't exceed half the length of the marriage. However, additional provisions allow short-term spousal support in order to:
  ○ Assist a spouse reentering the workforce
  ○ Equalize a property settlement
  ○ Compensate a spouse who made substantial contributions to the other spouse's education during the marriage

- Maryland: The Maryland Court of Appeals has approved a trial judge's reference to the AAML alimony guidelines, meaning that Maryland judges may use that formula.[2]

- Massachusetts: A 2011 alimony statute set period maximums for "general term alimony," according to 5 classes of marriage duration.[3]
  ○ Up to 5 years: up to 50% of length of marriage
  ○ 5 - 10 years: up to 60% of length of marriage
  ○ 10 - 15 years: up to 70% of length of marriage

---

[1] CRS Section 14-10-114, entitled, "Spousal Maintenance-guidelines," effective January 1, 2014.
[2] *Boemio v. Boemio*, 994 A.2d 911 (Md. 2010)
[3] As in many states, Massachusetts has additional provisions for short-term alimony in shorter marriages.

- ○ 15 - 20 years: up to 80% of length of marriage
- ○ More than 20 years: indefinite term

- <u>Michigan</u>: Michigan judges can choose between 2 sets of unofficial guidelines . . . or ignore them altogether.

- <u>New Jersey</u>: In marriages and civil unions of less than 20 years, the alimony term cannot exceed the length of the marriage or union. A rebuttable presumption ends alimony when the obligor becomes 67.

- <u>New York</u>: See http://www.nycourts.gov/divorce/legislationandcourt-rules.shtml for new formulas adopted in 2016.

- <u>Pennsylvania</u>: <u>Temporary</u> "spousal support" and "alimony *pendente lite*" ("APL") are calculated as follows:
  - ○ If there are no children, 40% of the difference between the obligor's net monthly income and the recipient's net income
  - ○ If there are children, the income differential is reduced by the amount of child support and the result is multiplied by 30%.
    Note: these guidelines apply only to spousal support awarded for the period before judgment is entered in a divorce case.

- <u>Texas</u>: Texas has a rebuttable presumption that spousal maintenance is unnecessary except if a spouse or dependent is disabled. Recipients able to rebut the presumption are still subject to maximums:
  - ○ 5 years, if the marriage lasted less than 10 years <u>and</u> the obligor committed an act of family violence
  - ○ 5 years for marriages between ten and 20 years
  - ○ 7 years for marriages between 20 and 30 years
  - ○ 10 years for marriages of 30 years or more

- <u>Northern Virginia</u>: An unofficial formula used in some Virginia counties provides that if one spouse's earnings exceed the other's by at least 50%, alimony is calculated at 30% of the higher-earning spouse's gross income minus 50% of the other's gross income. If the alimony obligor is paying child support, the percentage of the obligor's income drops from 30% to 28% and the amount of the recipient's income to be subtracted rises from 50% to 58%.

How to Calculate Spousal Support in Your Case

Whether or not your state is a formula state, you will still need to know more than what your state statutes say about spousal support in order to estimate the likely range of support in your case. You can start with the state-by state information and forms available at http://family.findlaw.com/divorce/spousal-support-alimony-forms-and-information-by-state.html. If the link to your state has changed, search for information regarding alimony on your state's court system or bar association website.

State statutes, whether or not they include guidelines regarding amount or duration, typically provide the following:

- The factors judges can consider in ordering spousal support. While most statutes include the factors listed below, there are still significant differences among them. Find out, for example, whether responsibility for breakdown of the marriage or other "misconduct" affects alimony awards in your state.
- Definition of terms such as "length of marriage," which in some states ends upon commencement of the divorce action but in others, not until the final judgment of dissolution.
- Availability of the different types of spousal support discussed above.

Remember that in addition to your state's statutes and the case law interpreting them, support orders can be affected by:

- Customs in particular county or "judicial district" courthouses
- Particular judges' tendencies or biases

Finding Your State's Divorce Laws

For quick access to your state's laws regarding alimony and other divorce-related topics, visit The American Bar Association's hyperlinked directory of state and local bar associations at: http://shop.americanbar.org/ebus/ABAGroups/DivisionforBarServices/BarAssociationDirectories/StateLocalBarAssociations.aspx.

If selecting your state doesn't work, search in your browser:

- [Your state's] judicial "system," "branch" or "department;" or
- [Your state's] bar association

An Old War (Horse) Story

Early in my career, I represented a husband who had won a Bronze Star as a helicopter pilot in Vietnam. We were assigned for trial to a traditional-thinking older judge whose chambers were ablaze with photos celebrat-ing his own military experi-

ence in World War II. And this old war-horse judge never tired of telling, or hearing war stories.

Accordingly, I elicited extensive testimony from my client about his military service. Such testimony would have served my client well with this judge under any circumstances... except maybe one.

Unfortunately, the judge's "traditional thinking" included an aversion to life styles that differed significantly from his. And my decorated veteran client was gay. Can you guess which one of the judge's partialities prevailed?

The more important point is that predicting outcomes of fi-nancial issues such as spousal support is difficult. It involves more than reading statutes and case law. Lawyers familiar with the back-grounds and predispositions of local judges can use that informa-tion for their clients' benefit. But there are no guarantees, which is one reason divorce lawyers routinely advise clients to settle.

Once you get to your state, you should be able to access plain language pamphlets and information regarding your state's divorce laws via the follow-ing type of path:

- "For the public," "public resources," "On-line help center," "Self-Help," or "FAQs; then...
- "Family Law," Family Matters," "Divorce," "Alimony," "Child Support," and similar topics

Then...

- An index of publications, videos, etc. or...
- A link to the state bar's Family Law Section or...
- A link to Lawyer Referral Services

Something Small in Texas

In Texas, where everything is supposed to be so big, spousal support isn't. Spousal support awards are often much less than in other states, and don't last as long. Texas law calls for 7 years of support after marriages of between 20 and 30 years, and 10 years after 30-year marriages.

Factors Affecting Alimony

The best source of information concerning the likely range of alimony and of local judges' tendencies in your case, is the local matrimonial bar. Because judges have a great deal of discretion even in states with statutory guidelines, predicting alimony outcomes can be difficult, as discussed above. What you can find out is what factors judges in your state are permitted to consider in making alimony decisions. Those factors typically include the following:

- Length of marriage (the single most important factor affecting alimony duration)
- Earnings and other sources of income
- Age and health of the parties
- Future earnings prospects based on employment history, education, and professional qualifications
- How being a child's primary caregiving parent affects the feasibility and desirability of that parent's employment
- Standard of living during the marriage
- The parties' assets and liabilities
- Tax consequences of an alimony award
- Each party's financial and non-financial contributions to the marriage
- Opportunities to acquire property in the future
- The recipient's financial and non-financial contributions to the marriage, including assistance with spouse's education or career
- Any other factors the court deems relevant

Judges are not required to consider all of the factors enumerated in their state's alimony statutes. Furthermore, they are usually free to give more weight to some factors than to others.[4] What can be valuable to learn is whether your state laws contain any absolutes such as whether or not there are circumstances that prohibit a spouse from paying or receiving spousal support.

Alimony No-No's: When Spousal Support is Prohibited

The following states prohibit alimony awards in specific situations:

- California: There is a rebuttable presumption that a spouse convicted of domestic violence within 5 years of the dissolution of marriage may be barred from receiving alimony.
- Georgia: Marital infidelity that caused the divorce bars the unfaithful spouse from receiving alimony unless the infidelity is forgiven or the spouses continue to live together.
- North Carolina: A "dependent spouse" who commits adultery is barred from receiving alimony unless the supporting spouse committed adultery as well.
- South Carolina: A spouse who commits adultery cannot be awarded alimony. In addition, habitual drunkenness, physical cruelty, or desertion may prohibit alimony if that conduct contributed to the breakdown of the marriage.

Determining the Amount of Income on Which to Calculate Spousal Support

In most states, income is the most important factor affecting the *amount* of alimony. In Chapter 11 we saw the importance of figuring out an obligor spouse's actual income when calculating his support obligation. We also saw how complicated it can be. If you skipped Chapter 11 (or fell asleep reading it), review the material there beginning on page 122.

Using the Alimony Tax Deduction

Not all spousal support "qualifies" for the alimony tax deduction. Strict adherence to complex IRS rules is required for the deduction to apply.

---

[4] Most state statutes that list factors don't prioritize them. A notable exception is California, which emphasizes "the standard of living established during the marriage." California Family Code sec.s 4320(d), 4330(a), and 4332.

Alimony saves taxes, particularly when the obligor can deduct the alimony in a substantially higher tax bracket than the recipient pays income taxes on it. To allow the recipient to share in the overall tax savings, the amount of alimony is typically increased or "grossed up" to include the taxes the recipient will pay on the alimony. Skillful attorneys can find a level that maximizes the after tax income of *both* spouses.

Alimony Deduction Requirements

For a taxpayer to qualify for the alimony deduction, the IRS requires the following:

- Payments must be made pursuant to a court order or written agreement signed by the spouses or their counsel.
- Payments made while the obligor and recipient occupy the same household are not considered alimony.
- Alimony "recapture rules" apply if alimony paid in the first post-separation year (the first calendar year in which the payer spouse pays alimony to the payee spouse *and* the parties live apart) exceeds the average of the payments in the second and third post-separation years by more than $15,000.
- Alimony "recapture rules" apply if alimony paid in the third post-separation year decrease by more than $15,000 from the preceding year.
- The 3-year recapture rules in the 2 preceding items do not apply to
  - *Pendente lite* alimony paid while divorce proceedings are pending
  - Where the amount of alimony is tied to the payer's income that varies widely due to factors out of his/her control
- Alimony cannot be reduced or terminated at a time that appears to be related to the expiration of child support.
- Alimony must end upon the recipient's death.

Whaaaaaat?
I know! IRS's alimony rules are about as unSimply Stated as it gets. The recapture rules in particular are traps for the unwary, and a good example of why you need the advice of a divorce lawyer, accountant or certified divorce planner or financial analyst.

Protecting the Alimony Deduction

Alimony can be a great tax-savings device. However, poor planning or poorly drafted alimony agreements can create a hefty back tax bill for the obligor. Use the following as a checklist to make sure your agreement complies with IRS regulations and maximizes the deduction benefits.

- Alimony agreements must
  - Be in writing
  - Be signed by each spouse or his/her counsel
  - End or "terminate" upon the recipient's death
- Involve qualified professionals (which includes CPAs, certified divorce planners, and matrimonial lawyers) in negotiating and drafting alimony agreements to avoid the alimony "recapture rules" mentioned in the above "Alimony Deduction Requirements" list. Under those rules, IRS can disallow the deduction and re-compute the obligor's taxes without it, plus interest and penalties. IRS Publication #502 provides a form for calculating whether and to what extent you risk recapture.
- If you have been paying or receiving *pendente lite* alimony during a year in which you and your STBX are still married on December 31st, ask your tax advisor about filing separate tax returns. Normally, you should avoid "Married Filing Separately" tax filing status. However, tax savings from alimony, which cannot be claimed on a joint tax return, may outweigh the usual disadvantage of filing "Married Filing Separately."
- If you are the alimony obligor in circumstances where annual alimony amounts are expected to vary depending upon your income, acknowledge in your settlement agreement that you and your STBX expect that your income (and thus the alimony you pay) will vary, and why.
- Be aware that if alimony is modified or terminated (other than because of remarriage or death), or pre-paid within the first three post-separation years, you must structure any such changes to avoid the recapture rules.
- In the event that alimony "recapture rules" do come into play, avoid the obligor getting hammered by IRS by using "safety net" language in your agreement that spreads the financial responsibility between the parties.
- Make sure that alimony is not reduced upon the occurrence of a "contingency related to a child," especially if you combine alimony and child support into a single "unallocated alimony" payment that is entirely deductible to the payer. Contingencies related to a child include the child attaining majority or a specified age, marrying, dying or graduating high school. If you have more than one child, consider whether unallocated

alimony is worth the risk of running afoul of complex IRS regulations relating to overlapping "danger periods."
- Keep good records of all payments made and retain them for at least 3 years in case of an IRS audit.
- Consider having alimony paid by automatic withdrawal and direct deposit. It simplifies record keeping and can alleviate pain for the obligor and worry for the recipient.

Protecting Your Rights Regarding Spousal Support

Nominal Support

In most states, if no spousal support is awarded at the time of the divorce, a party cannot return to court to seek it in the future. An order of "nominal support" or "nominal alimony," usually in the amount of $1.00 per year, preserves a party's rights to seek alimony in the future. It is used when a receiving spouse has a need for support but the paying spouse has no current ability to pay it. This occurs, for example, in cases where the primary wage-earning spouse is:

- Unemployed
- Earning less than he/she has earned in the recent past (especially applicable to self-employed spouses)
- Earning less than he/she is capable of earning in the current job market and has actually earned at some point in the past

If you are the spouse entitled to spousal support in such circumstances, make sure that you receive:

- At least nominal support, and/or
- Additional property settlement to compensate for the lack of support

Modification of Spousal Support

Generally, spousal support is modifiable if the parties' circumstances have substantially or "materially" changed since the original support award or most recent post-judgment order. If you believe such a change has occurred, you must do the following:

- File a motion or application (check your state's judicial or bar website for forms) stating facts or reasonable belief of the existence of a ground for modification in your state.
- Request in the motion that any order be retroactive to the date of its filing, or (where state law permits) to the event such as loss of employment that triggered the modification claim.
- Prepare a financial disclosure statement (and file it with the motion if required).
- Have the motion served in the same manner as the original divorce pleadings[5].
- If your ex-spouse requests a continuance, condition your consent upon a written agreement that any order entered will be effective retroactively
  - To the date of the originally scheduled hearing, or
  - If permitted by state law, to the date of the filing of your motion or application.

What Changes in Circumstances Are Necessary For Modification?

A change in circumstances must be substantial in order to justify modification of support. Such changes can include:

- Loss of employment
- New employment
- Changes in either party's income
- Changes in either party's health
- Changes in either party's needs
- Cohabitation (see page 192)
- Change in custody
- Loss of child support
- Retirement

State law varies in defining the standard for modifying spousal support. For example:

- <u>California</u> is an exception to the general rule tying modification to changed circumstances. Instead, it is the life style during the marriage that determines whether alimony continues beyond the original term.

---

[5] Some states permit post-judgment motions or applications to be served on the opposing party or counsel by regular mail if filed within a certain period after entry of judgment.

An increase in the obligor's income cannot be the basis for an increase in support "except in unusual circumstances."[6]

- <u>Connecticut</u> falls between Kentucky's tough standard and North Carolina's broader one by requiring a "substantial change in circumstances."
- <u>Kentucky</u> requires "a showing of changed circumstances so substantial and continuing as to make the terms unconscionable."[7]
- <u>New Jersey</u> differentiates between "durational" alimony of finite length and "permanent" alimony of indefinite length (usually after long-term marriages only). Substantial, continuous changed circumstances are grounds for modification of both amount and length of permanent alimony but generally only the amount of durational alimony.
- <u>North Carolina</u>'s statute simply requires "a showing of changed circumstances" by either party.
- <u>Vermont</u> requires that the changes in circumstances be both important and unanticipated.

The ability of a court to order, or parties to agree to non-modifiable spousal support distinguishes it from child support, which is always modifiable. Spouses can agree to prohibit or limit modification of spousal support in many ways, including the following:

- Prohibiting the obligor from seeking to reduce support below a specified dollar amount or percentage of the obligor's income
- Prohibiting the recipient from seeking more than a stated amount of support or percentage of income
- Prohibiting either party from seeking to modify the duration of support
- Prohibiting either party from seeking modification until after a certain date

Note that spouses considering eliminating all modification may find themselves with unintended results because
- Courts scrutinize non-modification provisions carefully, so any ambiguity will be interpreted to allow modification.
- A ban on modification could be disastrous if either spouse becomes disabled.

Thus, exceptions should be included in agreement provisions barring or limiting modification, to cover the following situations:

---

[6] N.J.S.A. 2A:34-23c.
[7] Kentucky Revised Statutes sec. 403.250 (7/13/90)

- Either spouse has serious unresolved health issues
- Where termination of spousal support would disallow the alimony deduction under IRS recapture rules; for example, if the recipient cohabited, triggering alimony termination during the first 3 years of support
- Either spouse becoming disabled

⚠ What to Do If You Cannot Fulfill Your Support Obligation

Losing your job or being out of work due to illness or disability does not automatically suspend your alimony obligation. If you cannot pay your support obligation, you must take steps to protect yourself:

- Ask your Ex to agree in writing that you are not obligated during the period of unemployment, disability, etc. and that your Ex won't oppose a court order incorporating that agreement. Then file a motion to amend or revise the judgment in accordance with that agreement (or "stipulation"), attaching the signed original. Don't delay, because until a court order is entered in accordance with such an agreement, the existing order remains in effect.
- If your Ex won't agree to any change in your obligation, immediately file a motion for modification that requests a reduction or suspension of alimony retroactive to the date of the filing of the motion.

The "Second Look"

Duration of spousal support can be one of the toughest issues to settle and is frequently the last obstacle to settlement. When that happens, lawyers and mediators sometimes salvage a settlement by putting off a resolution of the duration issue until a future date. They accomplish that with a "second look" provision in a scenario such as the following:

- Settlement negotiations stall over the issue of spousal support. The obligor has made a final proposal regarding length of support. The recipient wants at least the possibility of receiving support for longer, without being required to prove the substantial change in circumstances required in modification proceedings.

- As a result, the parties craft a second look provision stating that at the end of the term to which the obligor has agreed, they will return to court (perhaps trying ADR first) to determine whether and for how long support will be paid thereafter, and in what amount.
- To avoid any "gap" in support, the provision also provides that any additional support will be retroactive to the end of the term stated in the original agreement.

Cohabitation

In all states, spousal support can be terminated, modified and/or suspended if the recipient cohabitates with another person.[8] However, there are numerous important differences among state cohabitation laws, including:

1. How cohabitation is defined, for example,
   ○ Whether it must last more than a certain length of time
   ○ The types of arrangements it covers; i.e., it must be more than spending weekends together but need not be full-time residence sharing
2. Whether the cohabitation alone is sufficient to justify termination, modification, etc., or whether the cohabitation must also change the alimony recipient's needs
3. Whether the statute gives judges alternatives to terminating support outright, such as modification or suspension while the cohabitation continues, so that
   ○ Judges are not forced to make "all-or-nothing" decisions
   ○ Recipients are not barred from future support

Statutory Definitions of Cohabitation

In most states, cohabitation sufficient to terminate or modify spousal support means more than simply sharing living space. It requires a relationship

---

[8] However, cohabitation at the time of the divorce doesn't necessarily preclude an award of spousal support. *In re Marriage of Vandenberg*, 229 P.3d 1187 (Kan. Ct. App. 2010)

that resembles a marriage. Some states also require that the cohabitation must alter the recipient's financial needs or circumstances. Below is a sampling of statutory definitions of cohabitation:

- California: Unless the parties agree otherwise in writing, there is a rebuttable presumption that a supported party cohabiting with a person of the opposite sex has a decreased need for spousal support.[9]
- Connecticut: The support recipient must be "living with another person under circumstances which the court finds should result in the modification, suspension, reduction, or termination of alimony because the living arrangements cause such a change of circumstances as to alter the financial needs of that party."[10]
- Massachusetts: The spousal support recipient must have "maintained a common household" with another person for at least three continuous months.[11]
- North Carolina: ". . . the act of two adults dwelling together continuously and habitually in a private heterosexual relationship, even if this relationship is not solemnized by marriage, or a private homosexual relationship."[12]
- Virginia: "Habitual cohabitation" in a relationship analogous to a marriage for at least one year, unless (1) otherwise provided by stipulation or contract or (2) the recipient proves by a preponderance of the evidence that termination of such support would be unconscionable.[13]

"Hard Cases Make Bad Law"

There's a saying among lawyers that "hard cases make bad law." In other words, cases that tug at judges' heartstrings can lead to decisions based upon emotion rather than established law.

Many settlement agreements create those hard cases by providing that spousal support terminates upon cohabitation. That's a bad idea in states that also allow modification or suspension of support upon cohabitation by a support recipient, because it forces a judge into an all-or-nothing choice: a "hard case." And *that* can lead to a finding of no cohabitation despite compelling

---

[9] California Family Code §4323 (a)(1)
[10] Conn. General Statutes §46b-86
[11] Chapter 208 Massachusetts General Laws §49(d)
[12] North Carolina General Statutes §50-16.9(b)
[13] Code of Virginia §20-109

evidence of it, if the judge feels that ending spousal support forever could create a hardship for the recipient or the recipient's children.

A better option is to provide that, upon cohabitation, the obligor may seek any of the remedies provided for in the cohabitation statute.

> **"Hard *Time* Makes Ridiculous Law."**
> If "hard cases" foster bad law, "hard time" apparently leads to even worse law: In Florida, a judge terminated an incarcerated woman's alimony on the ground that she was cohabitating with her cellmate. (*Craissati v. Craisatti*, 997 So. 2d 458 (Fla.Dist. Ct. App. 2008)

Cohabitation Statutes That Require Economic Impact

In many states, cohabitation that doesn't affect a spousal support recipient's needs, will *not* justify a change in the existing order. Those states include:

- California
- Colorado
- Connecticut
- Florida
- New Jersey
- Ohio

Cohabitation Statutes Containing Alternative Remedies

States with cohabitation statutes providing for less drastic remedies than termination, such as suspension or modification, include:

- California
- Connecticut
- Florida
- Massachusetts
- New York
- Virginia

Spousal Support by Automatic Direct Deposit

Consider providing for automatic deposit of spousal support in your settlement agreement. It offers benefits for both parties by
- Creating reliable documentation of payments
- Allowing the recipient to count on receiving support payments on time
- Avoiding disputes over late payments, cash payments, etc.
- Relieving the obligor of the pain of writing monthly checks

Enforcing Obligations and Protecting Rights Under Spousal Support Orders

Spousal support recipients can protect their rights in a number of ways:

- The Uniform Interstate Family Support Act (UIFSA). UIFSA aids enforcement of out-of-state spousal and child support orders, as well as orders made by courts in your state against obligors who have left the state.[14] Enforcement is sometimes facilitated by judges from two states agreeing on a "home state" that will maintain authority or "jurisdiction" over the case. (See Chapter 11.) Note: UIFSA has been amended, so different states apply different versions of it.

- Wage Orders or "Garnishment." Many states allow support recipients to elect a "wage garnishment" or "wage order" by which employers deduct support from the obligor's paycheck. If you are a recipient where there is a history of failure to comply with temporary orders, consider a wage order at the conclusion of the case.

- Life Insurance Provision. Require in your agreement that your Ex maintain life insurance naming you as beneficiary, until spousal support terminates. You attorney, accountant, or an actuary can calculate the "present value" of the necessary amount of insurance. Your agreement can provide for one or more "step-downs" in the amount required as the years go by and the remaining support obligation is reduced.

- Security Orders. Where there is reason to believe the obligor may not comply with a spousal support order, some states allow recipients to request that the court order the obligor to provide security for payments.

---

[14] While jurisdiction to modify *child support* orders can move to a "home state" that is more logical in view of ex-spouses moving away, UIFSA provides that *only the court issuing a spousal support order* may modify that order. UIFSA 2008 sec. 211.

- <u>Attorneys' Fees Provision</u>. Most state statutes provide that attorneys' fees can be awarded in contempt proceedings. But those awards are usually up to the judge and require a finding that the obligor is in contempt of court. If you are a support recipient, provide in your settlement agreement that the obligor must pay your reasonable attorneys' fees if you are awarded past due support even if the obligor is not held in contempt.

- <u>Interest and Penalties</u>. Support recipients may seek language in their settlement agreements providing for interest and even an additional monetary penalty to be assessed for willful (and perhaps repeated) failure to honor the support obligation.

- <u>Motions for Contempt</u>. Support orders, whether resulting from a judge's decision or a settlement agreement incorporated into a divorce decree, are enforceable by the court's contempt power. Motions for contempt get you speedy access to court to collect arrearages. The contempt power includes the authority to assess attorneys' fees and ultimately to imprison obligors who are chronically and willfully in arrears.

- <u>Obtaining a Judgment Regarding Arrearages</u>. If you are a support recipient and the obligor has run up a substantial arrearage, you can seek a judgment in the amount of the arrearage so that interest will accrue.

- <u>Maintaining Accurate Records</u>. Spousal support recipients and obligors should keep records of all payments made. Documentation will be necessary in proceedings to collect arrearages, and in case of an IRS audit.

Who Needs a Lawyer?

Probably you. Careful drafting of settlement agreements is crucial to avoid problems later on. Here are some examples of problems that poor drafting can create:

- In Iowa, money paid to a support recipient to pay for health insurance was modifiable alimony, not non-modifiable property settlement.[15] SOLUTION: Make sure that any continuing payments in your settlement agreement are clearly designated as spousal support (or alimony), child support, or property settlement. Each of the three should be in separate provisions.

---

[15] *In Re Marriage of Johnson*, 781 N.W.2d 553 (Iowa 2010)

- A Virginia court has concluded that a husband's obligation to pay the wife's health insurance premiums did not constitute alimony and thus did not end upon her remarriage.[16] SOLUTION: Same as above.

- Where IRS disallows an obligor's alimony deduction, the recipient receives a windfall of suddenly tax-free income and the obligor is socked with back taxes plus penalties and interest. SOLUTION: A "safety net" provision requiring renegotiation of the alimony amount in the event of unintended tax consequences.

- As a general rule, ambiguous language in a provision prohibiting modification will be construed as allowing it. SOLUTION: This is another example of the wisdom of having your agreement prepared by an experienced matrimonial lawyer.

---

[16] *McKoy v. McKoy*, 687 S.E.2d 82 Va. Ct. App. 2010)

 Yes, there *IS* a quiz! Test what you have (or haven't) learned.

1. The term "cohabitate" is
   A. Lawglish for "cohabit," lengthened by lawyers to make themselves sound important
   B. Lawglish for "cohabit," lengthened by lawyers who get paid by the letter
   C. One of those words like "co-dependency" that they have a field day with at AA meetings
   D. A word to describe unmarried individuals living together as married persons

2. The term "interest and penalties" can be used as:
   A. A way for IRS to punish us for not understanding divorce tax rules that only some accountants and a handful of lawyers actually do understand
   B. The title for a timeline showing the decline of your marriage
   C. Incentives in a separation agreement to encourage timely payment of support

3. Unscramble the following key phrases from this chapter!
   A. laminon lamiyon
   B. necods kolo
   C. telatubber ternoppimus

CHAPTER 13

Property Distribution

"Sir, if you were my husband, I would poison your drink."
"Madam, if you were my wife, I would drink it."

— A conversation between
Lady Astor and Winston Churchill

The Split-Up Split Up

Property distribution is the process by which you (by agreement) or a court (by a divorce judgment or "decree") distributes between you and your STBX

- What you own (property or "assets") and
- What you owe (debts or "liabilities")

⚠ The Difference Between "Marital" and "Non-Marital" Property

Nearly all states distinguish between "marital property," which is subject to distribution between divorcing spouses, and "separate property," which is usually not. State laws vary widely, of course, but the following definitions apply in most jurisdictions:

- "Marital property" is property acquired by one or both spouses during the marriage.
- Non-marital or "separate property" includes
  - Property acquired by one of the parties prior to the marriage which has not substantially changed in value during the marriage because of the efforts of one or both spouses such as renovating the marital residence or growing a small business
  - Property acquired with the proceeds of sale or trade of separate property
  - Property acquired by will, trust, or gift at any time

General Rules of Property Division

Many judges approach marital property distribution as follows, subject to state law[1] and (mostly in equitable distribution states) considerations of fairness or "equity:"

- In longer marriages, judges often first consider dividing *marital property* equally. While most states don't include inherited property or assets owned before the marriage as marital property, the value of such assets can still be "in the pot" when it has been so "conmingled" with marital property that there is no way to separate it.
- In short-term marriages (often considered to be approximately 5 years or less), especially 2nd marriages or those with no children, equitable distribution courts[2] often consider returning the parties to their situations prior to the marriage.
- Unless state law makes it impossible, judges often attempt to leave each party self-sufficient or at least in a position to become self-sufficient.

Types of Property Distributed in Divorce

Family courts have the authority or "jurisdiction" to divide up the following kinds of property upon divorce:

- Marital residence
- Second homes and other real estate interests including real estate investment trusts ("REITs")
- Bank, money market, and trade union accounts
- Investments, including securities such as stocks, bonds, and partnership interests
- Ownership of businesses including professional practices
- Automobiles, boats, RVs, and other vehicles
- Personal property valuables such as antiques, collectibles, and artwork
- Retirement accounts, including pensions, savings plans (401(k) plans, IRAs, etc.)
- Vested stock options (and sometimes "unvested" options that an employee owns if he/she stays with the company for a certain period of time) and stock ownership plans ("ESOPs"), and other deferred compensation programs available through employment

[1] As discussed below, 3 of the 9 "community property states," require a 50/50 division of marital property.
[2] See the discussion below of the differences between "community property jurisdictions" and the majority of states (and the District of Columbia) that are "equitable distribution jurisdictions."

- Trusts that a spouse controls or in which the spouse has a "legal interest"
- Higher education degrees and professional licenses
- Club memberships
- Debts owed to a spouse such as legal judgments
- Intellectual property such as inventions, books, and music that a spouse has written with some track record or realistic expectation of production or publication
- Income tax refunds
- Digital assets such as domain names, websites, and social media accounts
- Lottery, contest, and gambling winnings
- Miscellaneous assets (e.g., frequent flyer points, timeshares, etc.)

Types of Property <u>Not</u> Distributed in Divorce

Generally, the following are *not* divided in a divorce:

- As discussed above, separate, "non-marital" property owned by a spouse before the marriage which did not substantially change in value during the marriage due to the efforts of a spouse, such as renovating the marital residence or growing a small business. However, there are some exceptions, namely
    - Connecticut and Massachusetts, which don't recognize the distinction between separate and marital property
    - Indiana, in which the distinction is not determinative
    - New York and Ohio, in which judges have included property acquired before the marriage
- Property acquired <u>after</u> the "marriage termination date," which is variously defined as one of the following
    - The date of legal separation
    - The date of physical separation
    - The date of entry of the divorce decree
- Mere "expectancies" such as revocable trusts and provisions naming a spouse as a beneficiary of a will of a person who is still alive and thus able to change the provision
- Children's assets, such as education accounts ("529 accounts," etc.), and Uniform Gifts to Minor Act (UGMA) accounts, and Uniform Transfers to Minor Act (UTMA) accounts
- Most unvested stock options and other employment benefits that employees don't own until after a certain number of years

> ### Assisted Reproductive Technology
> As assisted reproductive technology ("ART") continues to develop, disputes over control or ownership of genetic material have begun to appear in divorce cases. The emerging rule is that the divorcing party who does not wish to procreate will win a dispute regarding ownership and disposition of stored genetic material. But this is obviously a developing area of the law, so stay tuned!

Factors Affecting Property Distribution

About two thirds of state statutes list the factors a judge may consider in dividing property. In the other states, those factors have been established by case law made by judges in deciding cases. Judges generally have broad discretion as to which of the following factors they wish to apply and how much importance or "weight" to give them.

- The parties' ages
- Health issues that might affect employability and cause post-divorce assets to be dissipated
- Length of marriage
- Whether the marriage is the parties' principal marriage that has produced children, as opposed to
  - A marriage subsequent to the principal marriage
  - A brief first marriage
- Life style
- Amount and sources of income, including regular gifts or trust income
- Earning capacity based upon
  - Occupation
  - Education
  - Vocational skills
  - Employability including impact of long term absence from the work force
- Whether one spouse will receive child support
- The size of marital estates in exceptional circumstances such as
  - Very substantial assets attributable principally to the efforts of one spouse, the other spouse receives less than 50% where 50% would substantially exceed the amount needed to maintain the life style established during the marriage

　　° Very insubstantial assets where the spouse with less earning capacity receives more than 50% of the property in order to "stay afloat"
- Contributions to the accumulation and preservation of assets
- Non-financial contributions such as raising children, managing the household, and "sweat-equity" in projects such as renovation of the family home
- Financial or non-financial contributions to the other spouse obtaining a professional license or degree
- Reasonable opportunity to acquire property in the future
- Contributions to the children's higher education
- The parties' respective liabilities
- The parties' needs
- "Economic misconduct" such as squandering assets or transferring them to family members, friends, or paramours
- Whether a spouse's "personal conduct" such as infidelity caused the breakdown of the marriage (except in some states where this factor applies only to alimony or in states such as Colorado where it is irrelevant to either alimony or property distribution)
- In some states, extraordinary value of non-marital property

What You Need to Know About Your State's Property Distribution Laws

Matrimonial lawyers are the experts on how your state's law applies to your case. Here are the questions to ask a local lawyer:

- Is your state a "community property state" or an "equitable distribution state"? (see below)
- When is your marriage considered to be over for purposes of determining ownership and valuation of property?
- Is property acquired during cohabitation prior to the marriage "in the pot" for purposes of property division at divorce?[3]
- Does "marital property" always exclude inheritances, gifts, or property acquired before the marriage?
- Can separate property be divided if it changes form or is con-mingled with marital property?
- Does your state presume a 50/50 division of marital assets?

---

[3] In New York and Ohio, for example, there is case law for the proposition that portions of property acquired "in contemplation of marriage" may be treated as marital property.

- Can professional licenses and higher educational degrees be assigned a value for purposes of property division?
- Is there a state statute that lists factors to be used in property division?

You can learn more about your state's divorce laws using the resources provided in Chapter 17.

Ship Ahoy!
Be wary of on-line charts claiming to summarize state divorce laws. Charts are useful for sailors, but not so much for summarizing divorce rules. Too often, they ignore legal subtleties . . . or are just plain wrong.

Equitable Distribution States vs. Community Property States

The biggest difference among the states regarding property distribution is the distinction between the 41 "equitable distribution" jurisdictions and the remaining "community property" states listed in the section below on community property.

Equitable Distribution

In "equitable distribution" jurisdictions
- Judges generally have broader discretion to divide property than community property judges, who usually divide marital property equally.
- "Marital property" can sometimes include inherited property or property acquired before the marriage. (See "all-property states" below.)

When dealing with long-term marriages, lawyers and judges often start from a 50/50 division of marital assets and make adjustments as they feel the circumstances require. For example, a spouse who has been the primary earner but whose earnings have temporarily (or intentionally) declined at the time of the divorce, may be called upon to take less than 50% of the assets to make up for the reduced spousal support allowed by his/her decreased earnings. Such flexibility is considered part of the "equity" in equitable distribution.

However, even among equitable distribution states, there are significant differences in property distribution rules, exemplified by the following:

- Presumptions[4]
    - In Indiana and Ohio, marital assets are distributed equally unless an even split would be unfair.
    - New York, New Jersey, Connecticut, and Pennsylvania have no such "50/50 presumption."
- Legal title isn't controlling in "all-property states." In some equitable distribution states known as "all-property" or "kitchen sink" states, it doesn't matter which spouse is the legal owner of an item of property. These states include
    - Connecticut
    - Indiana
    - Kansas
    - Massachusetts
    - Michigan
    - Minnesota
    - Mississippi
    - Montana
    - New Hampshire
    - North Dakota
    - South Dakota
    - Oregon
    - Vermont
    - Washington
    - Wyoming
- Some states divide both marital and non-marital property. In several states, even non-marital property such as inherited property and property acquired prior to the marriage can be divided between spouses. These states include
    - Connecticut
    - Massachusetts
    - North Dakota

---

[4] Lawglish reminder: A legal presumption allows a court to assume a fact to be true or requires a court to reach a certain conclusion until evidence disproves the fact or the appropriateness of the conclusion.

Courts in these states will nevertheless often award a larger portion of an inherited asset to the inheriting spouse. Similarly, judges can take into consideration whether property was acquired by one spouse before the marriage and reduce the portion awarded to the other spouse in a manner that the court feels is equitable given the applicable property division criteria.

- "Con-mingling" (Lawglish for "mixing together") can convert non-marital property into marital property. Con-mingling occurs, for example, when money inherited by one spouse is deposited into a joint bank account. In order to establish that funds or other property that has been con-mingled with the other spouse's separate property or with marital property, it's necessary to use bank records, etc. to "trace" the property back to one spouse.
  Equitable distribution state laws differ on the impact of con-mingling of marital and non-marital property. For example,
    ○ In Florida, con-mingling non-marital property, such as inherited property or property acquired before the marriage, converts it into marital property.
    ○ In Ohio, con-mingling converts separate property to marital property only if there is no way to identify the original separate property.
    ○ In Connecticut, Massachusetts, and North Dakota where both marital and non-marital property can be divided, con-mingling is not an issue.

Note that the "equitable" in "equitable distribution" means "fair." It does not necessarily mean "equal." Equitable distribution judges have broad discretion in apportioning property and debt. For example, even in Connecticut, a judge dividing most of a couple's property evenly might assign only 15 or 20% of a spouse's recent inheritance to the other spouse.

Note also that "equitable distribution" means different things in different states. In Ohio, it means that marital assets are distributed equally unless an even split would be unfair. New York, New Jersey, Connecticut, and Pennsylvania have no such "50/50 presumption." In fact, although Ohio is considered an equitable distribution state, many of its laws resemble more closely those of community property states.

Community Property

Nine and a half states are known as "community property" states. Alaska is the "1/2"—an equitable distribution state that allows couples to elect community property treatment. The other community property states are:

- Arizona
- California
- Idaho
- Louisiana
- New Mexico
- Nevada
- Texas
- Washington
- Wisconsin

In community property states, there are two kinds of property—"separate" and "community" property. While state law varies even within community property states, some general principles apply.

Community Property Principles

- "Community property" includes earnings produced by the labor of the spouses, and property purchased with those earnings, between the date of the marriage and the end-date of the marriage. Gifts, inheritances, and certain trust assets are not considered community earnings or property.

- "Separate property" includes inheritances or gifts received by a spouse during the marriage, and assets owned by a spouse prior to the marriage, including the portion of retirement benefits that vested prior to the marriage. It can also include earnings from separate property and personal injury awards to one spouse. In some states, even if the asset has changed forms, such as cash used to buy a car, the car remains separate property. Spouses have no claim to each other's separate property.

- The "end-date" of the marriage after which property acquired is considered separate, is most often defined as the date of dissolution of the marriage. However in California, the marriage end-date occurs when the spouses physically separate.

- Community property is considered jointly owned, and it is divided in two basic ways.

- ○ In California, Louisiana and New Mexico, community property is divided equally.
- ○ Courts in Arizona, Idaho, Nevada, Texas, Washington, and Wisconsin are not quite as rigid; while an equal division is presumed or used as a starting point, a more equitable division can be considered.

- Some community property states adjust property division where
    - ○ A spouse is disabled
    - ○ Marital property is "wasted" by irresponsible spending
    - ○ Marital property is concealed
    - ○ There is disproportionate earning capacity between the spouses
Note that in California, there is less "wiggle room" than in some other community property states for a judge to inject fairness.

- In community property states such as Arizona, Texas, and Wisconsin, it is presumed that property possessed by either spouse during the marriage is community property. Thus, a spouse claiming separate property bears the burden of proving it.

- Creditors can reach <u>community property</u> to pay debts that either spouse has incurred regardless of which spouse created the debt, or for whose benefit. However, note that the <u>separate property</u> of the spouse who did NOT incur the debt is generally NOT available to satisfy it.

Alaska is an equitable distribution state that nevertheless allows couples to elect community property treatment. That might be what comes from staring too long into the sun, trying to see Russia.

Circumstances That Complicate
Community Property Distribution

- Separate property such as cash becomes community property when it is con-mingled with community property and can't be separated out or "traced" to its separate source.
- A portion of the increase in value (appreciation) of property such as a business owned by one spouse prior to the marriage, where the appreciation is the result of the efforts of both spouses during the marriage, can be considered community property.
- Determining the end-date of the marriage after which assets acquired and debts incurred by one spouse are no longer owned/owed by both. In states where the marriage end-date is defined as separation, that date can be disputed, especially if neither spouse moved out of the family home.
- Premarital agreements can negate the effect of a state's community property laws, but the validity of such agreements is often disputed.

Dealing With the Family Residence

Some property issues—covered in the remainder of this chapter—are common to both equitable distribution and community property states. They include how to deal with the "former marital residence."

Where there are no children, the home is often sold as soon as possible. However, a home with children requires balancing continuity in the children's lives with financial realities. The feasibility of keeping the home until older children leave the nest, should be considered.

Financial issues regarding the family home include:

- Whether the home expense can be afforded once the spouses have separated and have the cost of two households rather than one

- ⚠ If the home is to be sold, whether it should be kept in joint names to preserve the full $500,000 capital gains tax exemption available to joint owners vs. $250,000 for a single owner

- What if any contributions the "out-spouse" must make, for example, to major repair and improvements necessary to preserve its value

- How long the out-spouse must wait for his/her share of the proceeds of sale

- Whether an overall tax savings can be realized by the out-spouse paying tax deductible property taxes and assessments

- Whether the out-spouse will be entitled to share in any appreciation in the residence's value after the divorce
- Whether the home can be refinanced in order to
  - Lower monthly payments
  - Remove the "out-spouse" from the mortgage and thus facilitate his/ her purchase of another residence
  - Allow the resident spouse to buy out the other spouse's share in the house at market value established by a procedure spelled out in the settlement agreement

⚠️ *Protecting Your Interests Until the House is Sold*

If the marital residence has not been sold by the time of the divorce, your settlement agreement should include protections for both parties by specifying the following:

- How the proceeds of sale will be divided
- A date by which the house must be listed for sale
- That the parties cooperate in marketing the house so as to sell quickly and upon the best possible terms
- Which ex-spouse is responsible for which house-related expenses
- How specific decisions will be made regarding
  - Setting the initial listing price
  - How often and by how much the listing price can be lowered
  - How the realtor and any successors will be chosen
  - What offers a spouse must accept (for example, offers within 5% of the listing price) if the other spouse wishes to accept
- That the court have "continuing jurisdiction" to resolve disputes regarding the marketing and sale of the house
- That a spouse who conveys title to the home at the time of the divorce will be protected by a mortgage note and deed, or other filing on the land records, establishing precedence over any subsequent claims or liens

Dealing With a Professional Practice or Closely Held Business

Perhaps the most difficult asset to value in divorce is a small "closely held" business or professional practice. If the business is considered marital property, the non-business owning spouse may receive property of comparable value such as a retirement plan or a larger share of the marital residence.

Operating businesses have two main value components:

- "Tangible" assets such as
  - Equipment
  - Inventory
  - Buildings
  - Accounts receivable
- Intangible assets (also referred to as "good will")

Good Will

"Goodwill" is the value of an operating business, over and above "tangible assets." Goodwill typically reflects the value of intangible assets such as:

- A well-regarded brand name or professional reputation
- Customer loyalty
- Advantageous location
- Proprietary information and technology
- Copyrights and trademarks

There are three kinds of good will:

- Enterprise Good Will: The business's intangible assets described above
- "Pure" Personal Good Will: Good will derived from skills, knowledge, and reputation of an individual member of the business that cannot be transferred to the entity or to other individuals
- Transferrable Good Will: Good will which is personal in nature but can be transferred to the entity or to another individual through training, etc.

Commercial Real Estate Appraisals
The appraisal of commercial real estate is based on "highest and best use" and thus differs from that of other business interests such as an ownership interest of a company. The commercial real estate appraiser should:
- Be licensed as a "general" (not "residential") appraiser in the state where the property is located
- Be prepared to produce an appraisal report certifying that the appraisal complies with the Uniform Standards of Professional Appraisal Practice (USPAP)
- Preferably, have advanced credentials such as "MAI" or "SRPA" from the Appraisal Institute

Valuation

A business appraiser is usually needed to determine a small business's value. Appraisers can also determine the "real income" (as opposed to income reflected on tax returns) that the business yields to its owner. Before hiring an appraiser, find out the following:

- The business appraiser's credentials such as certification as a business appraiser (CBA) or accredited senior appraiser (ASA)
- Whether the appraiser is familiar with the valuation methodology that has been approved by your state's family courts
- The appraiser's knowledge and experience valuing the same or similar type of business
- How often the appraiser has given expert testimony and whether transcripts of that testimony are available to opposing counsel
- The number of articles and books the appraiser has written on the subject that could be used against him on cross-examination

There is a lack of consensus among the states on how to value a business's good will. Many courts use the fair market value (FMV) standard, which is the amount that a hypothetical able and willing buyer would pay a willing seller when both have the necessary facts and neither is under any compulsion to make the deal. However, applying the FMV standard involves complications:

Beware double dips! (see below)

- In most states (California is an exception), only "enterprise goodwill" is marital property and it can be difficult to differentiate between "personal goodwill" and "enterprise goodwill."[5]
- Where a spouse does not control a company, the value of his/her interest may be reduced by a "minority discount" due to the inability to control the company and a "marketability discount" due to the inability to sell a minority interest in it.

---

[5] Many experts feel that only another valuation method, the capitalization of excess earnings method, can accurately separate out "personal goodwill" from Entity or Practice Goodwill.

What Is a "Double Dip" and What's So Bad About Something That's So Good at Baskin Robbins?

A "double dip" can occur when one spouse receives assets in the property settlement based on the other spouse's solely owned business, and also receives support derived from the business's income. This happens most often with medical, law, and other professional practices as follows:

- Spouse A's sole practitioner law practice provides all of A's earned income
- The value of the practice, based entirely or nearly entirely upon A's earnings, is included in the total value of the assets to be divided between the spouses
- Spouse B receives assets in exchange for A keeping the practice
- But Spouse B also gets spousal support based on A's law income, thus giving B *both support and property in exchange for the same asset*

Small Business: To Appraise or Not to Appraise

Before hiring an appraiser, the following questions must be answered:

- Is the business likely to have enough value to justify the cost of an appraisal?
- Does the goodwill of the business (for example, a sole practitioner lawyer's practice) consist essentially of personal good will that is usually not considered marital property, thus rendering a valuation useless?
- Where the sole owner of a business is to pay alimony based on his/her income from the business, will that constitute an impermissible "double dip?"
- What standard of value should be used?
- Can the spouses agree on an appraiser to hire jointly (as is commonly done in mediation and colla205borative divorce), rather than engage in a costly battle of "hired guns"?
- Is a Certified Business Appraiser (CBA) or Accredited Senior Appraiser (ASA) available?
- Is the owning spouse's interest a minority interest that will reduce its value?
- Does the fact of a minority interest, restrictive language in governing documents such as Bylaws, the Operating Agreement or the Partnership Agreement, make it difficult or impossible to sell the interest? Does this then trigger a marketability discount that would further reduce its value?

Valuing Small Businesses in Community Property States

Even in community property states where a spouse owned a business prior to the marriage, the value of the business may nonetheless include marital property under these circumstances:

- Joint funds are invested in the business
- Joint contributions have increased the value of the business
- Non-financial contributions to the operation or growth of the business by the non-owning have increased the value of the business

Dividing Retirement Plans

Retirement plans are one of the largest assets to be distributed in divorce. Federal law ("ERISA") provides for the division of "qualified" retirement plans[6] by a Qualified Domestic Relations Order or "QDRO" (pronounced "kwah-dro"). Portions of retirement plans accumulated prior to marriage are usually excluded from distribution.

There are two main kinds of retirement plans:

- Defined contribution plans
- Defined benefit plans

Defined Contribution Plans

These retirement plans consist of
- Contributions by employees of a percentage of their compensation
- Matching contributions from employers
- Earnings and appreciation on those contributions.

The most common types of defined contribution plans are
- 401(k) savings plans
- SEP IRA's
- Profit sharing plans
- Keogh Plans
- 401(3)(b) tax sheltered annuity plans ("TSA's")
- Stock ownership plans ("ESOP's")

---

[6] Military, government, and many teachers' pensions are not "qualified" plans and are governed by other laws.

Defined contribution plans have the following features:

* Their value is calculated simply by adding
  ○ The contributions of the employer that have vested
  ○ The employee's contributions, if any
  ○ Accrued earnings
* Some plans allow employees "hardship" borrowing against the plan.
* An employee leaving his/her company can "roll over" funds from a 401(k) plan into an IRA account. Care must be taken in such circumstances, however, that the funds move directly from the 401(k) to the IRA to avoid taxes and a 10% penalty.

From the Bizarro-World Law Dictionary

Intellectual Property – (1) The product of creative or intellectual endeavor that has value and/or income producing potential. (2) A house with a Smart Car parked in the driveway. (3) What they gave out the day your spouse's lawyer was absent. (4) An elitist egghead hang-out such as a library, museum, or Starbucks.

Defined Benefit Plans

If you receive statements from your employer showing an estimated monthly benefit you will receive upon retirement, you have a defined benefit plan. Commonly known as "pensions," these plans are characterized by the following:

* Participants can depend upon receiving a known or at least calculable amount from retirement until death.
* Unlike defined contribution plans, employees become entitled to or "vested" in their benefits only after a specified number of years (often 5) of working for the employer.
* After a certain number of years of employment, employees also qualify for benefits at an "early" retirement age, commonly age 55. Electing early retirement trades receiving benefits sooner for receiving lower monthly amounts, similar to Social Security.
* The benefit amount is calculated according to
  ○ Length of "service" (employment)
  ○ Age at retirement
  ○ Level of earnings

• Unless otherwise elected, an employee's *current* spouse gets a death benefit when the employee dies. Divorcing spouses wishing to receive death or survivor's benefits must so provide in a QDRO.

Handling Defined Benefit Pensions

Defined contribution plans are relatively simple to handle in divorce because the value on the account statement is the value of the plan.

Defined benefit plans are much more difficult to value. In property settlement, they can be handled in 1 of 3 ways:

• Each spouse retains his/her own pension/retirement plans and thus no division of retirement assets occurs.
• The spouses agree to evenly divide the future benefits when the pension goes into "pay status."
• A portion of one spouse's pension is assigned to the other spouse.

If the third option is chosen as to a substantial pension, an actuary should be hired to determine its "present value." This will allow the pension's value to be expressed in "today's dollars" and thus be comparable to the values of other retirement assets owned by the parties such as IRAs and 401(k) plans.

The present value of a pension is the amount that, if invested today at a reasonable investment rate of return, would produce the same benefit that the employee will receive under the plan. The calculation applies mortality rates and a "discount rate" (a kind of reverse interest rate) to the benefits to determine that value.[7]

Many employers and securities firms that administer retirement plans provide on-line forms and do-it-yourself instructions on preparing and submitting QDROs. Except with the simplest 401(k) savings plan, it is *not* a good idea to prepare a QDRO yourself.

---

[7] Some employers provide defined contribution plan statements that include a present value. On-line "pension calculators" are also available. Without knowing the discount rate and other assumptions used in the calculation, it is impossible to know if the values are valid. In addition, if you go to trial, you may need the actuary who has calculated the value to testify as an expert witness.

The Risks of Do-It-Yourself QDROs

Here are some reasons why you may not want to prepare your own QDRO, even if the plan administrator furnishes a form that seems easy to fill out.

- QDROs must strictly comply with often complex retirement plan rules.
- Many pension plans allow for participants to make choices or "elections" regarding matters such as
  - Whether the non-employee spouse (referred to as the "alternate payee") will be entitled to a survivor benefit upon the employee's death
  - What happens if the employee dies before retirement
- A professional experienced in QDRO preparation can communicate knowledgeably with plan administrators regarding drafting questions, review procedures, elections, and valuation.

 The Retirement Account No-No

Make sure that divorce-related transfers from IRAs or other retirement accounts go directly into another qualified retirement account. If retirement money is transferred to a non-retirement account, it can be taxed as income.

Steps to Dividing Non-IRA Retirement Plans[8]

- Retain a lawyer or actuary with experience in QDRO preparation, to prepare the necessary QDRO(s).
- The preparer will then read the retirement plan summary and determine what if any elections (e.g., survivor's benefits) must be made.
- Once agreement is reached regarding issues such as survivor's benefits, the preparer submits the QDRO to the plan administrator for "pre-approval." This avoids a judge signing an order that the plan administrator later rejects because it doesn't comply with the plan's rules.
- After the plan administrator pre-approves the QDRO, it is submitted to the court for signature.
- The preparer then sends the signed QDRO (which is now a court order) to the plan administrator who is required to distribute to the alternate payee according to its terms.

---

[8] QDROs are not required for the transfer of funds in IRAs.

Saving Tax Dollars in Property Settlement

Taking Advantage of Special
Divorce Tax Rules Re: Property

She's *Baaack*!
Remember this poor soul suffering from the alimony recapture rules in Chapter 12? The tax material below is just as bad. If your case involves substantial assets or alimony, do yourself a favor. Consult a CDFA, CFDP or a CPA to help you with the tax stuff. (See Chapter 6.)

Divorce property settlements present both tax-saving opportunities and tax pitfalls. First, the opportunities:

- Transfers of property exceeding the amount an individual can gift to another individual tax-free, called the "annual gift tax exemption" normally trigger gift tax. However, pursuant to Internal Revenue Code §1031, property transfers made "incident to a divorce" and within 6 years of it, are not taxed.
- Early withdrawals (prior to age 59 ½) from retirement plans normally trigger income taxes plus a 10% penalty. A withdrawal made in a divorce settlement does not incur the 10% penalty, provided that it is made pursuant to a qualified domestic relations order ("QDRO").
- A taxpayer can exclude up to $250,000 of capital gains from tax on the sale of a principal residence. The taxpayer must have owned and used the property as a principal residence for 2 of the 5 years preceding sale. Taxpayers filing joint tax returns can exclude twice as much; $500,000 of capital gains on a principal residence owned by one or both of them if during the 5-year period preceding sale, *each* of them used it as a principal residence for at least 2 years.

  Sales of principal residences pursuant to divorce settlements often don't occur until after the divorce, sometimes years later. Because divorced taxpayers cannot file joint returns, special rules allow *both* ex-spouses to exclude $250,000 of capital gains from tax if:

º They continue to own the residence jointly

º The ex-spouse granted use of the property by a divorce or separation decree or agreement has used the property as a principal residence for 2 of the 5 years preceding sale.

⚠ What Are Capital Gains Taxes, When Must I Pay Them, and How Are They Calculated?

Capital gains taxes are owed on the profit or "gain" you earn when you sell property or "capital assets." Capital gains taxes are associated most frequently with the sale of stock, bonds, mutual funds, art, collectibles and real estate. Gain is determined by subtracting the "cost basis" (the original purchase price plus transaction fees and commissions, and the cost of "capital improvements" to real estate) from the selling price. The difference is the "capital gain."

"Short-term capital gains" (for assets you have owned for 1 year or less) are taxed at regular federal income tax rates. However, "long-term capital gains" (relating to assets you sell after owning them for more than 1 year) are subject to federal tax at the more favorable rate of 15% except for higher income tax-payers who may pay 20% plus an additional 3.8% "net investment income tax." In addition, 41 states and The District of Columbia have their own capital gains taxes.

Capital gains taxes upon sale of a former marital residence that has grown substantially in value can be a major issue in divorce. Careful planning with a tax professional is necessary to take advantage of the special rules for divorcing spouses.

Protecting Yourself Against Hidden Tax and Other Costs

You can lose the benefits of divorce tax breaks if you fail to adhere strictly to IRS requirements regarding them. Talk to your lawyer or a CPA about taking these steps to protect yourself:

• Tax-free property transfers pursuant to IRC §1031 (tax-free transfers incident to divorce) must occur within one year of your divorce. However, if your property settlement calls for a transfer that cannot occur within that period due to legal or business impediments such as restricted or minority stock, state those conditions in your agreement. You should still receive §1031 treatment if the transfer occurs

º Promptly after the impediment is removed, and

º Within six years of your divorce

- If you are a non-resident alien (to whom IRC §1031 does not apply), during settlement negotiations, you should reduce the value of assets you are receiving by any capital gain taxes you will be obligated to pay on the transfer.
- When dividing up stocks and bonds, find out the cost basis for each to determine their real "after-tax value." In this way, you can avoid receiving assets with "hidden tax" costs that will arise when you go to sell the security.
- Keep records regarding asset cost bases in case of an IRS audit. In the case of your home, this includes documentation of improvements that increase the cost basis and thus decrease the amount of taxable capital gain.
- Find out whether any mutual funds or other securities funds you are to receive in settlement contain penalties or "back-end fees" if you sell them prior to a specified date.
- In settlement negotiation, avoid trading non-retirement assets (e.g., your ownership interest in your home, savings accounts, etc.) for "pre-tax" retirement accounts [SEP IRAs, 401(k)s etc.] Income taxes are generally owed upon withdrawal from retirement accounts and thus they carry "hidden costs."

Allocation of Debts

The other part of property division is the allocation of responsibility for debts. Several issues can complicate debt allocation:

- The allocation of debts between spouses by a family court is not binding upon third parties such as mortgage lenders and taxing authorities that can still seek payment from either or both parties. In other words, even if your agreement provides that only one of you is responsible to pay the mortgage, the lender can still pursue either or both of you if the mortgage goes into default.
- In community property states, all debts of either spouse can be satisfied from the couple's community property regardless of which spouse incurred the debt. This may change if the couple moves from a community property state to a non-community property state, since generally the place of domicile determines debt obligations.
- Pay close attention to how much debt is to be your responsibility. The allocation to you of a sizeable debt can deprive you of the full value of the property settlement you thought you were getting.

> ⚠️ **Indemnification Provisions Regarding Debts**
> Make sure your settlement agreement provides:
> - That your spouse "indemnify" and "hold you harmless" in the event that he/she fails to pay a debt required by the agreement. The indemnification should cover anything you are required to pay toward the debt as well as all expenses you incur in connection with it including reasonable attorney's fees.
> - If you are a support recipient, state that the indemnification clause is in the nature of child (or spousal) support and thus not dischargeable if your Ex files for bankruptcy.

Pets

Chuck would be unhappy to learn that state laws generally do not distinguish pets from other personal property. Technically, that makes them subject to distribution in the same way as vehicles or furnishings. In practice, however, judges often consider special factors regarding pets.

For example, custody of pets usually follows that of the children. Where there are no children, judges are likely to consider the following factors:

- Whether one of the spouses owned the pet before the marriage
- Which spouse feeds and primarily cares for the pet
- Which spouse will have more time and resources to care for the pet and will be able to provide the best environment for it

Modification of Property Distribution

Unlike spousal and child support, property distribution is modifiable only if one of the following occurs:

- Modification is sought within a specified period after the divorce (for example, 4 months in Connecticut; 30 days in Illinois)
- The property distribution has been procured through fraud
- Both parties want to correct a mutual mistake

Yes, there *IS* a quiz! Test what you have (or haven't) learned.

1. **"Equitable distribution" is**
   A. The bonuses The Equitable Life Insurance Co. pays its fat-cat partners out of your exorbitant life insurance premiums
   B. The division of what, if any, property is left over after the divorce lawyers get paid
   C. Just more Lawglish that makes something simple like "splitting stuff up" sound complicated

2. **An "alternate payee" is**
   A. The guy who cashed the paycheck he stole from your gym locker
   B. A substitute juror who gets kicked off a jury for taking a bribe
   C. A former spouse who has received an assignment of benefits from your pension

3. **"Present value" is**
   A. What you made on Stub Hub selling the opera tickets your Aunt Eunice gave you for Christmas
   B. What the Buddhist guy at work says he gets out of meditating
   C. A calculation of the current value of future monthly pension benefits, which allows you to compare the pension's value with the value of other assets

CHAPTER 14

Scared Witless to Star Witness: A Testimony Primer

"I was gratified to be able to answer promptly, and I did. I said I didn't know."
— Mark Twain, *Life on the Mississippi*

Will I Have to Testify?

One of the best things about alternative dispute resolution (ADR) is that you don't have to go to court, except for a brief "uncontested hearing" at the end of your case. So if your divorce is on track to be resolved through ADR, you won't have to testify. And you can skip this chapter![1]

Even if your case is court-based, it too will most likely settle. But you may have to testify along the way in one of the following situations:[2]

- Temporary ("*pendente lite*") court proceedings to obtain court orders that remain in effect until your divorce is final. *Pendente lite* hearings cover matters such as
  - Temporary spousal support, child support, or child custody/access
  - Other matters such as requests for attorneys' fees or exclusive possession of the family home
  Note that *pendente lite* hearings are limited in scope. For example, *pendente lite* support hearings focus primarily on current income and spending, while hearings on children's issues usually exclude financial matters.
- Depositions during which opposing counsel questions you at his office. Depositions are part of the discovery process through which a party to

---

[1] As discussed in Chapter 5, one form of ADR—arbitration—involves a proceeding that resembles a trial at which the parties testify. If you are headed for arbitration, you do need to read the material in this chapter.
[2] My audio book *Become Your Own Star Witness* is an in-depth primer on testifying in family cases. Visit www.WitnessTutor.com to listen to an excerpt and purchase an mp3 or 2-CD set.

a lawsuit obtains information and documents from the other party. A court stenographer records the questions, answers, and lawyers' objections, and prepares a transcript of the proceedings. Questions about any matter that might lead to admissible evidence are permitted at depositions, so the questioning can cover a broad range of topics.

- Trial, where you can be questioned regarding all financial or child-related issues. Occasionally a case settles even after trial has begun. This can occur when counsel is surprised by how skilled a witness the opposing party is, and decides not to risk an unfavorable decision. Note that if you go to trial, you will be asked about previous "statements," such as

  - Your previous testimony at a deposition or *pendente lite* hearing
  - Documents that you produced during discovery
  - Your financial disclosure statement
  - Other documents that you prepared, received, or were responsible for such as
    - Tax returns
    - Loan applications
    - Emails on-line posts and other correspondence

Conquering Courtophobia: Road Trip!

If you're like most people, you might feel just a bit anxious at the prospect of answering questions from a potentially hostile lawyer under oath in front of your STBX, a judge, a couple of lawyers, various courthouse personnel and an assortment of other folks awaiting their turn in the Legal Funhouse. A great way to bring down your anxiety level is to take a road trip to your local courthouse before you testify.

When you get there, do the following:

- Find out at the Clerk's Office where family cases are being heard.
- If possible, choose a courtroom with a hearing similar to what yours will be, or at least where a "contested" hearing or trial is taking place so that you can observe witnesses testifying on both direct and cross-examination.
- Locate the "Family" or "Court Services" Office. Many courts require a meeting with a Court Services Counselor to try to resolve *pendente lite* matters before a judge will hear them.
- Ask an assistant clerk, bailiff or dozing lawyer about the best places to park so that you don't kick off your Big Day in Court panhandling for quarters for a parking meter.

Your Star Witness Makeover

⚠️ Your performance as a witness can substantially impact how quickly and favorably your case is resolved. Effective testimony at a pretrial hearing or deposition can dampen the other side's enthusiasm for a trial and thus increase your leverage during settlement negotiation. Effective testimony at trial earns points with the judge that can translate into favorable court orders.

That's why we're spending a whole chapter on your star witness makeover.

What Should I Wear to Court?

Court attire should be neat, conservative and reflect respect for the court. Wear what you would wear to a job interview. Leave the chewing gum home and wear only the most modest jewelry. Martha Stewart went to jail after showing up in court with a $20,000 handbag. Enough said.

Your appearance should also match your case "story-line." If you are reentering the workforce but claiming you're too old for your former field, let your age show. If your spouse accuses you of serial infidelity, avoid your most flattering outfits.

Types of Examination of Witnesses

There are essentially 4 types of questioning or "examination" of witnesses:

- Direct examination Questions asked by the attorney who calls a witness in court. In divorce trials, the parties typically answer questions from their own lawyer on "direct."
- Cross-examination
  - In court, examination of opposing parties or other "hostile" or "adversary" witnesses, such as experts retained by the opposing party. "Cross" is used to test the witness's credibility, reliability and the accuracy of his/her testimony on direct examination.
  - At a deposition, examination of the opposing party or adversary witness for the purpose of gathering information in preparation for settlement negotiation and/or court proceedings.
- Redirect examination Questions asked in court by the initial examiner regarding matters covered on cross-examination. Redirect is used to "rehabilitate" a witness's credibility and/or to revise inaccurate, damaging

or confusing testimony. The "scope" of redirect examination is limited to matters about which the witness has testified on cross-examination.

* <u>Re-cross-examination</u> Additional cross-examination by opposing counsel, limited to the scope of redirect.

The four Commandments of Testimony

The "Four Commandments" of testimony discussed below are the building blocks to your success as a witness.

I. Listen Carefully to Each Question in Its Entirety and Be Sure That You fully Understand It.

Careful listening is a MUST when you testify, whether on direct or cross-examination. That means listening to the *entire* question.

Next, be sure you understand the question fully. If you don't, say so! You won't be required to answer questions you don't hear or understand.

You might not hear or fully understand a question because:

* Your attention might have strayed due to emotion or fatigue
* Some questions are incomprehensible. (Lawyers are asking them, so confusion is always just around the corner.)

If you didn't hear or understand a question in its entirety, you can
* Ask that the question be repeated or rephrased
* State that you don't understand the question

II. Answer Each Question Accurately, Concisely, Responsively, and in a Way That Is fair to You.

Nothing angers judges more than a dishonest witness. Running a close second, however, is a witness who gives long, unresponsive answers. Unfocused, rambling testimony can hurt your case in several ways:

* On direct examination, that kind of testimony
    ○ Disrupts the flow of your story
    ○ Drives the judge—and your lawyer—nuts
    ○ Gives opposing counsel additional cross-examination opportunities
* On cross-examination, such testimony provides the cross-examiner
    ○ New areas of questioning
    ○ Additional opportunities to find inconsistencies in your testimony and question your credibility and reliability as a witness

Pearls of Witness Wisdom: Questions About Documents

If you are asked about a document, ask to see it *before* answering the question. Take as much time as you need to carefully review the document.

Documents most frequently asked about are:

- Your financial disclosure statement
- Tax returns
- Business records if you own or operate a business
- Documents regarding spending such as bank, credit card and on-line account records for PayPal Amazon.com, etc.
- Statements for pension benefit and other employment related benefits and "perks"
- Employment agreements
- Loan applications
- Emails, texts, social media posts, etc. especially where child-related issues or reason for the breakdown of the marriage are in dispute

The "Fairness Exception"

Note the phrase, "in a way that is fair to you" at the end of Commandment II. I call this the "fairness exception." It applies when a concise response without explanation creates a misimpression that is damaging or "prejudicial" to your case.

Don't forget the testimony commandments!

The "fairness exception" most often applies to questions that lack a time period or other *context*. If you are asked a question without the necessary context

- Ask for a time period, place or other circumstance that's needed to avoid confusion or a misimpression; or
- State in your response when or where you said or did what you've been asked about, and if necessary, explain why that context matters

Placing Questions in Context

Below is an example of how the "fairness exception" works. Consider the following exchange at a *pendente lite* hearing between the husband and Attorney Fox, the wife's lawyer:

ATTORNEY FOX: Mr. Sherwood, you feel that your wife should be employed at least part time, correct?

MR. SUREWOOD: Yes, I do.

ATTORNEY FOX: But that's now that you're divorcing her. Before the divorce began, you told her that she didn't have to work, correct?

MR. SUREWOOD: Yes, but that was before Nicky, our second child was born and our expenses went up. At that point, I asked her to consider working part time.

Attorney Fox's 2nd question relates to a statement Mr. Sherwood made *sometime* in the past. Answering that question "yes" would have been concise and responsive, but would have left a misimpression. Realizing that, Mr. Sherwood had the choice of:

- Asking that the question be rephrased to include a time period, or
- Adding an explanation to his "yes" answer

He chose the 2nd option, a "Yes, but" answer that explained the yes by supplying the necessary context.

III. Don't Be Argumentative, Sarcastic or Witty, or Try to Outsmart the Examining Lawyer.

Losing your cool at a deposition suggests to opposing counsel that you'll make a poor witness at trial. That can increase counsel's willingness to go to trial and thus make it more difficult to negotiate settlement.

Losing your cool at trial can accomplish several things (none of which are good), namely:

- Presenting you in a bad light to the judge
- Causing you to lose the focus necessary to follow the testimony commandments
- Strengthening your spouse's case. For example, if your spouse contends that your bad temper helped destroy the marriage, arguing with opposing counsel:

° Makes that contention more believable
° Bolsters your spouse's credibility

Witness Graduate School
Learn more about testifying in family court cases from my audio book, *Become Your Own Star Witness*. Visit www.WitnessTutor.com.

The Argumentative Witness

You have the right as a witness to insist upon clear, unambiguous, and understandable questions. But don't argue unnecessarily with your cross-examiner. The methods above allow you to obtain clarification of the question or explain a "yes" or "no" answer without being contentious.

It's particularly important to keep your cool in court. Judges want testimony to be

* Presented in an efficient and understandable way on direct examination.
* Tested in a meaningful way on cross-examination, despite the fact that it may annoy or antagonize you as the witness. If you have a lawyer, ask her to grill you ahead of time on topics that make you feel uncomfortable or vulnerable, to help you remain calm when answering difficult questions.

Judges do *not* want to listen to bickering witnesses and lawyers.

Staying Out of the Judge's Dog House

Judges particularly dislike seeing the following in the courtroom:

* Witnesses who lie
* Witnesses who give rambling, unresponsive answers
* Witnesses who quibble with the attorneys questioning them
* Witnesses who chew gum, slouch or "lounge" on the witness stand
* Witnesses who wear overly casual or revealing clothing such as T-shirts, flip-flops, low-rise pants or mini-skirts.
* Non-testifying parties who react out loud to their spouse's testimony
* Non-testifying parties whom the judge can hear talking to their lawyers
* Anyone with a cell phone!

IV. Prepare Effectively for Your Testimony.

Witness preparation is one of the most important—and neglected—aspects of effective testimony. To help you remember how to prepare yourself to testify, try using an acronym that's so tasteless, you'll have difficulty forgetting it:

The Key to Effective Testimony: B.U.R.P.

- **Breathe**: Practice relaxation techniques once or twice a day during the weeks preceding your testimony.
- **Update**: Avoid difficulties on the witness stand by periodically updating and checking your financial disclosure statement for accuracy.
- **Road Trip!** Visit the courthouse prior to testifying to watch contested hearings and familiarize yourself with the terrain (see below).
- **Prepare by:**
  - Going over your "statements" regarding your finances, including your financial disclosure statement, interrogatory responses, testimony transcripts, and documents such as loan applications and tax returns.
  - Meeting with your lawyer to go over both your direct testimony and the cross-examination you should expect. Ask your lawyer to focus on issues on which you feel vulnerable or uncertain.
  - Periodically reviewing the testimony commandments as your hearing or deposition approaches.

Be a Proactive Client!

Busy lawyers too often neglect to prepare their clients to testify. If your lawyer hasn't arranged to meet with you regarding testimony you are expecting to give at a hearing or deposition, take the initiative and schedule the meeting yourself. And tell your lawyer you want to do more than *discuss* your testimony: You want to *practice* it by having her fire questions at you and evaluate your responses to them.

If your lawyer hasn't prepared you to testify, take the wheel!

Understanding the Cross-Examiner's Goals

The testimony commandments apply both to direct and cross-examination. Concise, responsive answers on direct will help present your story in a methodical way that's easy for the judge to follow. Similar responses on cross will portray you as credible and reasonable.

However, cross-examination in court can be very different from cross at a deposition. Understanding the differences between the two can help you testify more effectively.

The Cross-Examiner's Goals in Court

In court, cross-examination typically comes after your lawyer questions you on direct exam. It is used to:

- Try to make you acknowledge facts unfavorable to you or favorable to your spouse
- Cast doubt on your testimony by challenging your memory and understanding ("reliability") or your honesty ("credibility")
- Cast doubt on your entitlement to the financial and other orders ("relief") that you are seeking

---

Pearls of Witness Wisdom: "Prior Statements"

If you are asked about a statement you made in the past (including statements contained in documents), you can request that the question be rephrased to locate your statement in time and place. This is crucial, especially if you have said different things about a topic at different times.

The Cross-Examiner's Goals at a Deposition

Lawyers use depositions to prepare for trial and settlement negotiations. Their goals at depositions are to:

- Gather relevant information
- Ask questions designed to learn what you will say at trial, and to "lock in" testimony that might be helpful to your spouse at trial
- Authenticate documents that you have authored or that relate to you
- Size up your skills as a witness

Avoiding "Yes" and "No" Responses

In court, skilled cross-examiners use "leading questions" nearly exclusively. Leading questions contain the cross-examiner's version of facts or conclusions with which the witness is simply asked to agree or disagree. They are actually more in the nature of statements than questions. As a result, cross-examiners using leading questions are actually the ones testifying.

The following are common types of leading questions:

- "So you didn't tell your husband that you got a bonus, *did you*?
- "You quit your job to try to get more support, *didn't you*?
- "The cash your father gave you was never intended to be a loan that had to be repaid; *isn't that a fact?*"
- "*The fact is* you have another savings account that you opened to try to hide money from your wife, *correct?*"

Responding "yes" to, or otherwise agreeing with a leading question is often the most damaging answer you can give. Once you give such an answer, the cross-examiner's version of the facts becomes your testimony. So be sure that *everything* in a question is accurate before answering "yes."

Your cross-examiner may try to insist upon "yes or no" answers to leading questions. You don't have to go along. When a "yes" or "no" response would be incomplete or misleading, respond with one of the following:

- "No, I can't answer that yes or no."
- "I can't answer yes or no without an explanation."

Taking Advantage of "Why?" Questions

In law school, baby lawyers are taught 3 rules of cross-examination:
- Don't.
- Don't ask a question to which you don't already know the answer.
- Never ask "why?"

These rules are intended to avoid harmful testimony in response to questions a lawyer does not have to ask . . . other than to show off his cross-examination skills. As you can imagine, lawyers routinely ignore these rules.

If you are lucky enough to be asked "why" you said, did or thought something, be ready to respond with *your* version of the relevant facts. This does not mean you should give a long rambling answer. It means that if the reasons you said, did or thought something are important *and* responsive, don't hold back. You might not get another chance.

- "That question can't be answered that simply."
- "I can't answer simply yes or no, the way you've phrased the question."

Standing Up to the Cross-Examiner

You can stand your ground on cross-examination in ways other than refusing to answer ambiguous questions "yes" or "no." For example:

- Refuse to answer definitively when you are almost, but not completely, sure of the answer. Instead, respond with one of the many alternatives available:
  - "I think so, but I'm not completely sure."
  - "That sounds right, but I can't swear to it."
  - "I don't believe so, but I'd have to check [a document] to be sure."
  - "I believe so, but I'm not 100% sure."
  - "I don't know."
  - "I don't remember."
  - "I'm not [exactly] sure."
  - "I don't recall that specifically."
- If you are being questioned about a document, ask to see it and review it carefully before responding.
- Take advantage of the witness's magic word that stops cross-examiners in their tracks. The word is "speculation." For example, responding, "I'd

"SPECULATION":
The Witness's Magic Word!

just be speculating if I answered that question," will force counsel to move on. Judges prohibit speculation because it has no "probative value."

What Lawyers *Cannot* Ask You

There are some limitations on what lawyers can ask:

- <u>At a deposition: harassing or overly burdensome questions</u>. Any question that might lead to admissible evidence is permissible at a deposition. Because financial orders are based upon a wide range of factors, there's very little that's irrelevant. Note that relevance is narrowed somewhat at trial where judges generally don't allow "fishing expeditions" for minor scraps of information.
- <u>In court: impermissible questions</u>. Each state has complex rules of evidence designed to enhance the reliability of testimony and other

evidence. For example, most statements made by a witness who is not a party and who is not present in the courtroom is considered "hearsay" and cannot be quoted or referred to by a witness in his/her court testimony. Similarly, witnesses who are not experts in the field about which they are testifying are generally not permitted to offer opinions.

There are also numerous exceptions to evidentiary rules that complicate their application. That's one reason why you need experienced trial counsel in a court-based case.

Courtroom Decorum

Earlier in this chapter we noted behavior that can land you in the judge's doghouse.[3] Below are a few more things you should know about what to do and what *not* to do in the courtroom.

When You Are Testifying in Court

Keep in mind the following when you testify:

- You must speak loudly enough to be heard by the lawyers, the court stenographer, and most importantly, the judge. Courtroom microphones are generally for recording, not amplification. You have to supply the volume yourself.
- During your testimony, a lawyer may ask you a question to which the other lawyer objects. When that happens, don't answer unless the judge "overrules" the objection. If the judge "sustains" an objection to a question, you may not answer it. Simply wait for the next question. (This differs from depositions where no judge is present, and you must answer even questions to which an objection has been made—unless your lawyer advises you not to.)
- If there's no drinking water on the witness stand, ask for some.
- If you start to feel overwhelmed to the extent that you can't concentrate on the questions, say so. Judges are generally sensitive to the emotional nature of family cases, and will give you an opportunity to regroup.

---

[3] Judges nearly always decide financial and child-related issues in divorces. In Georgia and Texas, juries can decide all issues in a divorce case, though the cost of jury trials is quite often prohibitive. Colorado, Illinois, Louisiana, Maine, Nevada, New York, North Carolina, Tennessee, and Wisconsin permit juries to decide limited issues such as grounds for, or entitlement to divorce; issues that are rarely litigated in the era of no-fault divorce.

- The witness stand is located beside the judge, though usually at a slightly lower elevation. You'll spend the great majority of your time facing the lawyer who is questioning you. However, it's not a bad idea to make brief, occasional eye contact with the judge especially to emphasize important testimony.
- ⚠️ Take your time! Skilled cross-examiners sometimes employ a fast-paced rhythm to try to unnerve witnesses and keep them from giving sufficient thought to their answers. If that happens, you can slow the pace by doing one of the following:
    - Saying something to the effect of:
        - "Let me think about that for a moment."
        - "I have to think—I want to make sure I'm being accurate."
        - "Give me a moment; I'm trying to recall."
    - Asking if you can refer to a document in evidence that will help you answer the question
    - Asking that the question be repeated
    - Taking a drink of water

When You *Aren't* Testifying in Court

During testimony by your spouse or other witnesses, you can provide valuable assistance to your lawyer, as follows:

- Pay close attention and take plenty of (legible) notes. You know more about your marriage than your lawyer, so you may pick up on something that she doesn't.
- If you wish to bring something to your lawyer's attention, communicate with her in writing, not verbally, so that she doesn't miss important testimony.
- If you've maintained a divorce binder as discussed in Chapter 7, keep it at the ready for quick access to key documents.
- Don't let emotion prevent you from performing the tasks above. And don't react to testimony, no matter how provocative it is.

Talking to the Judge

Judges sometimes ask witnesses a question or two. If your judge does that, don't feel intimidated. Answer the questions as thoroughly as you can. Make eye contact and convey respect, both verbally and with body language. As with any questions you are asked in court, if you don't understand them, say so.

If the judge appears dissatisfied or confused by an answer you give, try to remedy the situation. Encourage the judge to ask you for clarification with something like:

- "I may not be understanding your question."
- "Am I being clear?"
- "I feel like I'm not helping you."

In certain situations such as uncontested hearings (see page 28), a judge may speak directly to parties while they are seated at counsel table. If that happens and a response is called for, be sure to stand up when "addressing the court."

Getting Through a Courthouse Day

A typical court day begins between 9:00 and 10:00 A.M., suspends for lunch at 1:00 P.M., resumes at 2:00 and ends at 5:00. Many judges take mid-morning and mid-afternoon recesses.

Of course, your day will be much longer than the court's hours—starting with the moment you wake up thinking, "Oh, ===! Today's the day!" Leave yourself extra time in the morning to be sure that you can get to court on time without having to rush. Pace yourself through the day to avoid fatigue, because testifying in the highly focused manner described in this chapter burns a lot of energy.

Try your best to get a good night's sleep the night before. Avoid insomnia triggers like alcohol, caffeinated beverages, sugary snacks, and glowing electronics. If all else fails, choose something incredibly boring to read. Like the pension material in Chapter 8.

On the Road to Witness Stardom

You will be better prepared than the vast majority of witnesses if you:

- Master the testimony commandments
- Visit the courthouse ahead of time to observe contested family hearings
- Practice your testimony before your hearing or deposition[4]

---

[4] If you don't have a lawyer to help you prepare, write out questions about the matters that concern you the most, and have a friend fire them at you. Then grade yourself (and have your friend grade you as well) according to how well you followed the testimony commandments. Repeat, until you get it right.

So, relax. Or at least try to. No one is perfect and you won't need to be as a witness. Don't worry if you make a mistake here or there while testifying. Concise, thoughtful testimony will impress a judge in court, and render an attorney who takes your deposition more eager to settle your case.

 Yes, there IS a quiz! Test what you have (or haven't) learned.

1. **You can begin conquering courtophobia by:**
   A. Embracing the tiger
   B. Taking the tiger by the tail
   C. Getting trashed at a karaoke bar and singing "Eye of the Tiger"
   D. Getting over this thing you have about tigers, and visiting a local court-house prior to your court hearing

2. **You can tell that you are watching cross-examination when:**
   A. The witness begins speaking in tongues.
   B. The lawyer is more obnoxious than any of the Real Housewives of New Jersey. Except maybe Teresa.
   C. A lawyer wearing a tuxedo concludes his cross-examination with, "I'm through with dis guy!"
   D. Mostly "leading questions" are being asked, which allows the lawyer to be the one actually testifying and simply asking the witness to agree or disagree with the fact or conclusion contained in the question.

3. **Rate the texter below, who is texting from the courtroom, for compliance with the material in this chapter:**

CHAPTER 15

Same-Sex Marriage and Divorce

*"At his best, man is the noblest
of all animals; separated from
law and justice he is the worst."*

— Aristotle

Same-Sex Marriage

On June 26, 2015, the United States Supreme Court ruled that all states must recognize same-sex marriages, and that same-sex spouses are entitled to the same rights as heterosexual spouses. Writing for a 5-4 majority in the case of *Obergefell v. Hodges*,[1] Justice Anthony M. Kennedy based his ruling on the entitlement of same-sex spouses to "equal dignity in the eyes of the law."[2]

The Supreme Court has rejected what some call "traditional values."

The *Obergefell* decision will have far-reaching consequences, particularly in the 13 states that had not recognized same-sex marriage. Those consequences include the right of same-sex couples to divorce in each state, whether or not same-sex marriage was previously permitted there.

Same-Sex Divorce

Under the *Obergefell* decision, same-sex divorces will work the same as opposite-sex divorces. Nonetheless, certain issues and fact patterns will occur more often in same-sex divorces. And at least while state laws are

---

[1] 576 U.S. ___ (2015)
[2] Two years earlier in the case of *United States v. Windsor*, 570 U.S. ___ (2013), the Supreme Court had invalidated key provisions of the Defense of Marriage Act (DOMA) and granted to same-sex spouses the same rights enjoyed by opposite-sex spouses under federal law.

evolving in the wake of *Obergefell*, resolution of those issues is likely to be more complicated.

Same-Sex Property and Spousal Maintenance Issues

Because same-sex marriages didn't exist a mere dozen years before *Obergefell* (and were never sanctioned in 13 states), many same-sex couples lived together for long periods before they were able to marry. Many of those couples acquired substantial assets before marriage that they considered to belong to both of them.

Unfortunately, such circumstances could complicate property division issues at the time of divorce.

Most of the 42 equitable distribution jurisdictions in the U.S. consider property acquired before marriage to be non-marital property that upon divorce remains with the spouse that acquired it. In all 9 community property states, such property is also considered non-marital. (See Chapter 13 for details and exceptions.)

Issues in divorce relating to property acquired before marriage are not new. Certainly, heterosexual couples cohabit before marriage as well. But that cohabitation is by choice.

Pre-marital cohabitation for many same-sex couples has been due at least in part to prohibitions against marriage. Those prohibitions also led to quite lengthy periods of cohabitation, especially in states that never sanctioned same-sex marriage, or did so only shortly before June 2015. As a result, limiting marital property to that acquired after marriage creates significant potential for unfairness in same-sex divorces.

Consider 2 partners that have lived together for 15 years, then marry when their state law sanctions same-sex marriage. Three years later, the couple decides to divorce. A court that limits marital property to what was acquired during the last 3 years of an 18-year relationship could create a devastating injustice for one of the spouses.

Similar considerations apply to spousal maintenance. Let's say the same couple lives in a state where maintenance is typically awarded for half the length of marriages that exceed 10 years. A judge who ignores the 15-year cohabitation would award 1 or 2 years of maintenance at the most.

Using Prenuptial Agreements to *Avoid* Unfairness

Prenuptial agreements (also known as "premarital agreements") have traditionally been used to protect more affluent spouses from financial claims during divorce by their less well-off partners.

But "prenups" can also be used to try to avoid unfair results such as those discussed above. Long-term same-sex partners who weren't permitted to marry during part or all of their pre-marriage relationships can use prenups to
- Expand their state's definition of marital property
- Provide for spousal maintenance awards based on the length of the entire relationship

Keep in mind that prenups need not be one-sided. By way of example, let's consider again the couple that lived together for 15 years prior to a 3-year marriage that ended in divorce. The more affluent spouse may be willing to agree to spousal maintenance for longer than state law would allow after a 3-year marriage in exchange for a limitation on claims for property acquired by that spouse that became marital property due to con-mingling during the long relationship.

Of course, a prenup must be able to hold up in court. While it has become increasingly difficult to invalidate prenups in recent years, some courts still refuse to honor them when at least 1 of the following factors is present:

- The more well-to-do partner fails to fully disclose his/her finances
- The less affluent partner doesn't have access to professional advice
- The agreement is obtained through "duress" or "undue influence"
- The agreement is essentially unfair or "unconscionable"

A combination of good will and good planning can avoid the first 2 factors. And partners drafting a prenup to be *more* rather than *less* fair generally needn't worry about #3 or 4.

Broaching the subject of a prenuptial agreement can be a dicey matter, to say the least. It's difficult even for partners of many years to predict what reaction the suggestion might provoke. But those who are able to discuss—frankly and dispassionately—ways to avoid unfair results upon divorce may find it well worth their while to do so.

Child-Related Issues: Adoption and ART

While issues relating to adopted children and those conceived through assisted reproduction technology ("ART") arise in heterosexual divorces, they will come up more regularly for same-sex spouses with children. And controversies regarding those children are likely to be more complex in many same-sex divorces.

For example, let's say a same-sex couple decided to adopt a child in 2012 in a state in which same-sex marriage was not allowed. Though both partners wished to adopt, only one of them was permitted to do so under that state's law. Will the adopting parent be entitled to greater rights regarding the child if the couple later marries and then, following years of co-parenting, files for divorce?

Similar issues will arise regarding ART. Here's another example:

A lesbian couple marries in Massachusetts in 2004, the year in which that state became the first to sanction same-sex marriage. Several months later, the couple moves to a state that doesn't recognize same-sex marriage. In 2005, one of the spouses conceives through in vitro fertilization, and gives birth. In 2015, after 10 years of loving and nurturing their child equally, the spouses decide to divorce. Unfortunately, they are unable to agree on custody.

The family court is confronted with a number of thorny legal issues:

- Should the birth spouse have superior legal rights regarding custody and access solely because under the law of a state that didn't recognize same-sex marriage, she alone is listed on the birth certificate?
- Should the court apply by analogy the Uniform Status of Children of Assisted Conception Act under which a woman who bears a child (other than as a surrogate) is the child's mother, and the woman's husband is the father?
- Should the court apply by analogy the legal presumption that the husband of a woman who gives birth during marriage is the father?
- Should the court ignore birth certificates, common-law presumptions, and non-binding uniform acts, and instead base its decision solely on the best interests of the child ("BIC") standard?

Same-sex couples that marry and subsequently adopt, or conceive through ART after June 2015 will no longer be victimized by discriminatory laws. But they will still be forced to confront the issues faced by all couples where only one spouse is an adoptive or natural parent. And those issues can be further complicated in "blended families" where children of previous marriages are raised together by a parent and that parent's new spouse.

Unfortunately, prenuptial agreements are not as helpful in dealing with child-related issues as they can be with financial matters. That's because courts in every jurisdiction reserve the right to determine "ultimate" child-related issues such as custody, regardless of agreements the parents may reach. Thus, judges are free to ignore prenuptial agreement provisions that they consider to be inconsistent with BIC.[3]

Nevertheless, prenup provisions can affect custody and access determinations. For example, language acknowledging that both spouses have in the past, and expect in the future to participate equally in child-rearing can have an impact. The same is true of an acknowledgment of a child's close and loving relationship with both spouses and/or a statement of intention to continue to nurture the child's relationship with both spouses in the event of divorce.[4]

Moving Forward

As demonstrated by the examples above, changes in state laws will be needed to avoid the unique potential for unfairness that lurks in same-sex divorce. Those changes are likely to emerge slowly as judges struggle to resolve novel issues in the wake of the *Obergefell* decision.

In the meantime, same-sex spouses who can resolve matters themselves or through alternative dispute resolution will be able to avoid the uncertainties that will loom particularly large for them while the law develops.

My hope for those couples is the same as for all divorcing couples: a divorce that resolves issues fairly and efficiently.

---

[3] See page 141 for more on BIC.
[4] If the agreement contains additional provisions that affect "ultimate" child-related issues, make sure that it also contains a "severability" clause that preserves the remainder of the agreement in the event that such provisions are invalidated.

Yes, there *IS* a quiz! Test what you have (or haven't) learned.

1. **A main idea in this chapter is:**
    A. Civil unions would be likely to make employees more polite.
    B. Same-old-same-old same-sex marriages can get boring.
    C. The U.S. Supreme Court has eliminated distinctions between opposite-sex and same-sex marriage and divorce.

CHAPTER 16

Your Divorce Afterlife

"Life is not a matter of holding good cards, but of playing a poor hand well."

— Robert Louis Stevenson

Your Post-Divorce TBD List

You walk from the courthouse, freed at last from the clutches of the divorce process. After all is said and done, you've reached the finish line in one piece.

Except all is not quite "said and done."- Most likely, there are still some things for you to do. Try to take care of the matters be- low *at or before* your final hearing. But if you can't, address them as soon as possible after it. Keep copies of all correspondence regarding these tasks and make sure that all snail-mailed documents go via certified mail or other trackable means.

- Sign documents to transfer real estate, vehicles, etc. in accordance with your settlement agreement.
- Divide any savings or securities accounts per your settlement agreement.
- After cancelling any automatic withdrawals and making sure there are no outstanding checks, close all
  - ° Joint bank accounts,
  - ° Joint investment accounts
  - ° Joint credit cards (including accounts in your name for which your Ex had charging privileges)
  - ° Home equity and other loan accounts
- Change beneficiaries and survivor's rights per your settlement agreement for

- º Pension and other retirement plans including IRAs
- º Life insurance
- Make sure that any life insurance policies required to insure child or spousal support have been obtained or amended in accordance with your agreement and are in full force and effect. (If you are the recipient of support insured by a policy insuring your Ex's life, your settlement agreement should require notice to you of any lapses or beneficiary changes.)
- Revise or revoke any of the following in which your Ex has an interest or power to act on your behalf.
  - º Revocable trusts
  - º Living wills
  - º Powers of attorney
- Change email and other on-line passwords even if you don't think your Ex knows them because . . . you never know.
- Obtain a certified copy of your divorce decree from the Clerk of Court.
- If retirement assets are to be transferred by QDRO (see page 214), make sure that the QDRO is
  - º Prepared by a qualified lawyer, actuary or financial planner
  - º Submitted to the plan administrator for pre-approval
  - º Submitted to the court for a judge's signature
  - º Received back from the court containing a judge's signature
  - º Forwarded to the plan administrator (via certified mail)
  - º Acknowledged in writing by the plan administrator as being received, approved, and in effect
- If you will be obtaining COBRA health insurance through your Ex's employer, notify the employer of that election in writing within 30 days of the divorce.
- Make sure any other documents required by your agreement are signed and delivered to the appropriate entities.
- If your birth name has been restored, do the following.
  - º Download, fill out and submit a Form SS5, "Application for Social Security Card" at http://www.socialsecurity.gov to obtain a new card bearing your birth name
  - º Notify your employer, bank(s), insurance companies, the Post Office, retirement plan administrators, credit card companies, and utility companies
  - º Contact the U.S. Passport Office for a new passport
  - º Change car titles and registrations
- If you don't decide until after your final hearing to have your birth name restored, find out if you can file a post-judgment motion for restoration

in your dissolution case. Otherwise, you can make the change through your local Probate Court (known as "Surrogate's Courts" in New York and New Jersey).

- Obtain any personal property belonging to you that is in your Ex's possession, ASAP.
- Ask your tax preparer if you should change the amount of withholding from your paycheck with a new W-4 form in light of alimony or other changes resulting from your divorce.
- Set up direct withdrawal/deposit for support payments.
- Obtain from your lawyer any of your documents that you wish to have.
- Obtain a copy of your credit report (available free at www.AnnualCreditReport.com) to resolve any problems and to make sure the information used for your credit rating is accurate.

Taking Care of Your Children

Keep in mind that your divorce after-life will be a new world not only for you but for your children as well. Assistance in guiding your children's transition is available from numerous sources (See Chapter 17.), including:

- www.helpguide.org/mental/children_divorce.htm
- www.sesamestreet.org/parents/topicsandactivities/toolkits/divorce (for children through 8 years old)
- www.ourfamilywizard.com (avoids co-parenting conflict that traumatizes children, using on-line calendars, message boards, etc.)

A good deal of the parenting advice in this book applies both during and after the divorce. Start by telling your children that you love them. Then *show* them that you love them by following these rules:

- Be positive and reassuring.
- Keep involved in your children's lives—attending games and programs is more important than ever, especially for the parent not living with the children.
- Revise your Parenting Goal Statement with your Ex. If you didn't do one, it's never too late. (see page 145.)
- Avoid criticizing your Ex especially to or in your children's presence.
- Avoid arguments with your Ex, especially in the presence of the children, who often believe disputes are their fault.
- Never use the children to exchange messages with your Ex.

- Encourage your children to ask questions about the new state of things. Ideally, this should happen *after* you've agreed with your co-parent how to handle such questions.
- Don't contribute to children's "reconciliation fantasies" by implying that there might be one.
- Have your child see a professional if you notice signs of distress.
- Provide stability for your children by maintaining routines that are as consistent with those of your co-parent as possible. Prepare schedules so they will know where they will be.
- Review your parenting plan to make sure you and your Ex are fulfilling your respective responsibilities including
  - Requesting that all notices and bulletins are sent to both parents
  - Adhering to your parenting plan details such as consistent bedtime, homework, and curfew rules
- Get your post-divorce co-parenting off to a good start with amiable communication and constructive discussions about the items on this list.
- Read more on conflict management and cooperative problem-solving in "The *Talk to Strangers* Pocket Guide for Parents" at: www.ChildCustodyFilm.com.

Child Distress Warning Signs

Your children may experience lingering difficulties adjusting to their changed lives after your divorce. Be on the lookout for behavioral changes that can indicate anxiety, stress, insecurity, or depression such as:

- Altered sleep patterns or eating habits
- Declining performance in academics, athletics, or other activities
- Frequent and/or broad mood changes
- Acting out through anger, aggression, defiance, or other misbehavior with peers, teachers, or family members
- Withdrawal from family and friends
- Lethargy or disinterest
- Regression
- Becoming accident prone
- Excessive catering to parents that may signal a child's self-blame for the divorce

Taking Care of Yourself

If you possibly can, take some "R&R" time to help achieve closure on your marriage and the divorce process. Reflect upon how you are functioning and relating to those around you. To improve or "maintain," consider the following:

- Counseling to help you adjust to the new realities of your life
- Continued work on joint parenting with your Ex (as discussed in Chapter 10) in order to
    - Provide your children with a good model for dealing with conflict
    - Maintain consistency for your children regarding their routines and rules for bedtimes/curfews, homework, etc.
- Keeping stress and guilt levels down, and your wellbeing and self-esteem up by
    - Joining that yoga class or meditation group that you felt too busy to join during the divorce (See Chapter 17 for resources.)
    - Maintaining nutrition with a balanced diet including plenty of fresh fruits and vegetables, and staying away from soda and other sugar-laden products
    - Exercising regularly for cardio, core, etc.
    - Getting sufficient sleep (See the sleep tips on page 108.)
    - Joining a post-divorce support group locally or on-line (See Chapter 17 for resources to help you locate support groups.)
- If you are reentering the job market, look into
    - Taking a computer class (at a local library, college, etc.) to acquire or sharpen your skills
    - Catching up on developments in your field
    - Modernizing your resume and learning about key words and other techniques to get yourself past on-line "screening robots" to an actual interview

Try something new to get the juices going again!

- Get/Stay organized by
    - Checking out personal finance software such as MoneyDance or Quicken. Besides helping you organize, personal finance software can save you lots of bill-paying and tax preparation fun-time.
    - Managing your time efficiently with electronic "To Be Done Lists" synched to your phone, iPad, etc.
    - Handling paperwork with "one-touch" paper management techniques.

- ⁰ If you're a computer wiz, consider apps and hardware that scan and organize documents. If you're not a computer wiz, organize your correspondence, bills, and account statements in color-coded folders.
- Try something new and at long last, have some fun. Remember, laughing is actually healthy for you!

Take a Moment and Breathe

When you arrive at the end of your divorce journey, don't forget to congratulate yourself for reaching the finish line of an obstacle course no one wants to run. If you have children, congratulate yourself again for everything you did to make the divorce easier for them.

Then, take a little time to just... breathe. Reflect upon things you've learned during the past months that can be useful as you move forward. While you may have some wistful "the-way-we-were" moments in the future, be thankful for the opportunity to continue along your path free of the kind of dysfunctional relationship from which some people are never able to free themselves.

Kemba

Because you never know what new and exciting experience is just around the corner.

 Yes, there *IS* a quiz! Test what you have (or haven't) learned.

1. **The main idea of this chapter is:**
    A. It's not over 'til the Fat Lady sings, which will be me if I don't get to the gym.
    B. Soon I can forget I ever knew what COBRA and QDRO stand for.
    C. There are numerous details to be attended to after divorce.

2. **Unscramble the following key phrases from this chapter!**
    A. Stop-coverdi granpetin
    B. No-nile prutops prugos
    C. Mininangati tinnitruo

CHAPTER 17

More Divorce Resources

*"It is never too late to be the
person you might have been."*
— George Eliot

It would be impossible to list all, or even most of the worthwhile divorce resources available on-line and in book form, so this chapter does not attempt to do that. Instead, the sites and resources here represent a sampling of high quality general resources plus others that relate to specific issues and demographic groups.

To learn more about divorce law and practice in your state, always begin with your state's judicial branch or bar association site.

Come in out of the rain – there's plenty of help available!

Finding Divorce Professionals

Matrimonial Lawyers

Chapter 4 provides resources for locating matrimonial lawyers including additional details about the following:

- National Professional Organizations:
    - The American Bar Association Division for Bar Services/ Resources offers a database of state and local bar associations at http://www.americanbar.org/aba.html
    - The American Academy of Matrimonial Lawyers at www.aaml.org offers a searchable database of AAML members by location

- ○ The National Board of Trial Advocacy, a non-profit body accredited by the ABA to certify lawyers in family law trial advocacy: http://www.nblsc.us/
- ○ The International Academy of Collaborative Professionals maintains a member directory: http://www.collaborativepractice.com/

- **State Judiciary Websites**: These state court sites provide lists of lawyers certified in matrimonial law in those states that offer certification. They also can confirm that a lawyer's bar membership is in good standing and some provide the lawyer's bar disciplinary history if any.
  - ○ You can access your state's website with the links provided by The National Center for State Courts at
  - ○ http://www.ncsc.org/Information-and-Resources/Browse-by-State/State-Court-Websites.aspx
  - ○ To check out a lawyer's disciplinary history, visit http://hirealawyer.findlaw.com/choosing-the-right-lawyer/researching-attorney-discipline.html

- **Lawyer Referral Services**: The American Bar Association website, www.abanet.org, provides access to lawyer referral services. Generally, these services provide contact information for attorneys who are more moderately priced than those you would find, for example, through The American Academy of Matrimonial Lawyers that lists lawyers who are usually top-notch and nearly always top-dollar.
Lawyer referral services are maintained or authorized by state, county, and city bar associations in each state and U.S. territory. To find one nearby, select "Public Resource," then "Lawyer Referral Services," followed by the name of your state.

- **Lawyer Rating Services**: The most reliable of the rating services is Martindale Hubbell. Hard copies of the multi-volume set containing detailed information should be available in libraries and some local law offices. More limited information is available at www.martindale.com.

- **Law School Legal Clinics**: Most law schools maintain clinics offering free or nominal cost help from law students supervised by faculty members. A list of your state's law schools can be found at http://www.martindale.com/. Select "law schools" in the "search tools" drop-down box.

- **Special Interest Bar Associations**:
  - ○ American Association of Jewish Lawyers and Jurists: http://www.jewishlawyers.org

º Hispanic National Bar Association: www.hnba.com
º National Asian Pacific American Bar Association:
   http://www.napaba.org/
º National Bar Association: www.nationalbar.org (an association of
   African American lawyers and judges)
º National LGBT Bar Association: http://www.lgbtbar.org/
º National Native American Bar Association:
   http://www.nativeamericanbar.org/

º State Licensing Boards and Professional Organizations: If you are
   unable to access these entities through the national associations at
   the top of this list, search online using the key words below that are
   applicable to your inquiry:

º Your state's name, plus
º "State bar association," "unified bar," "county bar association," "judicial department," "courts," "lawyer referral," "licensing board"
   "psychiatrist," "psychologist," "psychotherapist," "family therapist,"
   "accountant" or "financial planner," plus
º "Association," "state," "board," and/or "licensing"

States With Private Bar Associations
in Addition to State Bars

A majority of jurisdictions have a single "unified bar" to which all licensed
lawyers must belong. Seventeen jurisdictions, however, have both
   • A bar administered by the state government to which all practicing at-
     torneys must belong (search the "judicial branch" of your state), and
   • A private bar association to which most attorneys belong though they
     are not required to (search your state's "bar association").

If you live in one of the states listed below, you can find authoritative information about divorce in your state on websites maintained by both the
state judicial branch and the private state bar association.

Arkansas, Colorado, Connecticut, Delaware, Illinois,
Indiana, Iowa, Kansas, Maine, Maryland, Massachusetts,
Minnesota, New York, Ohio, Pennsylvania, Tennessee, Vermont

Mediators, Collaborative Divorce Practitioners, Mental Health Professionals, Divorce Coaches, Analysts and Planners

The following national professional organization websites can help you locate qualified mediators, mental health professionals, divorce coaches, and divorce financial analysts and planners:

- Academy of Family Mediators: www.mediate.com (contains state directory of family mediators and mediation standards)
- Academy of Professional Family Mediators: https://apfmnet.org/
- Association of Family and Conciliation Courts: http://www.afccnet.org/ (offers resources for divorcing families)
- American Psychological Association: http://www.afccnet.org/
- American Psychological Association - State, Provincial & Territorial Psychological Association Directory: http://www.apa.org/about/apa/organizations/associations.aspx
- Association for Conflict Resolution: http://www.acrnet.org/ (mediators and other ADR practitioners)
- Association of Divorce Financial Planners: http://www.divorceandfinance.org/
- Institute for Divorce Financial Analysts: http://www.institutedfa.com
- International Academy of Collaborative Professionals (IACP): http://www.collaborativepractice.com/
- International Christian Coaching Association: http://iccaonline.net/courses/divorce-coaching

Information on Self-Representation and Legal Aid

- Resources for self-represented litigants are available at http://www.srln.org
- Lawhelp.org offers resources for your divorce in your area, including legal aid referrals: http://www.lawhelp.org/
- At http://www.martindale.com/ select "law schools" in the "search tools" drop-down box to find a law school nearby offering free or nominal cost divorce help.

Resources For Federal and State Family Law, and For Making Sound Divorce Decisions

- http://family.findlaw.com/divorce
- Cornell University's Legal Information Institute provides links to federal, state and uniform divorce-related laws: http://www.law.cornell.edu/states
- The Children's Rights Council website contains resources for parents as well as links to state government sites on which you can search your state's law: http://www.crckids.org/
- National Center for State Courts website contains links to your particular state's court website to find pertinent forms & information: http://www.ncsc.org
- Lawhelp.org offers resources for your divorce in your area, including legal aid referrals: http://www.lawhelp.org/
- http://public.findlaw.com/bookshelf-mdf/
- *The American Bar Association Guide to Marriage, Divorce & Families*: a general guide to many of the major issues and options in a divorce, for general background information
- *A Judge's Guide to Divorce: Uncommon Advice from the Bench* by Judge Roderic Duncan http://www.amazon.com/Judges-Guide-Divorce-Uncommon-Advice/dp/1413305687
- *Picture Your Divorce to See The Right Decisions* by Terry McNiff, Esq.: http://pictureyourdivorce.com/
- See parenting resources below

Parenting And Parenting Education Resources

There's plenty of on-line help for divorcing parents. The list below contains resources for all parents as well as for specific demographics or parenting issues. The second site is authorized in some jurisdictions to fulfill state parenting education requirements for divorcing parents.

- http://www.divorcedmoms.com – A wide range of articles for divorced and divorcing mothers
- https://www.onlineparentingprograms.com/ – An on-line parenting education program
- http://www.amazon.com/ – Putting-Kids-First-Divorce Relationships-ebook/dp/B01BK8YSRQ – *Putting Kids First in Divorce: How*

to Reduce Conflict, Preserve Relationships and Protect Children During and After Divorce by Jeremy Kossen and Mark Baer
- http://www.overcomingbarriers.org/ – Overcoming Barriers High-Conflict Divorce Family Camps
- http://iamachildofdivorce.com/what-is-custody-and-visitation/
- http://www.goodreads.com/book/show/8598798-don-t-alienate-the-kids-raising-resilient-children-while-avoiding-high – *Don't Alienate the Kids! Raising Resilient Children While Avoiding High Conflict Divorce* by Bill Eddy
- http://shop.americanbar.org/ebus/store – Enter "My Parents Are Getting Divorced" in the ABA bookstore search box
- www.sesameworkshop.org/ – Resources for parents and children ages 2 to 8 to help children understand and cope with divorce
- http://www.childcentereddivorce.com/kids/ – Unique approach to breaking the news about the divorce to the children
- www.childcustodyfilm.com – Film and resource site for Larry Sarezky's short film, *Talk to Strangers*, accompanying Parents' Guide and other resources for divorce professionals and parents
- http://www.amazon.com/exec/obidos/ASIN/1886230269/divorce-center-20 – *Parenting After Divorce: A Guide to Resolving Conflicts and Meeting Your Children's Needs* by Philip Stahl, Ph.D.
- www.familysupportamerica.org – Parenting advice, and information regarding child abuse, alcoholism, disciplining children, divorce, and other topics related to families
- www.Familyequality.org – An organization dedicated to family equality for lesbian, gay, bisexual and transgender parents, guardians, and allies

Appraisals and Valuation

Appraisals of property in divorce generally fall into 3 categories:

- "Personal property" such as collectibles, antiques, and artwork
- Real estate
- Business interests

In court-based cases in which valuation may be contested, an appraisal by a qualified expert may be necessary. Using such experts is preferable even in ADR cases or court-based cases on a settlement track. You can learn about the certification and training of experts from the organizations listed below.

- American Society of Appraisers: http://www.appraisers.org/ (search site for appraisers of particular types of property such as jewelry and machinery and technical specialties)
- Appraisal Institute: http://www.appraisalinstitute.org/ (worldwide real estate appraisals)
- Appraisers Association of America: http://appraisersassociation.org/ (for appraisals of collectibles, antiques, artwork, and other personal property)
- Institute of Business Appraisers: http://go-iba.org/
- International Society of Appraisers: http://www.isa-appraisers.org/

Locating More Experts and Consultants

Information about potential expert witnesses such as accountants, actuaries, appraisers and computer experts can be found on national organization websites:

- American Academy of Actuaries: http://actuary.org/
- American Board of Forensic Psychology: http://abfp.com/
- American Board of Vocational Experts: http://abve.net
- American Institute of Certified Public Accountants: www.aicpa.com
- ASIS International (computer forensics): www.asisonline.org
- International Association of Computer Investigative Specialists (IACIS): www.iacis.com
- International Society of Forensic Computer Examiners (ISFCE): www.isfce.com
- National Association of State Boards of Accountancy: http://nasba.org/stateboards/
- National Association of State Mental Health Program Directors (division roster page for Children, Youth and Family Division Members): http://www.nasmhpd.org/content/children-youth-and-families-division

If you are unable to access an association or board through the resources above, search online using key words applicable to your inquiry:

- Your state's name, plus
- "State bar association," "unified bar," "county bar association," "judicial department," "courts," "lawyer referral," "licensing board" "psychiatrist," "psychologist," "psychotherapist," "family therapist," "accountant" or "financial planner," plus
- Association, state, board, or licensing agency

Relaxation and Meditation

- One of the simplest ways to calm down and find the rhythm that will foster health, awareness and all that good stuff is through breathing meditation. Jon Kabat-Zinn's meditation CD/MP3 downloads are a good place to start. Zinn teaches and guides meditation practice that can take as little as ten minutes a couple of times a day: http://www.mindfulnesscds.com/
- Insight Meditation Society: http://www.dharma.org/
- Learn meditation technique via "Headspace:" https://www.headspace.com
- WebMD offers 10 relaxation techniques: http://www.webmd.com/balance/guide/blissing-out-10-relaxation-techniques-reduce-stress-spot
- To learn more about meditation and the Buddhist philosophy underlying it, check out *Listening to the Heart: A Contemplative Journey to Engaged Buddhism* by Kittisaro and Thanissara: http://www.namse-bangdzo.com/Listening_to_the_Heart_A_Contemplative_Journey_to_p/9781583948392.htm

Dealing With Domestic Violence and Impaired Spouses

In addition to the resources below, you can find local help for domestic violence by searching: [Your state, or your state and county] domestic violence resources. Try to conduct such searches outside the home. If you do use a home computer, delete the recent search history that your search engine keeps on your computer.

- http://www.womenshealth.gov U.S. Department of Health and Human Services site offering safety planning for abusive situations including safety packing lists, hotline resources, etc.
- The National Domestic Violence Hotline at 800-799-SAFE (7233) or TDD 800-787-3224. If you are concerned that your computer use is being monitored, you can call the hotline numbers for assistance.
- https://www.childwelfare.gov/preventing/ Resources on child abuse prevention, protecting children from risk of abuse, and strengthening families.
- http://www.goodreads.com/book/show/9996542-splitting *Splitting: Protecting Yourself While Divorcing Someone with Borderline or Narcissistic Personality Disorder* by Bill Eddy & Randi Kreger.

Support Groups and Post-Divorce Assistance

- http://www.divorcedmoms.com Extensive resources for dealing with both divorce and post-divorce issues
- http://divorcesupport.meetup.com locates support groups in your area
- About.com's blogs re post-divorce co-parenting: http://divorcesupport.about.com/od/relationshipwithyourex/?nl=1
- The National Association for Divorced Women & Children; and Post-Divorce Boot Camp for Women: http://www.freshstartafter-divorce.com/
- Faith-based support groups: http://www.divorcecare.org/
- Miscellaneous resources: http://www.thedivorceforum.com/

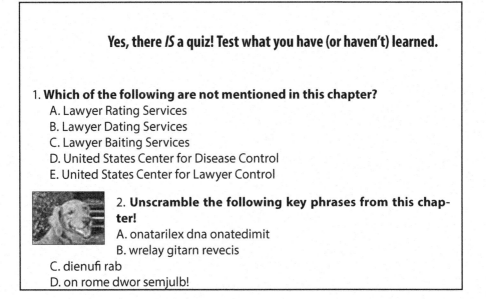

Yes, there *IS* a quiz! Test what you have (or haven't) learned.

1. **Which of the following are not mentioned in this chapter?**
   A. Lawyer Rating Services
   B. Lawyer Dating Services
   C. Lawyer Baiting Services
   D. United States Center for Disease Control
   E. United States Center for Lawyer Control

2. **Unscramble the following key phrases from this chapter!**
   A. onatarilex dna onatedimit
   B. wrelay gitarn revecis
   C. dienufi rab
   D. on rome dwor semjulb!

Appendix 1

Statutory Criteria Summary

[Note: You can download this Summary for printing at
http://divorcesimplystated.com/updates-materials/.]

Date of marriage: __/__/__

Marriage # for Wife (1st, 2nd, etc.): __

Marriage # for Husband (1st, 2nd, etc.): __

Wife's date of birth: __/__/__

Husband's date of birth: __/__/__

Wife's occupation: _____

Husband's occupation: _____

Ages of children: _____

Children's special needs: _____

Value of property currently in Wife's name: $_____

Property (with values) in Wife's name at time of marriage: $_____

_____

_____

Value of property currently in Husband's name: $_____

Property (with values) in Husband's name at time of marriage: $_____

_____

_____

Value of jointly owned assets: $_____

Wife's employer: _____

Wife's current total annual compensation (salary/wages/commissions/bonus):
$_____

Wife's current total annual compensation over the past three calendar years:
$_____

If Wife is self-employed, business's gross revenue/net profit from last filed tax return:
$_____(gross revenue) /$_____(net revenue)

Husband's employer: _____

Husband's current total annual compensation (salary/wages/commissions/bonus):
   $_____

Husband's current total annual compensation over the past three calendar years:
   $_____

If Husband is self-employed, business's gross revenue/net profit from last filed tax return: $ _____(gross revenue) /$ _____(net revenue)

Combined annual unearned income (interest, dividends, etc.)
   $_____/yr.

Other expected future sources of income or property such as trusts (source and est. amount):

Wife: _____$_____

Husband: _____$_____

Property (with estimated values) received by inheritance or gift during marriage:
Husband: $_____; Wife: $_____

Significant health issues:

Wife: _____

_____

Husband: _____

_____

Educational Level including degrees and dates:

Wife: _____

Husband: _____

If applicable, length of time currently out of the workforce:
Wife: _____Husband: _____

Do you have a prenuptial agreement? ____

If so, when was it signed? _____

Which if either spouse has been primarily responsible for child-raising? _____

Reasons for breakdown of marriage: _____

_____

Appendix 2

Initial Consultation Checklist

[Note: The following is a menu of questions from which to choose those that are most important to you. To maximize the usefulness of your consultation, bring 3 years of tax returns, a net worth statement, and your Statutory Criteria Summary. You can download this Checklist at http://divorcesimplystated.com/updates-materials/.]

Attorney/Client Relationship and Handling of the Case

1. Are you supportive of ADR? If I decided to mediate, would you act as my review counsel? What do you understand the role of review counsel to be?

2. Do you offer "unbundled legal services" and if so, how might that work most productively in my case?

3. How many of your divorce cases go to trial each year?

4. Do you have a policy of returning calls within a certain amount of time?

5. Will you be available to meet with me before any court proceedings or "four-way" negotiation session?

6. Do you prepare clients prior to depositions or court hearings by cross-examining them as you expect the other lawyer would?

7. How would you try to minimize the impact of the divorce on my children?

8. Is there anything I should do right away to protect my interests (for example, regarding joint bank accounts and credit cards, pending loan applications, upcoming pension elections, etc.)?

9. Are there things that I can get started on (financial affidavit, gathering documents, etc.) that will expedite my case?

10. Are there things that I shouldn't talk to my spouse about?

Attorney's Experience

11. How long have you been practicing family law?

12. What percentage of your practice is devoted to divorces?

13. Besides family law, what other types of law have you practiced?

14. What kind of relationship do you have with my spouse's attorney?

15. Are there any attorneys with whom you would prefer not to work?

Others Who May Become Involved in Your Case

16. In the event a lawyer or guardian is to be appointed for my child, will I be able to participate in the decisions regarding who you would recommend and what role such a representative would play?

17. What other members of the firm will be involved in my case? What experience do they have and what work will they be doing on my case?

18. Is your support staff experienced in family cases? What tasks do they perform?

19. Might an actuary, accountant, or lawyer outside your firm render services such as preparing qualified domestic relations orders? If so, who and what tasks do you envision them performing?

⚠20. Will you personally handle all substantive court proceedings and settlement negotiations?

Fees & Disbursements

⚠21. What is your hourly billing rate and the hourly rates of other lawyers who may work on my case?

⚠22. Will I be charged for non-legal clerical work such as bill preparation and scheduling of appointments?

⚠23. Will you be sending me a letter regarding your fees?

⚠24. Do you charge by the minute, increments of .1 hour, or in some other way?

Range of Likely Outcomes

25. Based on my tax returns, net worth statement, and statutory criteria summary, what can you tell me about the range of likely outcomes in my case regarding child custody/access, property settlement, child support, and alimony?

Miscellaneous

26. Do you use software such as Finplan to run alimony scenarios, calculate present value, etc.? Do you do that personally or does someone else in your office do it?

Appendix 3

CHILDREN'S BILL OF RIGHTS

WHEN PARENTS ARE NOT TOGETHER...

Every kid has rights, particularly when mom and dad are splitting up. Below are some things parents shouldn't forget – and kids shouldn't let them – when the family is in the midst of a break-up.

You have the right to love both your parents. You also have the right to be loved by both of them. That means you shouldn't feel guilty about wanting to see your dad or your mom at any time. It's important for you to have both parents in your life, particularly during difficult times such as a break-up of your parents.

You do not have to choose one parent over the other. If you have an opinion about which parent you want to live with, let it be known. But nobody can force you to make that choice. If your parents can't work it out, a judge may make the decision for them.

You're entitled to all the feelings you're having. Don't be embarrassed by what you're feeling. It is scary when your parents break up, and you're allowed to be scared. Or angry. Or sad. Or whatever.

You have the right to be in a safe environment. This means that nobody is allowed to put you in danger, either physically or emotionally. If one of your parents is hurting you, tell someone – either your other parent or a trusted adult like a teacher.

You don't belong in the middle of your parents' break-up. Sometimes your parents may get so caught up in their own problems that they forget that you're just a kid, and that you can't handle their adult worries. If they start putting you in the middle of their dispute, remind them that it's their fight, not yours.

Grandparents, aunts, uncles and cousins are still part of your life. Even if you're living with one parent, you can still see relatives on your other parent's side. You'll always be a part of their lives, even if your parents aren't together anymore.

You have the right to be a child. Kids shouldn't worry about adult problems. Concentrate on your school work, your friends, activities, etc. Your mom and dad just need your love. They can handle the rest.

IT IS NOT YOUR FAULT AND DON'T BLAME YOURSELF.

Appendix 4

Index of State Laws

As noted in the preceding pages, state laws differ significantly as to the rules governing divorce and related matters. State bar sites and the resources provided in Chapter 17 are good places to begin familiarizing yourself with your state's family law and procedure.

References are made throughout this book to various state laws. Those references acquaint the reader with some prevailing legal principles as well as variations among the states on certain aspects of family law. Perhaps most importantly, however, the references point out important aspects of state law about which the reader should become informed. As noted, the best sources of such information are matrimonial attorneys licensed to practice in the reader's state.

Below are the pages on which references appear to the laws of particular states and The District of Columbia.